The only British 18 inch gauge steam railway in passenger operation today is the superb Bicton Woodland Railway at East Budleigh, Devon. Much of the equipment used originates from the Royal Arsenal Railway at Woolwich, including BWR No.1 *Woolwich*, (Avonside 1748 of 1916) an oil-burning 0-4-0T seen here in its former blue livery.

(Richard Tarr)

An illustrated history of

18 INCH GAUGE STEAM RAILWAYS

Mark Smithers

OPC

Oxford Publishing Co.

Title page: Culverin seen in service circa 1920. Unlike *Hannibal*, this locomotive was latterly fitted with a fully enclosed cab in addition to the Neath spark arrester. The vehicle is a Superintendent Saloon probably constructed in the 1890s with a roof styled after the famous Spooner 'curly roof' luggage vans of the Festiniog Railway.

(The Locomotive)

Dedication

To my father, who supplied much help during the preparation of
this book, but did not live to see its publication.

A catalogue record for this book is available from the British Library.

ISBN 0-86093-499-3

Oxford Publishing Co. is part of the
Haynes Publishing Group PLC
Sparkford, near Yeovil, Somerset, BA22 7JJ

Haynes Publications Inc.
861 Lawrence Drive, Newbury Park, California 91320, USA

Printed in Great Britain by the Bath Press, Bath, Avon.
Typeset in Times Roman Medium

Contents

A rear three-quarter view of Beyer, Peacock 0-4-0WT No. 2817, *Dot* showing the firebox backhead. This locomotive, formerly used on Beyer, Peacock's works tramway, survives today in the Narrow Gauge Railway Museum, Tywyn.
(A. Neale Collection)

Acknowledgements

I would sincerely like to thank all of the people who provided assistance at all stages during the preparation of this Volume. The relevant information concerning the origins of the Plates and Figures is included in the appropriate captions. Further assistance with research was forthcoming from many sources and four organisations in particular deserve a mention in this connection. These are:

The Industrial Railway Society
The Lancashire & Yorkshire Railway Society
The London & North Western Railway Society
The Narrow Gauge Railway Society

In addition, I would like to thank particular individuals for valuable assistance with this project. These include Messrs G. Horsman, M. Swift, R. Fitzgerald, J.G. Vincent, J. Kimber, M. Billington, C.R. Weaver, R.W. Kidner, J. Brown, A. Neale, R. Link, E. Wade, A. Civil, C. Taylor, R. Thomson, N. Lee, A. Lowe, B. Lane, D. Boreham, W. Harry, A. Turner, M. Rutherford, B. Clarke, C. Veitch, P. Towers, F. Jux, J. Follett, R. Holdsworth, R. Dawe, W. Potter, R. Riley, R. Murmann, P. Nicholson, A. Hughes, B. Ewins and Dr P. Lee. Assistance was also provided by the National Railway Museum, Leeds Industrial Museum, the Royal Engineers Library, Chatham, the Bicton Woodland Railway, the Royal Arsenal, Woolwich and Chatham Historic Dockyard.

The photographs credited to *The Locomotive* magazine were taken by the late Major E.W. Taylerson and are courtesy of J. Townsend.

LNWR Crewe Works system locomotive *Dickie* photographed in the Old Works Yard. Unlike *Billy* the nameplate lacks a full stop and no steam brakes are fitted.

(Dutton Collection/LNWR Society 9953)

Introduction

From the earliest days of steam locomotive usage on railways, circumstances have arisen to favour the use of a track gauge less than the dimension of 4ft 8¹⁄₂in which came to be accepted as the normal standard throughout most of Europe and the United States of America. As was to be expected such railways tended to be of a specialist nature, serving one or at most a small number of locally based industries, with physical or economic limitations imposing the requirement for a narrower than usual gauge. By the early 1860s, the emergence of a market for industrial steam locomotives of gauges of 3ft and under had been noted and exploited by some private manufacturers. These included Fletcher, Jennings & Co. of the Lowca Foundry near Whitehaven and Manning, Wardle & Co. Ltd. of the Boyne Engine Works in Leeds, whose first locomotive of 1859 was a 3ft gauge 0-4-0 saddle tank.

Most of the better-known narrow gauge lines fell between the gauge limits of 1ft 11¹⁄₂in and 2ft 6in and these tended to be situated in Mid and North Wales. Although most entertained a significant proportion of industrial traffic, such as slate or agricultural produce, there was in most instances, a fair amount of passenger traffic which today supports the surviving lines in the form of tourists.

The subject of the present Volume, however, is a group of railways for which the perceived physical and economic limitations prevented the use of a track gauge as large as that used on the Festiniog Railway, and necessitated the use of a gauge dimension of 18 inches. From the point of view of purpose, these lines fell neatly into three groups, namely those serving railway workshops such as at Crewe, those whose purpose was of a military or military support nature, as was the case at Woolwich Arsenal, and those designed for use as a transport system for industrial users or large estates of the type exemplified by the Sand Hutton Light Railway in Yorkshire. All of the locomotives employed on these lines could rightfully claim to be functional entities in their own right rather than representations, scale or otherwise, of locomotives employed on larger gauge railways elsewhere. Railways with a 'miniature' outlook, such as the Jaywick Miniature Railway which closed soon after the outbreak of the Second World War, are specifically excluded from the scope of this work.

The lines and equipment featured herewith could, broadly speaking, be deemed to fall into the nineteenth century school of development although construction of similar equipment, often for use overseas, continued into the present century. Also, the First World War provided an opportunity for three manufacturers to embark upon construction of 18 inch gauge steam locomotives in significant numbers.

The earliest known steam railway of this basic type to be used in the United Kingdom was the system laid down under the direction of Mr John Ramsbottom from 1862 onwards, in the Old Works at Crewe. This successful application of steam motive power on a gauge of such a small dimension was to have a profound influence not only upon other users of similar railways, but also upon builders and users of larger narrow gauge lines. It preceded, for example, the introduction of steam locomotives onto the Festiniog Railway in North Wales.

The first followers of the lead set by the system at Crewe were the military and military service lines at Chatham and Woolwich which appeared in the late 1860s and early 1870s. As we shall see, the design of locomotives used on these railways differed greatly from those used at Crewe, largely as a result of two factors; the first of these being that loading gauge and curve restrictions were less onerous than those experienced at Crewe and the second being that major developments had taken place in narrow gauge steam locomotive design generally during the intervening years. From the point of view of rolling stock design, there was an additional requirement that some passenger vehicles be provided for the Chatham and Woolwich lines and so major advances were made in this field during the ensuing three decades.

The Crewe Works lead was more closely copied in 1887 at the then newly constructed Horwich Workshops of the Lancashire & Yorkshire Railway, but apart from a similar system dating from the same year, and using the same design of locomotive as that used at Horwich, at Beyer, Peacock & Co. Ltd's premises in Gorton, Manchester, no further steam operated 18 inch gauge lines were to be employed by major railway workshops in the United Kingdom. Several purely hand-worked systems existed however, and examples included those at Wolverton Carriage Works of the London & North Western Railway and at John Fowler & Co. Ltd at Leeds.

During the latter part of the nineteenth century and the first decade of the twentieth, a few home-based industrial users adopted steam haulage on railways of 18 inch gauge, the most well known probably being the line used by John Knowles Ltd of Woodville, Leicestershire.

As we have mentioned, the First World War proved to be an Indian Summer for the nineteenth century school of 18 inch gauge steam railway design and another military support line came into being in 1915 at the Royal Army Service Corps Depot in Deptford. Unlike the system at Woolwich Arsenal, this line conveyed rations rather than munitions but it still warranted the use of a dozen locomotives at the height of its activity.

The Woolwich system reached its zenith during World War One and the 18 inch gauge track there extended to approximately 100 miles, a feat not achieved by any other steam worked narrow gauge railway on the British mainland. The mixed gauge permanent way and the variety of motive power employed on the Royal Arsenal Railways at this time also ensured the system a unique place in British railway history, albeit one which has been neglected in more recent years.

The cessation of hostilities in 1918 brought the wider availability of internal combustion engines for civilian users, the expansion of the use of motorised road transport and, for a decade at least, a significant reduction in military service activity, factors which all combined to bring about the demise of the nineteenth century school of commercial 18 inch gauge steam railway.

The last major development in the story of predominantly commercial, as opposed to leisure orientated 18 inch gauge steam railways, was the opening of the Sand Hutton Light Railway in the early 1920s. This line is

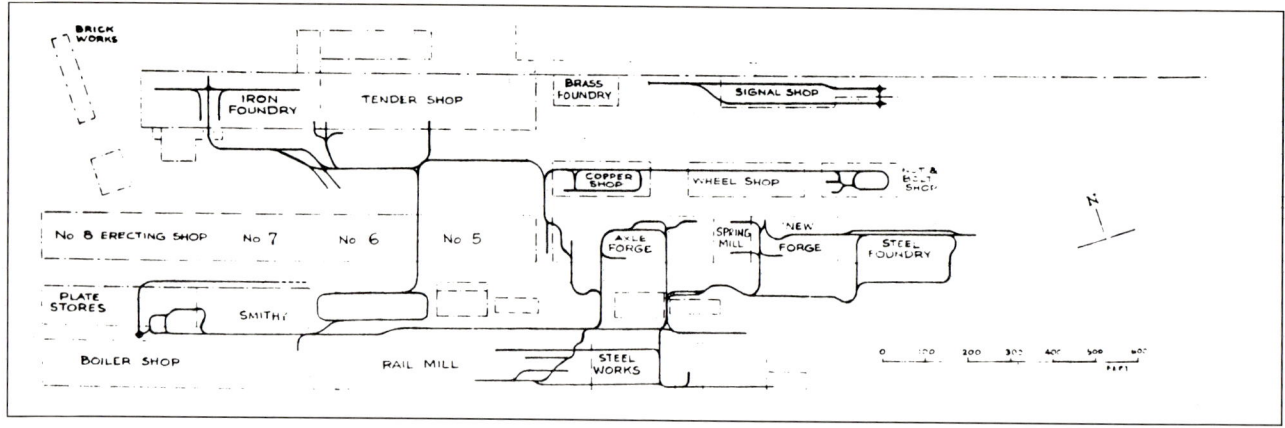

the bridge remained in use until the late 1920s while the bridge itself was demolished in 1939, having latterly been used for pedestrian access to the Works from the station.

After the 1920's reorganization of Crewe Works under LMS ownership, most of the narrow gauge trackwork in the Old Works disappeared with just two hand-worked sections being left in existence. One was in the Iron Stores, formerly the Forge, whilst the other was a new section on three floors in what had become the Signal Stores. This latter section utilised the hydraulic lift in order to transfer wagons from one floor to another. There was also at least one turnout and three turntables in the internal trackwork on this section, along with a further turntable which was connected to a section of track outside of the building. The section of trackwork in the Iron Stores was in use by 1933.

The largest section of 18 inch gauge trackwork was to be found in the Steel Works complex, which was rather inappropriately named as the complex eventually encompassed a wider range of activities than steel making. The earliest sections of trackwork were laid in the mid-1860s to serve the Bessemer converters then being installed but the track layout underwent a considerable amount of revision over the years. A layout representative of the period just before the beginning of the First World War is shown in an accompanying plan. Access to No.7 Erecting Shop was gained by means of a mixed gauge traverser although the narrow gauge track had been removed from this prior to the period represented in the plan.

An isolated section of narrow gauge track serving the Paint Shop enabled deliveries to be made from standard gauge vans to the Shop Stores. This section

A plan showing the locomotive-worked 18 inch gauge lines in the Crewe Steel Works complex in 1914. By this time, the narrow gauge track on the traverser between Nos 7 and 8 Erecting Shops had fallen out of use. By 1926 the stretch of line connecting the Axle Forge and the Smithy and the spur feeding the Tender Shop (this latter building is not to be confused with its Old Works namesake) had also disappeared.

(LNWR Society)

was always hand-worked and apparently never used locomotives. Access to the Paint Shop was gained by means of an archway, the bricked-up remains of which were still extant in 1985. In addition to the lines serving the Signal Shop, two further sections are known to have existed. The first of these ran from the central pointwork in the Iron Foundry out through the rearmost wall to a spoil tip. External access was gained by means of a simple hole, of sufficient size to accommodate a loaded wagon, which was subsequently bricked up but was still traceable in 1985.

The second of these sections served the new Machine Shop and No.9 Erecting Shop, being used to remove swarf from the former and transport components to the latter. As with the lines in the Deviation Works, this section did not employ locomotive haulage and remained hand-worked throughout its entire existence. Rails from this section became incorporated into grids covering steam heating pipes and as such remained extant into the early 1980s.

A small section of track remained in use for locomo-

This diagram shows the track layout in the Crewe Steel Works as correct for 1929. *Billy* spent its declining years in use on the surviving 18 inch gauge section.

(The Railway Engineer)

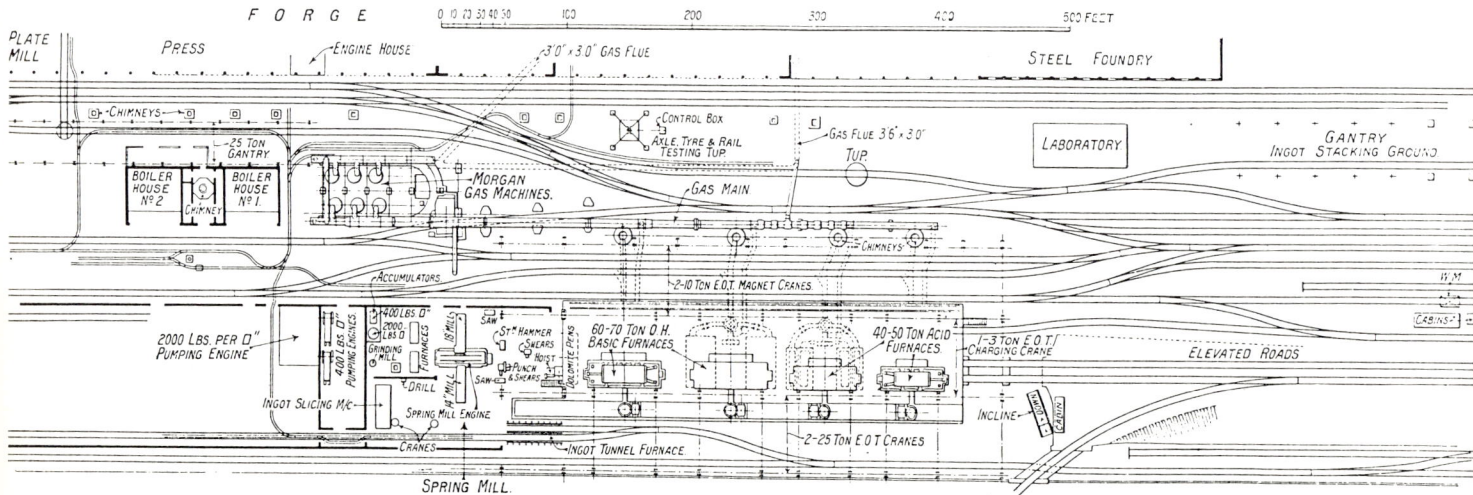

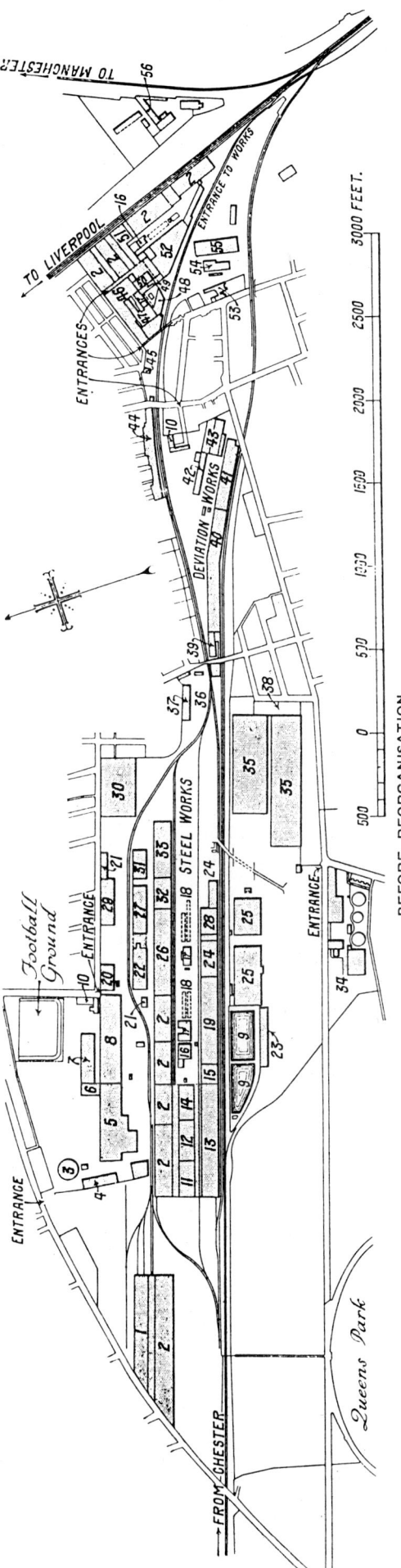

BEFORE REORGANISATION.

1. Fitting Shop. 2. Erecting Shops. 3. Brick Kiln. 4. Drying Shed. 5. Iron Foundry. 6. Pattern Shop. 7. Pattern Stores. 8. Tender Shop. 9. Cooling Ponds. 10. Dining Rooms. 11. Plate Stores. 12. Flanging Shop. 13. Boiler Shop. 14. Angle Iron Smithy. 15. Points and Crossings Shop. 16 Electric Power Station. 17. Boilers. 18. Gas Producers. 19. Rail Mill. 20. Brass Foundry. 21. Stores. 22. Coppersmiths' Shop. 23. Carriage Washing Shed. 24. Siemens Martin Furnaces. 25. Carriage Repairing Shops. 26. Axle Forge. 27. Wheel Shop. 28. Spring Mill and Ingot Stripping Shop. 29. Signal Shop. 30. Paint Shop. 31. Nut and Bolt Shop. 32. Iron Forge. 33. Steel Foundry. 34. Gas Works. 35. Carriage Store Sheds. 36. Store Yard. 37. Mortar Mill. 38. Clothing Factory. 39. Testing Shop. 40. Mill-wrights' Shop. 41. Joiners Shop. 42. Timber Shed. 43. Sawmills. 44. Locomotive Offices. 45. Pay Office. 46. Smiths' Shop. 47. Drop Hammers. 48. Iron Stores. 49. Millshop. 50. Spring Shop. 51. Valve Motion Shop. 52. Fitting Shop. 53. Hospital. 54. Locomotive Stores. 55. Out Station Shop. 56. Grease Works.

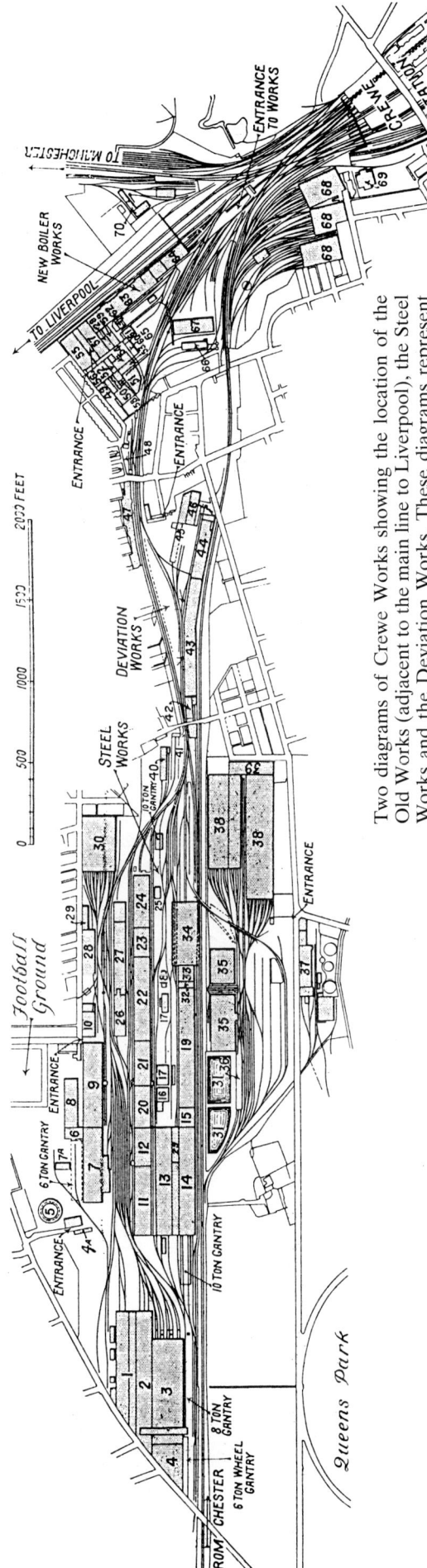

Two diagrams of Crewe Works showing the location of the Old Works (adjacent to the main line to Liverpool), the Steel Works and the Deviation Works. These diagrams represent the Works before and after the implementation of the 1920's Reorganization Scheme.

(The Railway Engineer)

AFTER REORGANISATION.

1. Fitting and Machine Shops. 2. No.9 Erecting Shop. 3. New Erecting Shop. 4. Machine Shop. 4a. Progress Office. 5. Brick Kiln. 6. Pattern Shop. 7. Iron Foundry. 7a. Chair Foundry. 8. Pattern Stores. 9. Tender Shop. 10. Brass Foundry. 11. Finished Part Stores, and Welders Superheater Element Tubes. 12. Mounting Shop. 13. Smithy. 14. Boiler Shop Repairs. 15. Points and Crossings Shop. 16. Electric Power House. 17. Boilers. 18. Gas Machines. 19. Rail Mill. 20. Tube Shop. 21. Frame and Cylinder Shop. 22. Axle Forge. 23. Iron Forge. 24. Steel Foundry. 25. Laboratory. 26. Coppersmiths' Shop. 27. Wheel Shop. 28. Brass and Finishing Shop. 29. Stores. 30. Paint Shop. 31. Cooling Ponds. 32. Millwrights' Shop. 33. Spring Mill. 34. 45- and 65-ton Steel Furnaces. 35. Carriage Repairing Shops. 36. Carriage Washing Shed. 37. Gas Works. 38. Carriage Store Sheds. 39. Clothing Factory. 40. Mortar Mill. 41. Stone Yard. 42. Testing Shop. 43. Millwrights' Shop. 44. Joiners Shop. 45. Timber Shed. 46. Saw Mills. 47. Locomotive Offices. 48. Pay Office. 49. Smiths' Shop. 50. Drop Hammer Shop. 51. Iron Stores. 52. Tube Shop. 53. Die Sinking Shop. 54. Spring Shop and Copper Store. 55. Boiler and Finishing Shop. 56. Roof Bar Shop. 57. Mounting and Assembly Shop. 58. Boilers. 59. Stay Shop. 60. Galvanising Shop. 61. Tin Shop. 62. Power House. 63. Flanging and Machine Shop. 64. Plate Stores. 65. Signal Shop. 66. Loco. Stores. 67. Stores. 68. Loco. Sheds 69. Electric Power House. 70. Grease Works.

tive hauled trains after the 1920's reorganization until final abandonment in 1932 following the Steel Plant's closure. This was worked by *Billy* until 1931 and by the Hudswell, Clarke diesel for the remainder of its existence.

Although strictly speaking outside the scope of the present volume, the purely hand worked line in the Deviation Works was not without interest. The Deviation Works buildings comprised the newest of the 19th Century complexes at Crewe and the narrow gauge system there dated from about 1870. The track was laid on three floors. The line on the ground floor (Joiners' Shop, Power Station and Boiler House) was connected to a line descending from the first floor (Sawmill) and the difference in levels necessitated the use of a capstan in facilitating the ascent and controlling the descent of wagons. The freewheeling of wagons from the Sawmill down to the doors close to the Boiler House occurred on occasions, although this practice was not officially approved.

In the basement of the Deviation Works there was an isolated section of narrow gauge track that was of particular interest in the fact that some of the rail at least was of the Vignoles' Patent variety. This rail appears to match the illustration in the Vignes Technical Study of 1878 and represented something of an advance on the plain rectangular section used initially for much of the 18 inch gauge permanent way. The third basic type of 18 inch gauge track in use at Crewe consisted of cast-iron plates and these can be seen in the illustrations of *Billy* and *Dickie* in the Old Works yard.

Largely unaffected by the withdrawal from service of the locomotives, the narrow gauge lines at the Deviation Works remained in use until 1967 with relatively few alterations in track configuration. As late as 1981, the layout in the Joiners' Shop remained traceable although even this formation has now been obliterated. The track surviving in 1981 included a four-way point, which was cast iron and hand- or foot-worked in accordance with normal Crewe practice. This still exists today in private storage.

The Locomotives and Stock used on the Crewe Systems

The locomotives constructed during Mr Ramsbottom's tenure of office were interesting in several respects, not least in the fact that their initial appearance preceded the use of steam locomotives on the Festiniog Railway, an event universally regarded as a major turning point in narrow gauge railway history. As has already been mentioned, *Tiny* was the first locomotive to be completed, being constructed by May 1862 and fully painted the following month. The locomotive differed radically from subsequent mainstream thinking in narrow gauge locomotive design, as lessons learned later on the Festiniog, the Talyllyn and the Festiniog & Blaenau lines had yet to make their impact at such an early stage. The basic design was still to have a major influence on the 18 inch gauge field, however, and for this reason, it will receive a considerable degree of coverage in this section.

The first major feature of note about *Tiny* was that the engine was, rather contrary to normal small gauge practice, fitted with inside cylinders. This was the result of the desire on the part of Ramsbottom to keep the overall width of the little locomotive to an absolute minimum. The widest point of the engine measured only 3ft overall and this was over the lifting lugs on the sides of the boiler. The cylinders were made to the dimensions of 4$\frac{1}{2}$in bore and 6in stroke, rather small when compared with most subsequent 18 inch gauge steam locomotives.

The main frames were continuous throughout their length between buffer beams and were mounted in the space bounded by the back-to-back limits of the wheels. The side frames were formed of iron plates of maximum depth 7in, thickness $\frac{3}{4}$in and pitched apart at 13$\frac{1}{4}$in. The guides for the axle boxes were formed by the cutting of the horn recesses directly into the frames which were strengthened on their inner faces at the boundaries of the recess (there being no castings for the horncheeks).

The wheels were 15$\frac{1}{4}$in diameter and consisted of cast iron centres with steel tyres (the treads were 3in wide). The wheelbase of the locomotive was 3ft.

The locomotive frames were secured together by the buffer plates, the boiler backplate and the slide bar support bracket (also attached to the boiler). The cylinders were attached to the main frames by means of flanges. A wooden buffer beam, sandwiched between plates, was fitted to the front end of the locomotive and this composite beam sported a central fixed eye which could accept a wagon towbar. Behind the boiler backplate, a similar eye was located and into this a towbar was engaged which passed through a slot in the rear buffer plate of sufficient width to allow the requisite arc of swing for the bar.

The pistons were of the wrought iron variety, forged in one piece with the piston rods, and the remote ends of the rods were screwed into the crossheads. The slide bars were of the single variety, with the bar mounted, as with normal locomotive practice, above the crosshead. Stephenson's link motion was used and the connecting rods were of interest in that only the big ends had separate brass bearings which were 1$\frac{1}{2}$in wide and 2$\frac{1}{4}$in bore. The equivalent figures for the axle bearings were a width of 2in and a bore of 2$\frac{1}{4}$in.

The suspension used on *Tiny* did not consist of the usual leaf or helical springing but instead consisted of pads of India rubber, 10in long, 2$\frac{1}{2}$in wide and 3in deep when fully loaded. The use of this material probably influenced Arthur Percival Heywood in the design of the suspension arrangements on his 15 inch gauge locomotives, particularly as he admitted that there was Ramsbottom influence in his boiler designs.

As Ramsbottom had been the first British main line locomotive engineer to use injectors it was not surprising that *Tiny* was equipped with a No.2 Giffard injector, mounted on the left hand side of the boiler backhead. There was a tendency in the early days of injector usage not to place sole reliance on them for water delivery (this practice continued on a number of standard gauge locomotives built by Manning, Wardle into the present century), and to provide an additional feedpump. *Tiny*, therefore, possessed a feedpump driven from the right hand crosshead. This pump could

An early photograph of circa 1873 showing *Nipper*, with original pattern chimney, alongside the LNWR 8ft 6in single *Cornwall*. This view emphasizes the relative size difference between the two locomotives.

(Courtesy The Railway Magazine)

The first locomotive built for use on the 18 inch gauge lines at Crewe: *Tiny*, designed by John Ramsbottom and built in 1862, stands in the Old Works complex. This view illustrates a number of features of the design, such as the inside frame and cylinder configuration, the forward mounted dome, the disc wheels and the cutting down of the chimney carried out during the locomotive's working life.

(LNWR Society Collection 1401)

not, of course, be operated when the locomotive was stationary and it is suggested that the injector was mainly intended, at least at the design stage, for use when the engine was not in motion. The type of feed-pump used on many Beattie/Beyer, Peacock locomotives on the LSWR during this period was an attempt to circumvent the same problem. The use of a feed-pump and an injector became standard practice on 18 inch gauge locomotives built for War Office home use requirements, right up to World War One. The last 'functional' 18 inch gauge steam locomotive for the home market was fitted with a feedpump and this was not completed until 1920.

The boiler used on *Tiny* was 2ft in outside diameter and 4ft 6¼in in length, being constructed in the form of two rings, butt-jointed together. Owing to the fact that the chassis was of the inside-framed variety, there would not have been sufficient space, given the low pitching of the boiler, for a depending firebox of generous proportions. Such a firebox was precluded in any case by the positioning of the rear axle. The firebox was therefore constructed in a cylindrical pattern with inside dimensions 2ft 5¾in length and 1ft 5¼in diameter.

The design and method of construction of this firebox was to be copied in a number of narrow gauge designs and even some standard gauge locomotives: for example the 15 inch gauge Heywood locomotives and the standard gauge preserved locomotives, LNWR No. 1439 and *Coalbrookdale No.5*. It was not totally new in concept as a peculiar Neilson single cylinder colliery locomotive design with a similar-pattern of

boiler had made its appearance by the late 1850s (ref Ahrons *The British Steam Locomotive 1825-1925*). The rear end of the firebox was flanged over to facilitate attachment to the firebox backhead (which extended from close to the level of the bottom of the main frames to the top of the coal bunker), whilst the front end was attached to the tubeplate. A firebrick bridge was constructed almost immediately behind the tubeplate with a loose brick incorporated at its lowest point. This enabled the ashes trapped in the lower forward part of the firebox space to be removed. The 14 firebars, each 16in long, were supported so as to slope downwards towards the firebrick bridge. The boiler's front tube-plate was 0.625in in thickness and there were 37 tubes of 1¾in outside diameter and 2ft overall length.

A major feature of interest possessed by *Tiny's* boiler was the exceptionally large proportionate size of the steam collector. This was 1 ft in diameter and stood no less than 3ft above the level of the top of the boiler. The reason for the necessity of this provision was the desire to avoid priming in a boiler where the amount of free steam generation and collection space would otherwise have been extremely limited. The proportions of this turret were such that it served not only for steam collection purposes but also to provide water space. The water gauge was mounted in such a position as to suggest that the safe working lower limit of water was almost coincident with the level of the top of the boiler and that the limits of water level fluctuation were largely contained within the turret. The turret was surmounted by a pair of Ramsbottom patent safety valves and the upper internal portion housed the regulator. This consisted of a brass cock activated by a bell-crank connected by a coupling rod to a similar bellcrank. This latter bellcrank was mounted on the forward end of the rod carrying the regulator handle. The other fittings on the turret were the uppermost connection to the gauge glass and the whistle.

The smokebox portion of the boiler barrel was 8½in

14

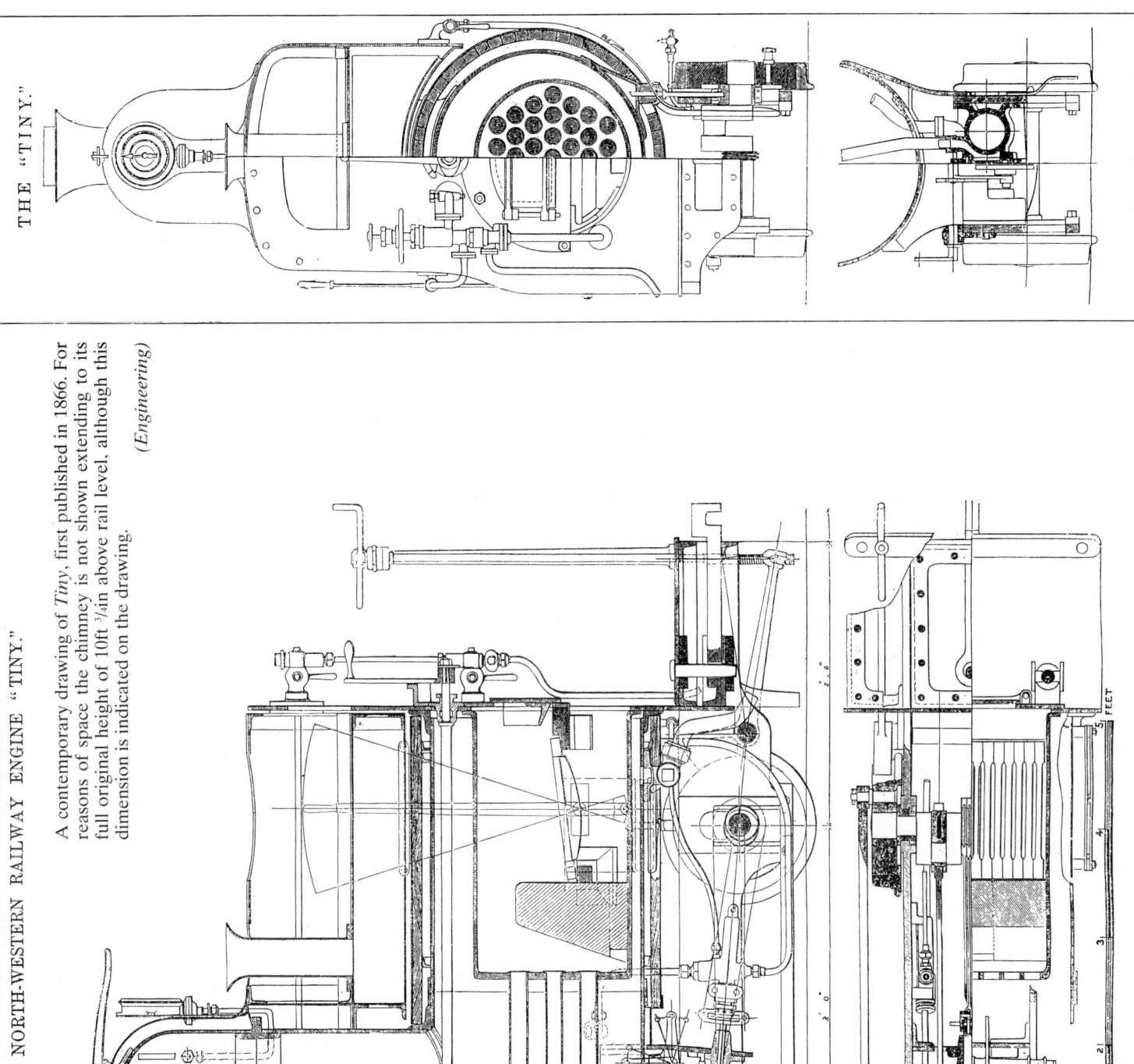

THE LONDON AND NORTH-WESTERN RAILWAY ENGINE "TINY."

A contemporary drawing of *Tiny*, first published in 1866. For reasons of space the chimney is not shown extending to its full original height of 10ft ¾in above rail level, although this dimension is indicated on the drawing.

(Engineering)

THE "TINY."

Nipper seen at Crewe in 1900, with traces of the lining applied to the tank sides. The lid on the tank filler is of the original convex pattern and immediately behind it is the hole for filling the coal bunker in the rear upper portion of the tank assembly. The lifting lug on the side of the boiler has been bent upwards.

(LNWR Society 990)

long and the chimney height, as originally constructed, was 10ft ³/₄in above rail level. The total heating surface was 37.67 square feet, made up of 30.27 square feet for the tubes and 7.40 square feet for the firebox.

Tiny proved so successful in operation at the Old Works that when the Steel Works were opened, there arose a demand for more locomotives of the same type. Over the ensuing few years four similar engines were constructed. In June 1865, *Pet* was completed and by 24th January 1867 *Nipper* and *Topsy* were in the Paint Shop, being outshopped in black livery by the end of the month. The last of this group to be completed was *Midge* in November 1870, but as with *Pet*, there is no record of the engine in the Paint Shop book.

The now preserved locomotive, *Pet* outside the Crewe Steel Foundry in the mid-1920s. Note the missing brake block and generally untidy appearance. All of the Ramsbottom locomotives were withdrawn from service in October 1929 as a direct result of the rationalisation of the narrow gauge trackwork following the reorganisation of Crewe Works by the LMS in the late 1920s. After a period of display at the old BTC museum at Clapham, *Pet* was transferred to the Narrow Gauge Railway Museum at Tywyn in 1967. The engine remains part of the National Collection.

(LNWR Society Collection 1403)

Topsy (partially dismantled) loaded onto a wagon. It is believed that this view was taken after the engine had been withdrawn. The aperture in the rear of the coal bunker can be seen here.

(LNWR Society 1402)

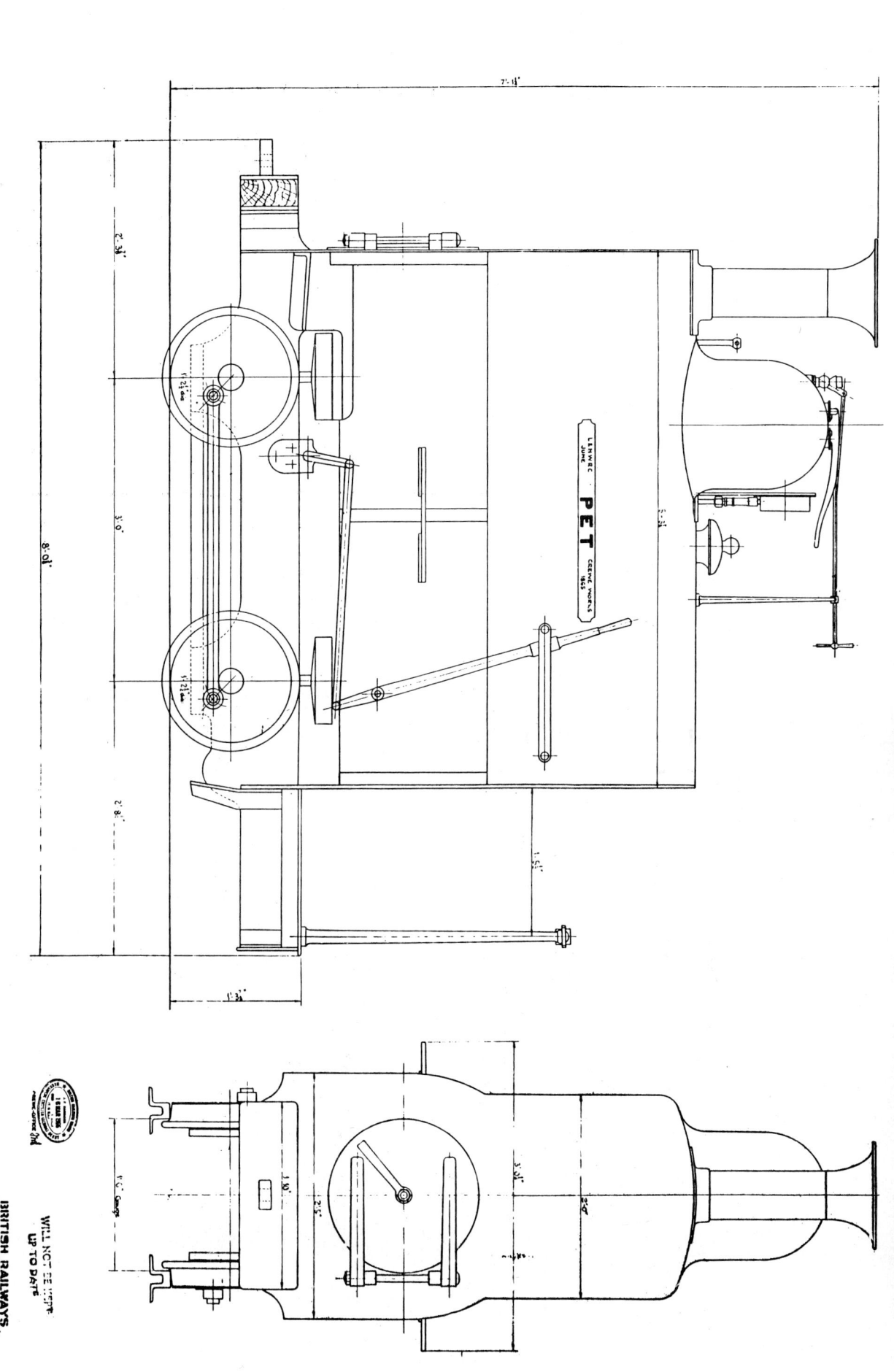

1·6 GAUGE TRAMWAY LOCOMOTIVE PET.

An official diagram of *Pet* prepared after the locomotive was withdrawn from service.

(National Railway Museum)

Unlike their contemporaries on the Festiniog Railway, the Crewe engines underwent few structural alterations over the years. The most obvious change was the cutting down of the chimneys as all of the locomotives had originally been built with chimneys the same height as the original dimension for *Tiny*, so as to direct the smoke and steam away from the drivers' faces. The final reduced height was 7ft 1¼in although drawings survive to show that some engines at least went through an intermediate stage of a chimney height of 7ft 7in. The reduction in chimney height was believed to have been carried out to allow passage through more restricted clearances.

The nameplates carried by the engines were straight as they did not need to follow the arcs of splashers. The lettering was of typical LNWR style, suitably scaled-down in size. No running numbers were allocated. In their early years, the locomotives were well kept with the lining on the tank assemblies being visible on a few (earlier) photographs. In the years between World War One and the reorganization, however, the standard of turnout deteriorated considerably and miscellaneous fittings disappeared. The entire class was withdrawn in October 1929.

The original five locomotives were sufficient for the LNWR company's requirements during the remainder of Mr Ramsbottom's period of office, but a few years later additional motive power was required. Mr F.W. Webb (who had been appointed to the post of Locomotive Superintendent in 1871) ordered the construction of a new locomotive, *Billy*, in 1875. This engine was named after the Senior Chargehand, Mr William Rylance, who supervised a number of special projects at Crewe, including the locomotive's construction. Although an employee of the Company for nearly forty years, until his death on St. Valentine's day in 1887, he always signed job sheets in the name of 'Wm. Rylance and Co.', a fact which led to the erroneous assumption over the years that *Billy* and the later engine, *Dickie* were constructed by an independent concern outside Crewe Works. In reality, both were very much Crewe products and this fact was proclaimed, as with the earlier 18 inch gauge locomotives, on the nameplates.

The design of *Billy* differed radically from the design of the earlier locomotives and the engine possessed a number of interesting features. From the

Nipper seen in the Steel Works in the 1920s in a generally unkempt condition. The lifting lug on the side of the boiler has been bent downwards in contrast to the 1900 view.
(LNWR Society 1399)

Two locomotives outside the Steel Foundry during their final years of operation. Note the missing smokebox door fastener on the leading engine.
(LNWR Society 1404)

The influence of John Ramsbottom's design of locomotive for use at Crewe can be seen in the Sharp, Stewart product (No. 2079 of 1870) for service on the 18 inch gauge line of the Ebbw Vale Steel, Iron & Coal Co. Ltd. The first locomotive completed for the 1 ft 10 in gauge Guinness Brewery tramway by Sharp, Stewart in 1875 was a wider gauge copy of *Little Dorrit*.

(Makers' Official Photograph Courtesy F. Jones).

An engraving of *Billy*, first published in 1876.

(Engineering)

point of view of boiler design, it could be seen that although the arrangements for the brick arch and fire-bars largely followed those of *Tiny*, there was no fire-box tubeplate of the type used on this latter engine. Instead, the cylindrical firebox merged with a hexagonal flue (the precise nature of the joint is unclear) which was fitted with transverse water tubes located between opposite faces of four sides of the hexagonal section. The firebox/flue assembly was bolted to the boiler so as to enable easy removal for cleaning purposes.

At the smokebox end of the flue, which was integral with the remainder, the blastpipe arrangements consisted of three nozzles exhausting into three separate chimneys. These passed through the steam dome into which, as with *Tiny*, the upper pipe from the gauge glass fed. As with the earlier locomotives, Ramsbottom pattern safety valves were used.

The peculiarity of the design did not end with the

flue configuration however, and another interesting feature was the fact that the controls for both the regulator and the reverser were constructed so that they could be operated from platforms at either end of the locomotive. Instead of the normal inside cylinder arrangement found on railway locomotives, a three-cylinder motor of the type produced by the marine engineer, Mr Peter Brotherhood, was fitted between the frames. It has been possible to trace most of the details of the mechanism fitted to *Billy* from Patent Specification 2003 of 1873. This shows a three-cylinder (single acting) engine with a rotary slide valve. As regards the reversing mechanism, it is likely that some variation of what was effectively the footplate controlled slip eccentric principle applied to the later *Dickie* was used. This proposition is also supported by the reverser details given in the Patent Specification.

Another feature of interest is what appears to be a

19

FIG. I.

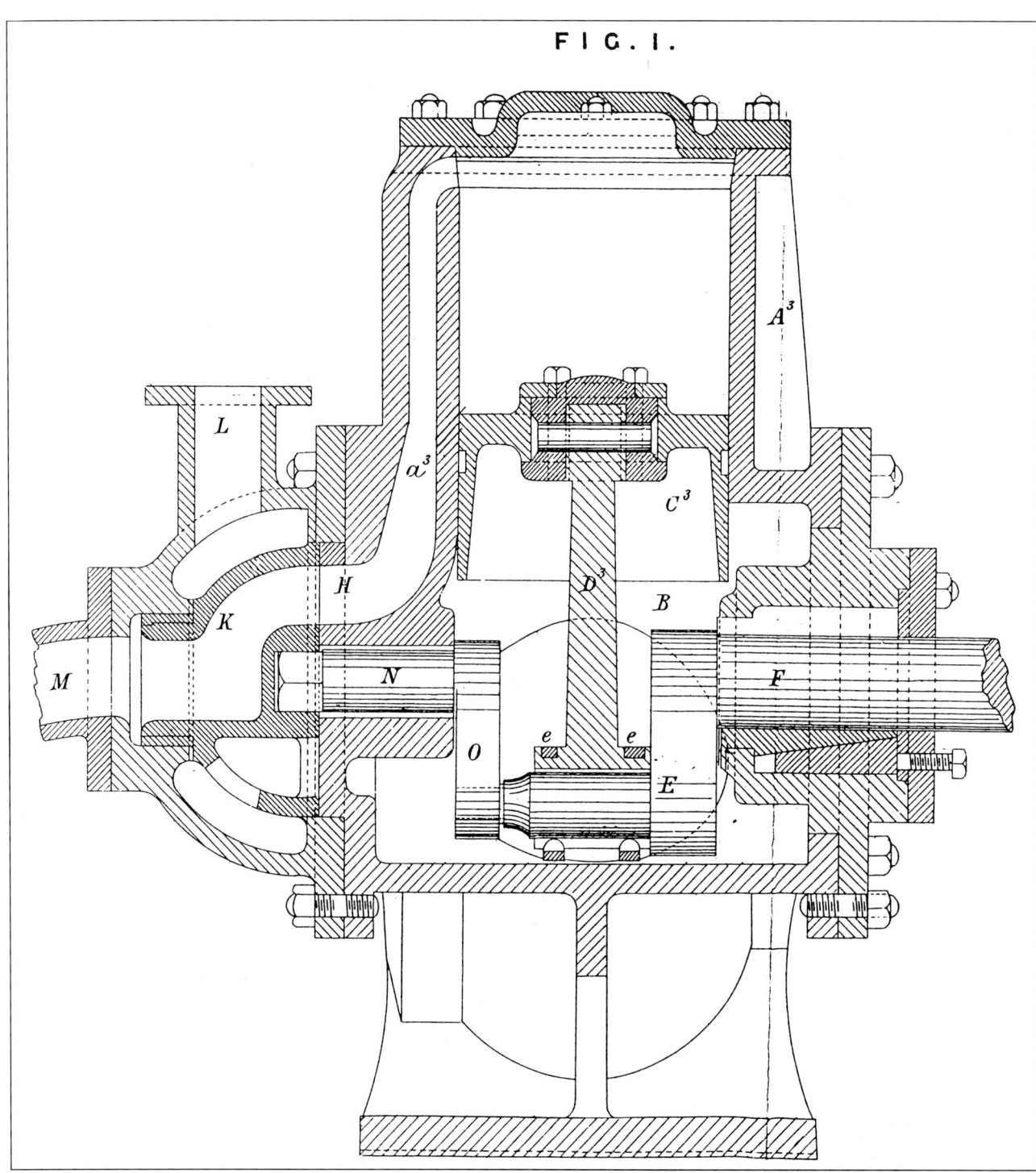

These views show the Brotherhood 3-cylinder motor used in inverted form on *Billy*. The use of a rotary slide valve enabled relative simplicity of construction at the expense of comparitively long steam and exhaust passages. The reversing mechanism can be seen to be an application of the slip eccentric principle with the valve being rotated manually between two stop pins in order to change the direction of rotation of the single crank.

From the diagrams, it can be seen that the engine could only be reversed by means of the handwheel shown. This would have been adequate for use on a stationary engine, as a power unit for a winch, for example, but not for use on most railway locomotives. In order to satisfy the requirement for footplate controlled reversing, a more sophisticated means of reversal was required and in the apparent absence of surviving drawings of *Billy* as built, it is submitted here that a variation of the arm, clutch plate and helical groove system, later

used on *Dickie* was adopted. This suggestion is supported by the appearance of the reversing levers on the original engraving of *Billy* which appeared in *Engineering* in 1876 where their position is consistent with the proposition that the shaft carrying the arm engaging in the clutch plate was mounted transversely rather than longitudinally as on *Dickie*. This clutch plate would have been mounted on a sleeve surrounding the slide valve rod. The sleeve would have engaged, via a helical groove, a dog on the slide valve rod and by this means, reversing would be effected when there was longitudinal displacement of the sleeve caused by pushing one of the reversing levers in the desired direction of motion.

No variation in the expansive working of the steam was possible with the steam motor used on *Billy* and this feature was persisted with on both *Dickie* and its Fox, Walker counterpart constructed for the War Office.

(Patent Specification 2003 of 1873)

FIG. 2.

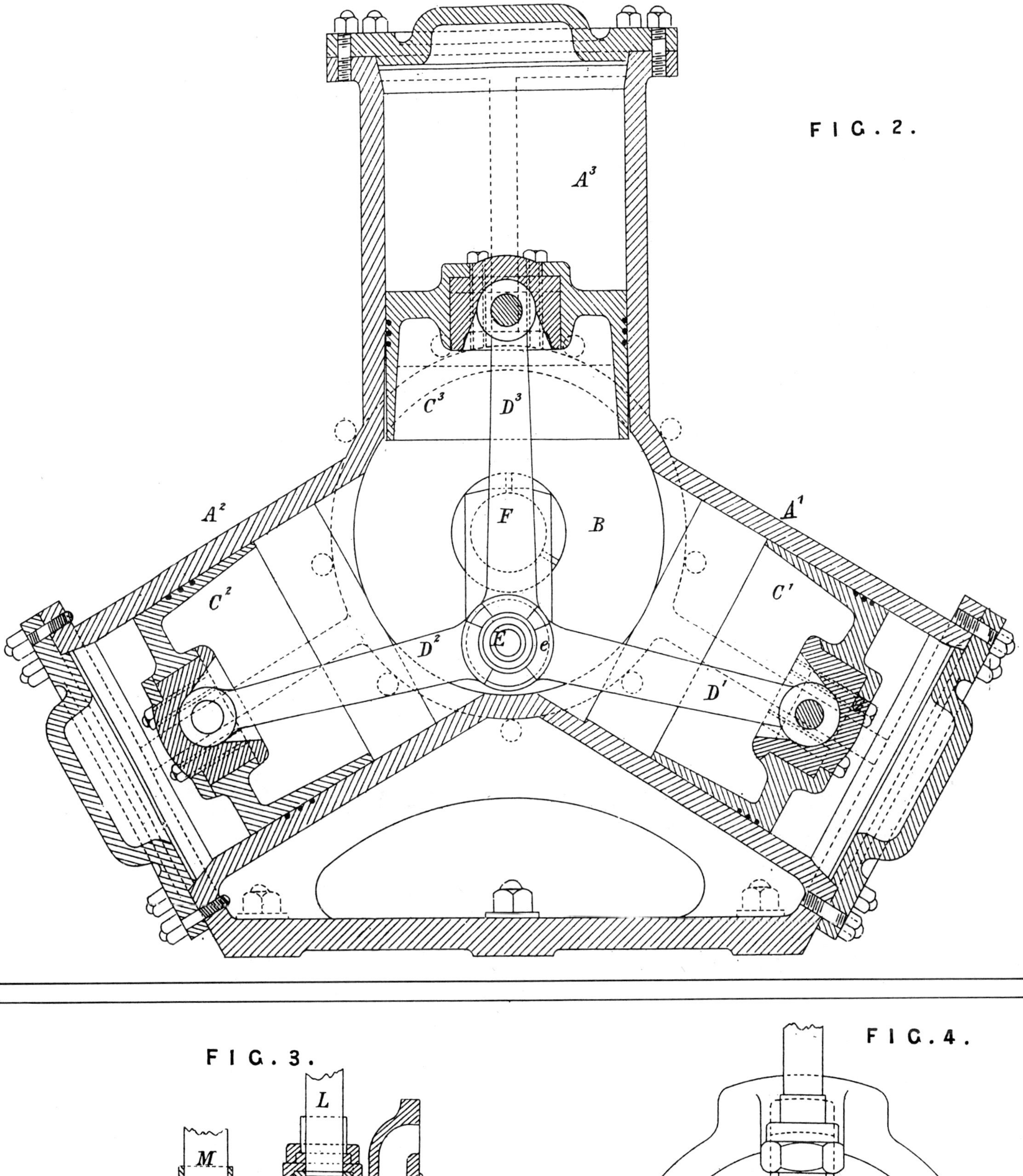

A^3

C^3 D^3

A^2 F B A^1

C^2 C'

D^2 E e

D'

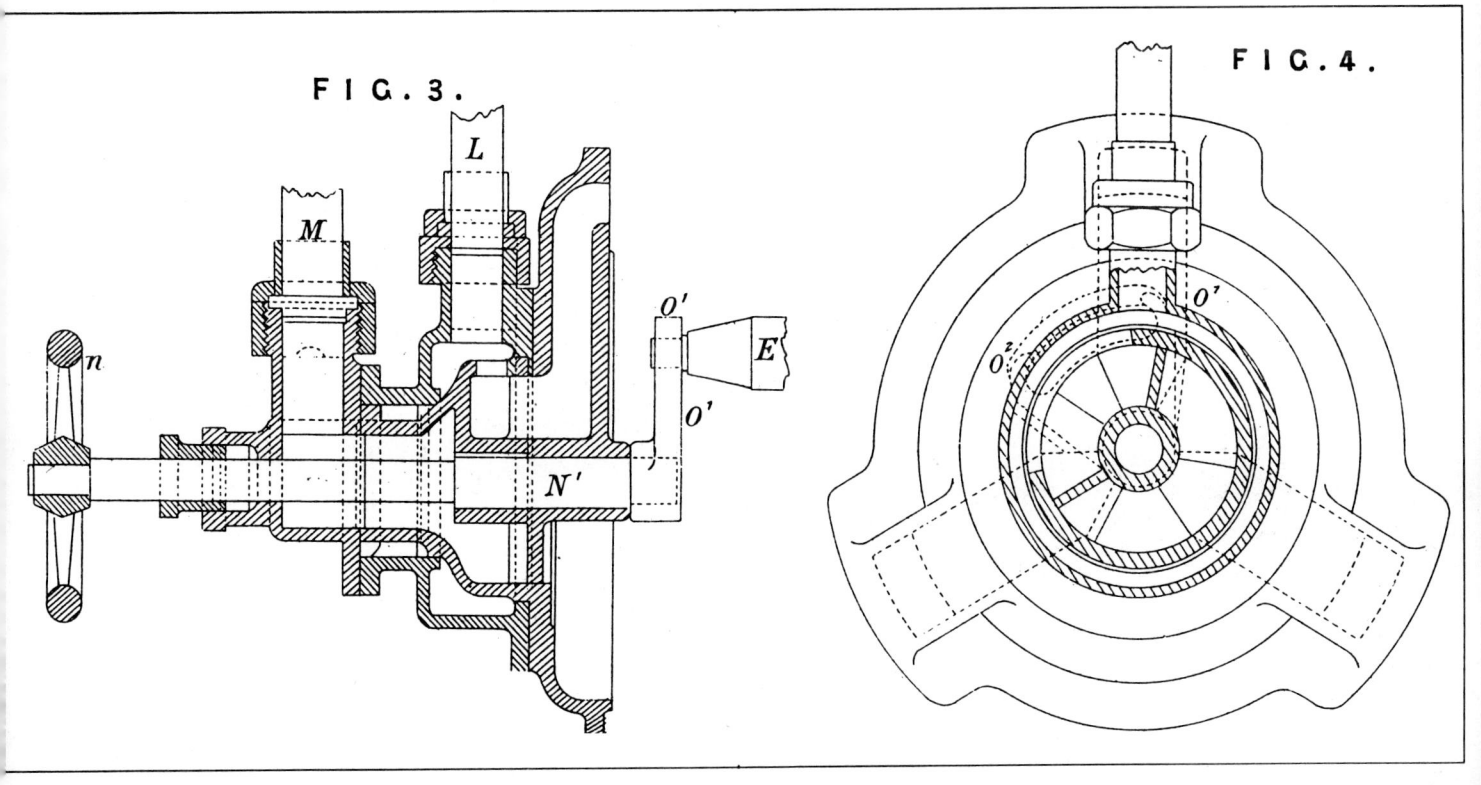

FIG. 3.   FIG. 4.

L

M

n O'

O' E O^2 O'

O'

N'

cylinder end cover visible on the engraving of *Billy*, shown in *Engineering* for 1st September 1876. The position of the cover suggests that the cylinders drove onto a longitudinal shaft (ie perpendicular to the customary axis of drive on a steam locomotive) and that this would account for the difference between the axis of the fulcrum of *Billy's* reverser from that found on the later *Dickie*. The reverser was operated by simply pushing the lever in the desired direction of travel. The water supply for *Billy* was carried in a well tank between the frames and not, as was suggested by the locomotive's outline, in side tanks (the side appendages being merely panels). As with the earlier locomotives, *Billy's* chassis was of the inside framed variety and continuous between the buffer beams.

The length of time which *Billy* ran in original condition cannot apparently be stated for certain, although it was featured in this form in both the Vignes' work of 1878 and in *The Engineer* the following year. There is, however, evidence to suggest that *Billy* was rebuilt shortly afterwards in the fact that two Brotherhood three-cylinder motors were used for experimental purposes in the 1880s for the generation of power for train lighting purposes. It is quite possible that the first of these came from *Billy*, although this is not currently known for certain.

The use of a locomotive which could be driven from either end was not confined to the 18 inch gauge works system and Webb also designed a class of standard gauge shunting locomotives which could also be driven in a similar fashion. These proved to be fairly successful and the last survivor of this class was not withdrawn until 1942.

The second of the Webb 18 inch gauge locomotives, *Dickie* was completed in May 1876, approximately ten months after *Billy*. The engine was similar to its predecessor in boiler, superstructure and wheel details but, as has been mentioned, differed considerably from the point of view of cylinder and motion design. Instead of the Brotherhood motor, two outside cylinders of 5½in bore and 6in stroke were fitted at the smokebox end. The boiler pressure for *Dickie* was 90 psi, that for *Billy* was not apparently recorded.

The additional feature of interest about *Dickie* was the design of valve motion. The function normally performed by eccentrics was performed by small flycranks on the extreme ends of a countershaft. From this countershaft, in the space between the frames, projected a short bar in a perpendicular direction so as to engage in a helical groove in a collar surrounding the bar. Attached to this collar were a grooved clutch plate assembly and a wide spur gear which meshed with

Billy as rebuilt to conform to the basic configuration of *Dickie*. The steam brake is of interest and may have been added partly to obscure the aperture in the main frame originally necessitated by the 3-cylinder motor. The suspension, at least in the engine's rebuilt form, was by means of four Thompson's cushion springs located in recesses cast in the axlebox guides. The cast iron tram-plates used for some of the 18 inch gauge system are visible in this view.
(Dutton Collection/LNWR Society 9954)

In May 1888 *Dickie* was involved in trials for canal boat haulage on the towpath of the Middlewich branch of the Ellesmere & Chester Canal at Cholmondeston near Nantwich. The trials took place along a mile length of 18 inch gauge track with the engine hauling a maximum of eight boats. With four loaded boats in tow a speed of 7 mph was achieved, although there was a tendency for the boats to veer towards the canal bank. This was aggravated by the attachment of the tow-rope to the bow-stud of the leading boat, rather than the mast-stud.
(LNWR Society 846)

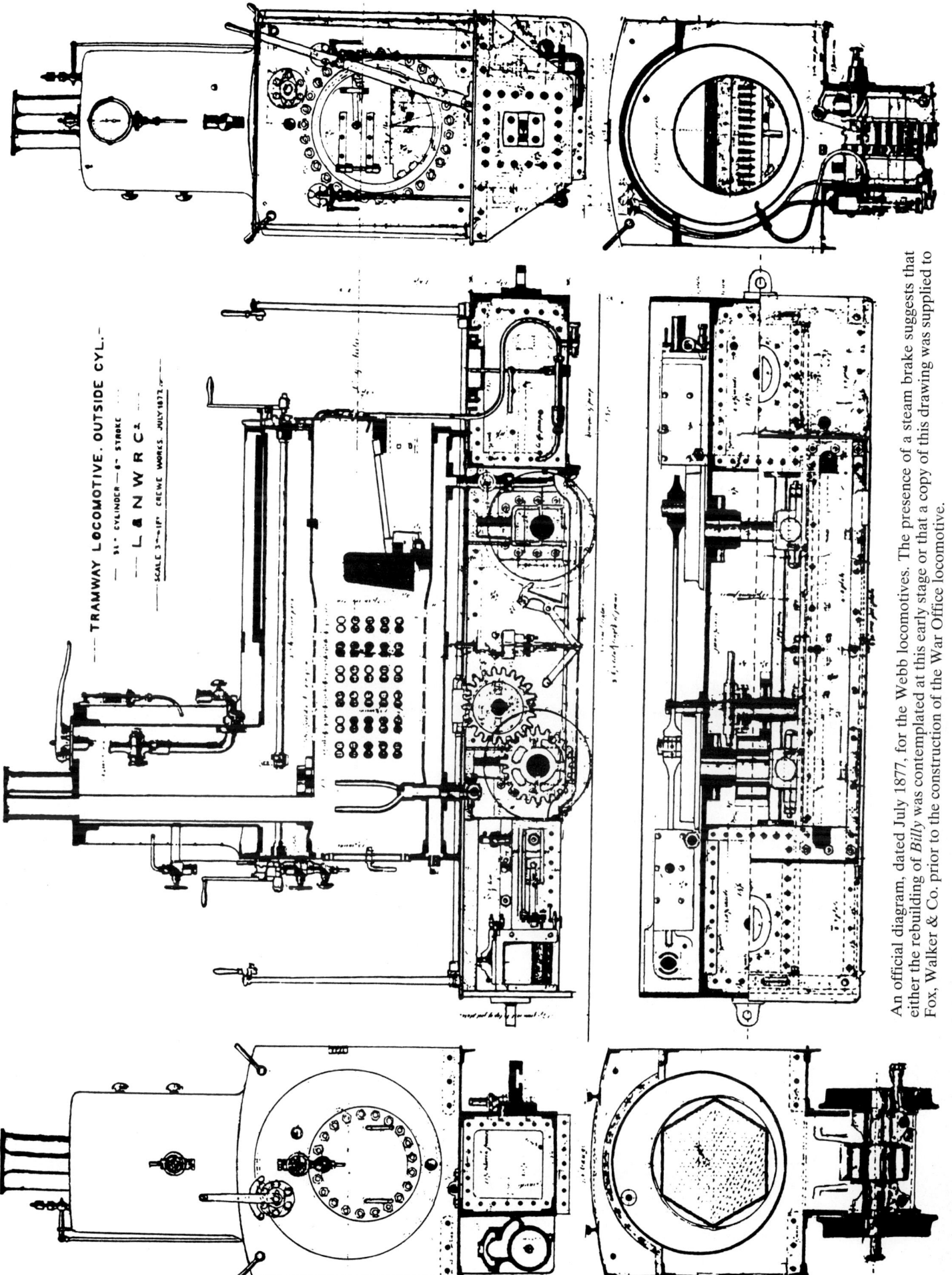

--- TRAMWAY LOCOMOTIVE. OUTSIDE CYL. ---

9½" CYLINDER — 6" STROKE

L & N W Rᶜ

SCALE 3—1FT CREWE WORKS JULY 1877

An official diagram, dated July 1877, for the Webb locomotives. The presence of a steam brake suggests that either the rebuilding of *Billy* was contemplated at this early stage or that a copy of this drawing was supplied to Fox, Walker & Co. prior to the construction of the War Office locomotive.

(LNWR Society)

another spur gear on the front driving axle. Engaging in the groove of the clutch plate assembly was an arm projecting from a long reversing shaft which was fitted with a lever at either end of the locomotive. Movement of the reversing levers from one position to the other therefore transmitted rotational motion to the countershaft and altered the position of the flycranks relative to the main cranks, but as with a slip eccentric, no variations in cutoff from either extreme allowed by the reverser could be obtained.

It is thought that *Dickie* was constructed for experimental comparisons with the cylinder arrangement used on *Billy* and that this was the reason behind the retention of the triple blastpipe in *Dickie's* boiler/smokebox design. Be that as it may, *Billy* was altered to match the chassis arrangement of *Dickie* with the exception of the addition of steam braking. As with the Ramsbottom engines, *Dickie* was withdrawn in October 1929, but *Billy* lingered on in the Steel Works until scrapped in 1931.

The replacement for *Billy* came in the form of the first diesel locomotive to be employed by the LMS. This was constructed by Hudswell, Clarke & Co. Ltd,

of Leeds as their No. D563 of 1930. This interesting machine was fitted with a McLaren-Benz three-cylinder engine rated at 20hp at 800 rpm. Transmission was effected via a multiple disc clutch, a Bostock & Bramley gearbox, a worm reduction and a final drive via a jackshaft to the wheels which were rod-coupled.

After the abandonment of the 18 inch gauge line in the Steel Works, the diesel locomotive, which carried the name *Crewe*, was transferred to the Horwich Works system which, as we shall see, retained locomotive haulage for more than three further decades, into the mid-1960s.

As with the Ramsbottom locomotive design, the Webb locomotive exemplified by *Dickie* was also copied and in 1878 the War Office ordered such an engine from the Bristol firm of Fox, Walker & Co. This engine (builder's No.386) probably saw service on an Irish fortification railway, as will be considered in a later section. From the technical point of view, there is little that can be said about the engine that did not apply to *Dickie* but it should be noted at this stage that its construction at Crewe was precluded by a court injunction taken out by the Locomotive Manufacturers

Billy seen towards the end of its working days in the Steel Foundry area. By this time the engine was in a bad state of repair having lost the cylinder covers, front driving controls and front handrail. This view also shows a loaded cast iron wagon, emphasising the preference for this type of wagon for use involving locomotive haulage in most instances. The engine appears to be propelling wagons in a 'push-pull' mode.
(LNWR Society Collection 1400)

A view of the right hand side of *Billy* taken at the same time as the previous illustration and showing what appears to be a crankpin-driven feedpump worked from the rear axle. *Billy* was finally withdrawn from service in January 1931, being replaced for a short time by a diesel locomotive.
(LNWR Society Collection 1398)

The Hudswell, Clarke diesel-mechanical locomotive (No. D563 of 1930) that replaced *Billy* in the Steel Works in 1931. After a short spell at Crewe, this locomotive moved to the works at Horwich where it survived until replaced by another diesel-mechanical locomotive in 1957.

(Maker's Official Photograph Courtesy R. Redman)

HUDSWELL CLARKE & CO. LTD., RAILWAY FOUNDRY, LEEDS.

D.20

DIESEL LOCOMOTIVE BUILT FOR LONDON, MIDLAND & SCOTTISH RAILWAY CO.

Association, preventing locomotive building by railway companies for external sale. The Fox, Walker engine is illustrated in an accompanying illustration which shows that it was fitted, along with the rebuilt *Billy* with steam braking.

Throughout the period of operation of the 18 inch gauge lines at Crewe works, the only type of rolling stock in use was of the four-wheeled variety for the conveyance of goods. There were never any bogie vehicles in the normal sense, nor was the conveyance of passengers over the narrow gauge lines officially sanctioned, although, as we have seen, this happened on the hand-worked Deviation Works system.

The method of haulage was exclusively by means of the use of towbars and no conventional buffing gear or link couplings were ever used. Two types of towbar were in use, one of which consisted of a bar of square cross-section with a forged vertical pin at each end. The bar was cranked so as to facilitate location of an

A typical wooden-framed wagon of 1866 adapted to carry a support for a boiler.

(LNWR Society Collection)

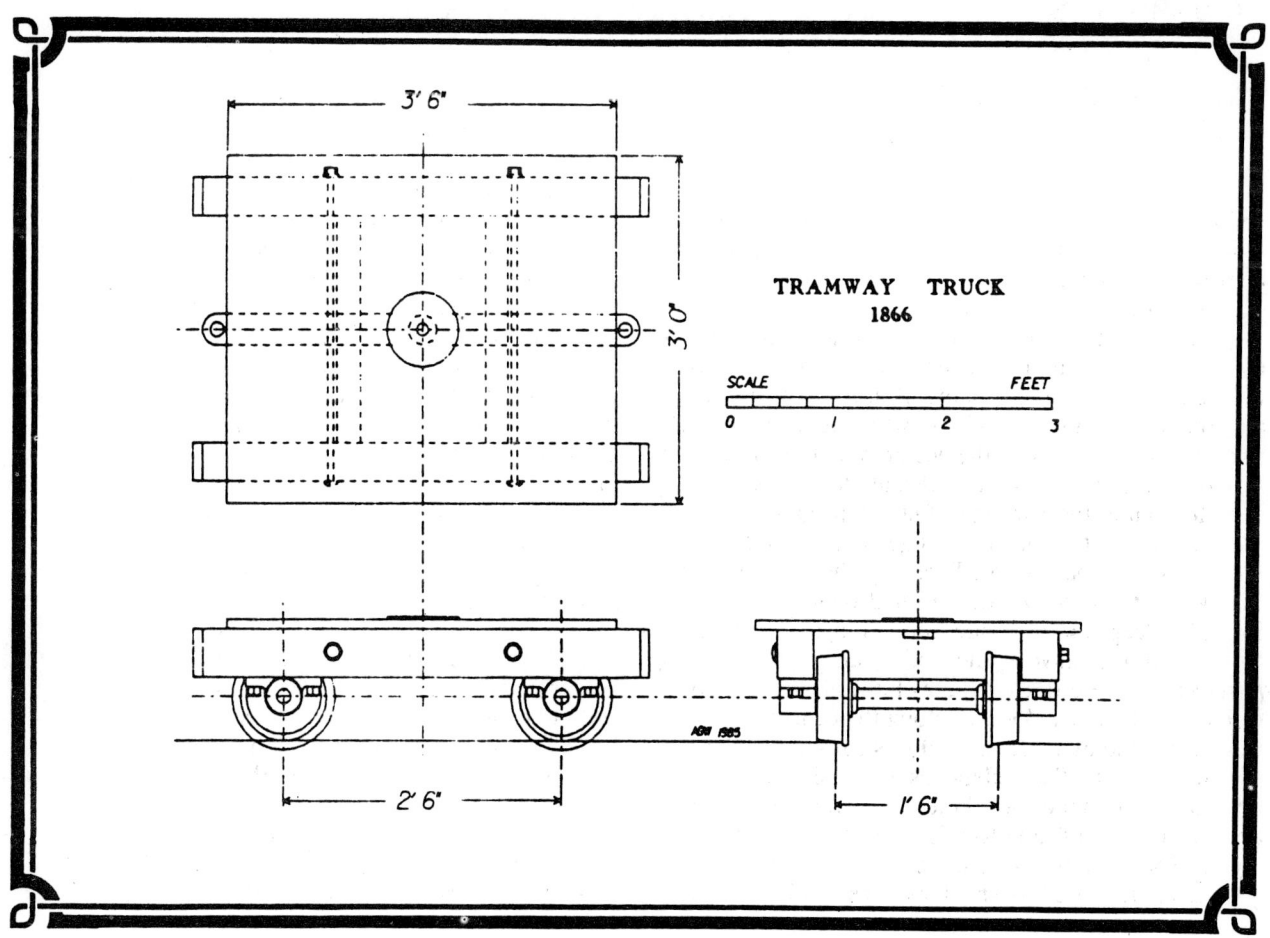

3' 6"

3' 0"

TRAMWAY TRUCK
1866

SCALE
0   1   2   3   FEET

2' 6"

1' 6"

25

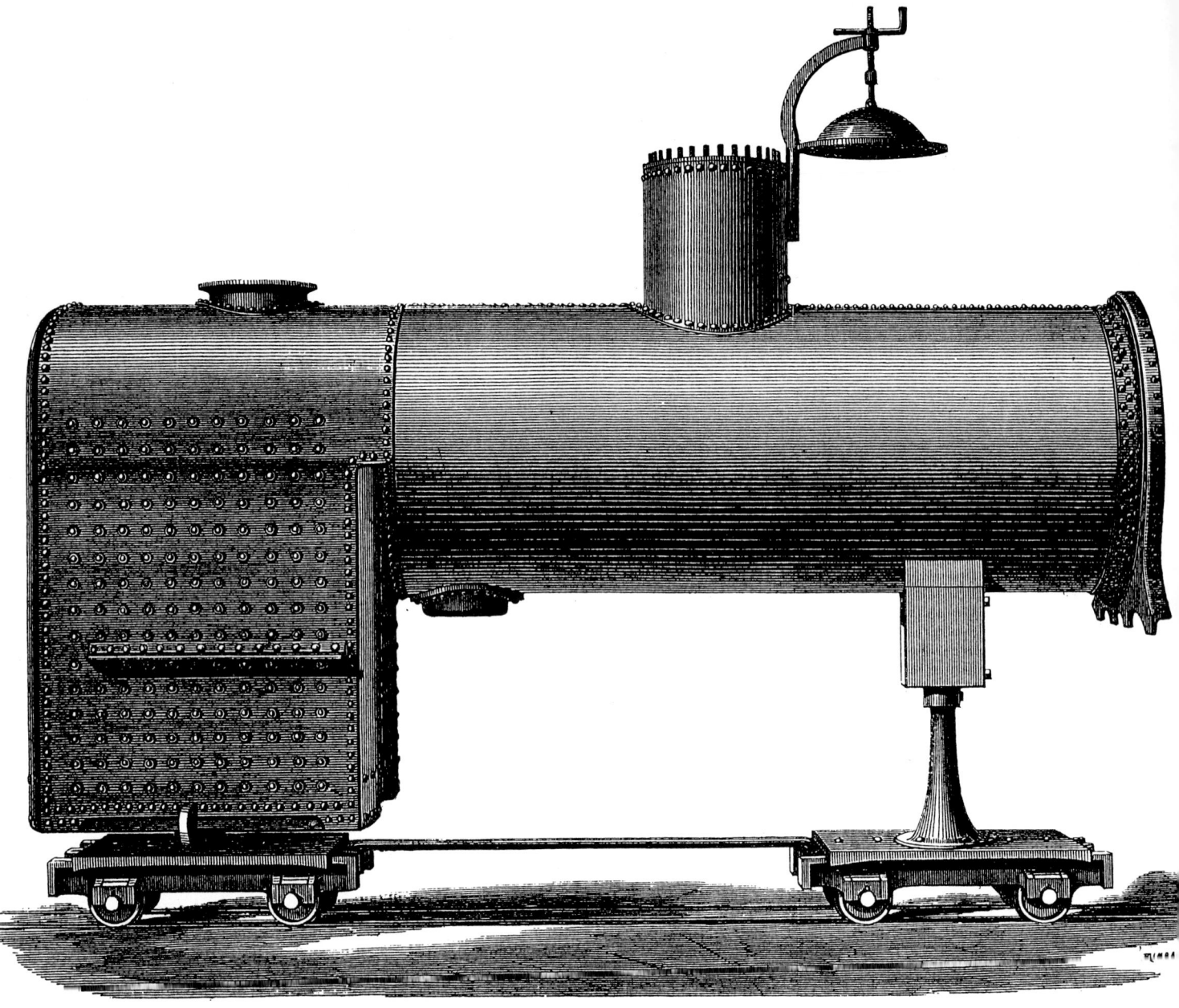

An engraving originally published in 1879 showing two cast iron wagons adapted to carry a locomotive boiler.

(Engineering)

end pin in the eye provided on a locomotive. The other type was simply a length of round bar with its ends bent downwards at 90 degrees. This variety of coupler was used for connections between wagons.

There were two basic varieties of wagon used on the Crewe Works system. The first type was primarily of wooden construction and some of these were fitted with an iron chequer plate platform with a central hole. The purpose of this hole was the accommodation of a cradle (for the firebox end) or a pedestal (for the smokebox end) to enable the carriage of standard gauge locomotive boilers on two narrow gauge wagons, linked by a long round section towbar. Typically, the main frames of this small variety of wooden framed wagon were 4ft 4in long, 5in deep and 4in wide. Steel hoops were screwed to the extreme ends of the main frames for stiffening purposes as these ends acted as buffers. A longitudinal iron or steel bar was located along the centre line of the wagon and the extreme ends of this bar carried the eyes for the towbar. The axleboxes were simple cast-iron bushes with an uppermost hole connecting to an oblique bore in the main frame to allow access for the lubricating oil. Solid cast iron disc wheels were used which were 8½in diameter, and the wheelbase was 2ft 6in.

Two hand-pushed variations on the above theme were found in the Deviation Works 1981. One of these had a wheelbase of 2ft 1½in and the corresponding dimension for the other was 2ft 10in There was also a larger type of wooden framed wagon employed in the Sawmill and Joiners' Shop section of the Deviation Works system. The main frames were 5ft 6in long, 10in deep and 3in wide. As with the smaller wooden framed wagons, the ends of the frames were strengthened so that they could serve as buffers. It was possible to fit detachable sides on these wagons, which were fitted with cast steel wheels sporting cruciform section spokes. The oiling holes in the sides of the main frames were equipped with hinged metal caps, presumably to exclude sawdust and wood shavings from the bearings.

The second major variety of wagon to be found on the narrow gauge system was essentially a cast iron version of the smaller type of wooden framed wagon and these could also be used for the transportation of boilers, although, as will be considered later, it is unlikely that this practice was commonplace. One known illustration exists of two Crewe wagons in this capacity. Official drawings of this type of wagon have recently been unearthed in the National Railway Museum's Drawings Collection.

The locomotive-worked sections of the Crewe narrow gauge system passed into history largely as a result of the inevitable rationalisation which followed the reorganization of the Works in the late 1920s. The general run down state of maintenance which prevailed amongst the locomotive stock during this period may also have been a factor which influenced the decision on the part of the LMS authorities not to proceed with locomotive working on the 18 inch gauge system. In the end it was the Deviation Works layout, which remained hand-worked throughout its entire existence, that was to remain in use for the longest period. Most traces of the old narrow gauge system at Crewe Works have now been eliminated although a number of relics are preserved elsewhere. The most significant of these is the second of the Ramsbottom locomotives, *Pet* of 1865 which was laid aside in the Paint Shop after withdrawal in 1929 and officially preserved.

The survival of the four-way point from the Deviation Works has already been noted and in addition, five wagons and a number of track sections, both of the rectangular and of the Vignoles' pattern, survive in private hands, currently awaiting a suitable display venue. It is unfortunate that *Billy* was not retained after withdrawal as an example of the Webb design of locomotive, along with a cast iron wagon. The saving of these items would have preserved a completely representative collection of equipment used on a system which greatly assisted in the commercial advancement of the narrow gauge steam railway during the formative years of the nineteenth century.

The Horwich Works System

The Crewe Works system inspired other 18 inch gauge lines at a number of sites elsewhere in the United Kingdom. Although chronologically this represents a forward leap of over two decades, it is appropriate to follow the discussion of the Crewe system with a consideration of the railway which was in many respects its closest copy, namely that at the Horwich Works of the Lancashire & Yorkshire Railway.

The Horwich Works 18 inch gauge system first came into being when the Works itself was opened in 1887 under the direction of the Locomotive Superintendent, Mr John F. Aspinall. By 23rd September 1887, when the new Works were featured in *The Engineer*, approximately 2³/₄ miles of 18 inch gauge works railway had been completed on the site. Almost a decade later a plan of the Works, which accompanied an Aspinall Paper for the Institution of Civil Engineers, showed the 1896 course of the narrow gauge system. There was also a drawing in *The Engineer* showing the design of pointwork used on the narrow gauge system.

As with parts of the Crewe, Chatham Dockyard and Woolwich Arsenal systems, the pointwork consisted of a cast iron body with blades which could be operated by an engine driver, or an assistant, with a wooden pole. The Horwich system was discussed shortly after its opening in a Paper of 1888 prepared for the Institution of Mechanical Engineers which was primar-

ily concerned with the tramways serving the Guinness Brewery in Dublin. In his contribution to the proceedings, Mr Aspinall stated that the permanent way employed on the 18 inch gauge lines was of a calibre of 24lb/yd and that the maximum radius of curvature on his narrow gauge system was 13ft. His views were of interest in that they displayed a considerable degree of influence on the part of Ramsbottom, and that the limitation on the maximum radius of curve which could be employed, was a major factor in the determination of the choice of gauge, an observation made on several occasions before and since. In addition to the 24lb/yd rail mentioned by Aspinall, it should also be mentioned that much of the internal straight portions of track consisted of cast iron tram-plates of similar nature to the pointwork depicted in *The Engineer*.

Unlike the practice followed at Crewe of constructing works railway locomotives within the railway's own shops, Mr Aspinall decided initially upon the use of a private contractor to supply locomotives for use on the Horwich system. The choice fell on the Gorton firm of Beyer, Peacock & Co. Ltd and in 1887 they supplied three 18 inch gauge locomotives for use at Horwich in addition to constructing a further example for their own use. The three locomotives supplied to Horwich bore the names *Dot*, *Robin* and *Wren*, illustrating a very similar naming policy for works locomotives to

A cast iron point of the type used at Horwich. The basic similarity to the early design used at Chatham Dockyard will be noticed, although there are two important differences. The first of these is that the body of the point is cast in one piece and the second is that the blades are actually linked by a tie-bar situated beneath the level of the rails.

(The Engineer)

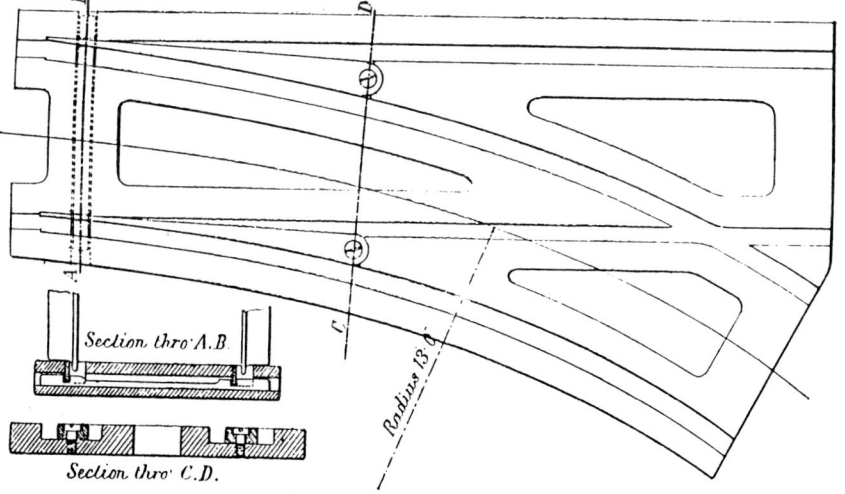

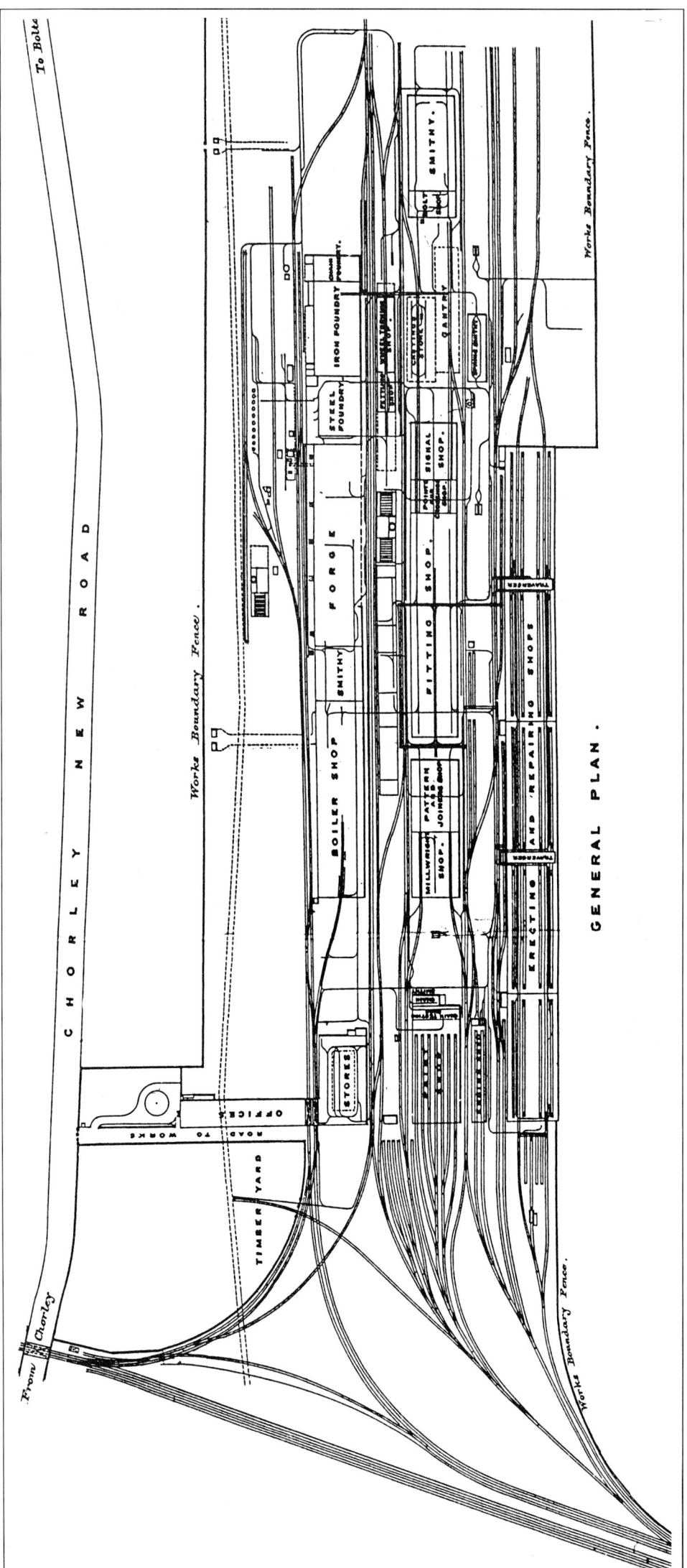

GENERAL PLAN.

Horwich Works as illustrated in Aspinall's Paper for the Institution of Civil Engineers in 1897. This plan shows the course of both the standard and narrow gauge lines in the Works area, (the thin single black line denotes the narrow gauge configuration). At this time the narrow gauge track extended to approximately 6½ miles and five locomotives were in use.

(The Institution of Civil Engineers)

the one that was in use at Crewe.

So successful did the 18 inch gauge system prove to be in use at Horwich that it was considerably enlarged over the ensuing three decades and at its peak, around the time of the First World War, there was a track length of approximately 7 miles in use. As with Crewe, however, the period following the cessation of hostilities in 1918 brought a protracted era of decline and by 1948, the maximum compliment of eight steam locomotives had been reduced to one, in company with the Hudswell, Clarke diesel transferred from the Steel Works at Crewe. In 1957, the Hudswell diesel was replaced by another from Ruston & Hornsby & Co.

Ruston & Hornsby 416214 of 1957, 4-wheel diesel, better known by its Horwich Works running number, ZM32. It is seen here when still retaining its original black and yellow 'wasp' livery, but following re-gauging to 2ft. It is now preserved in BR blue livery at the Narrow Gauge Railway Centre, Gloddfa Ganol.

(Peter Nicholson)

Ltd given the number ZM32, but although the surviving steam locomotive was not withdrawn from service until 1962, the remaining parts of the narrow gauge system soon fell into disuse. The Horwich system earned one important distinction however, in giving BR its smallest working steam locomotive.

The Locomotives and Stock Used at Horwich

The basic boiler configuration of the Horwich locomotives was similar to that used at Crewe in the fact that a non-depending firebox was used. The similarity of the Horwich boilers to those of Ramsbottom's *Tiny* was referred to in the Institution of Mechanical Engineers 1888 Paper concerning brewery railways, but it is significant to note that Aspinall declined to refer to this pattern of boiler as a 'Ramsbottom' boiler. The reason for this refusal was that it is often difficult to trace the true originator of any particular idea, a problem often encountered by railway historians today.

The design of the locomotives used at Horwich in their original condition is depicted by the earliest official diagram, and by the simplified plan prepared for the Institution of Mechanical Engineers in 1888. The boiler diameter was 2ft 3in outside and the overall length between backhead and smokebox front plate was 5ft 2in. The boiler and smokebox barrels were combined in a single structure and a flange on the rear of the firebox provided the means of securing the latter to the backhead. The iron firebox was 2ft 3 in long and 1ft 5in inside diameter and there were 55 tubes of 1.375in in outside diameter.

The boiler was fed by a single injector mounted on the rear left hand side of the footplate, just behind the backhead. The sole reliance on a single injector on

An official photograph of *Robin*, a Beyer, Peacock locomotive of 1887 as originally built for the Horwich Works system. Note the lifting lugs (as per Crewe practice) on the sides of the boiler, the pressure gauge and steam manifold behind the dome and the solitary injector on the left hand side of the footplate.

Dot and *Robin* were builder's Nos 2823 and 2824, whilst *Wren* is No 2825.

(L&YR Society Courtesy J.B. Hodgson)

these locomotives is of interest, particularly when comparison is made with the arrangement adopted on the LNWR's *Billy* (rebuilt) and *Dickie* some years earlier. It should be noted, however, that these last-named locomotives, as depicted in the 1877 Crewe diagram previously described, each possessed a crankpin-driven feed pump. No photographs confirming the fitting of two injectors to either *Billy* or *Dickie* have ever been traced. A view of *Billy* towards the end of its working days shows that no injector was fitted to the left hand side of the engine at this time and the Vignes' Technical Study, compiled in 1877 states that *Dickie* had only one injector as built.

One feature of the Horwich trio which differed from the other Beyer, Peacock 18 inch gauge locomotive (No.2817) was that whilst the latter was provided with an ornate capped chimney as built, the Horwich engines were constructed with chimneys of the plain stovepipe pattern. The method of operation of the blower pipe was unorthodox in that the control handle was not located at the driver's end of the locomotive, as was to be expected, but instead it was placed a few inches behind the chimney. The backhead fitting carrying the firehole door was of cast iron and a single water gauge was fitted. The lower mounting of this gauge was fitted onto the right hand side of the backhead. A steam manifold was located behind the dome and this component facilitated steam distribution to the injector, pressure gauge and steam brake. Unlike the basic design of Mr Ramsbottom's locomotive, *Tiny*, the dome on the Horwich engine did not act as an additional water space but purely as a steam collector. The dome was surmounted by a pair of Ramsbottom safety valves and a whistle.

As a result of the use of a non-depending firebox it was possible, as with the Crewe Works locomotives, to utilise a set of main frames which were continuous between buffer beams and mounted between the inner faces of the wheels. It was decided, however, not to copy *Tiny*, which had inside cylinders and link motion, and it was also felt unwise to directly follow the lead set by *Dickie* which combined outside cylinders with a valve mechanism not allowing for variable expansion.

The decision was therefore taken to combine the best features of the two main Crewe designs and adopt an outside cylindered configuration using a link motion, in this case the Allan straight link variety rather than the Stephenson/Howe motion found on *Tiny*. The cylinders used on the Horwich Works locomotives were 5in bore with a stroke of 6in and the wheels were 1ft 4¼in diameter. The boiler pressure was somewhat greater than that used on *Dickie*, namely 170 psi.

The contribution made by Mr Aspinall to the 1888 Institution of Mechanical Engineers Paper was fairly detailed in its nature and a number of additional dimensions were given. The wheelbase of the Horwich locomotives was 2ft 9in, the length of the main frames between buffer beams was 7ft 4¼in and the extreme width over buffer beams was 3ft. The tube heating surface was given as 36.12 sq ft and that of the firebox was 10.42 sq ft. The grate area was 1.78 sq ft.

The steam brake cylinder was located on the right hand side of the locomotive below footplate level and immediately forward of the well tank. The piston in the brake cylinder actuated a rod whose motion would cause radial displacement of the intermediate brake lever about a low set fulcrum. The rod actuating the brakes on the rear axle was connected to the intermediate lever above this fulcrum whereas its counterpart for the front brakes was connected below the main fulcrum. The steam brake cylinder was single acting and the brakes were returned to the off position by means of a helical spring.

The original three locomotives sufficed for the needs of Horwich Works for approximately four years, until enlargement of the narrow gauge network necessitated additions to the available motive power. In 1891, therefore, two further locomotives were constructed, bearing the names *Wasp* and *Fly*. *Wasp* is illustrated in its original condition. The major policy change which had occurred since 1887 was the decision on the part of the L&YR to construct these two locomotives at Horwich, rather than to place a repeat order with Beyer, Peacock. Apart from comparatively minor details, however, the design of *Wasp* and *Fly* was identical to that of the Beyer, Peacock locomotives. These loco-

An official works photograph showing the left hand side of Beyer, Peacock 0-4-0WT *Dot* (No. 2817 of 1887) which was constructed for the Maker's internal 18 inch gauge system. The design was substantially similar to that of the L&YR locomotives but differed with regard to certain small details.

(A. Neale Collection)

An official photograph of the right hand side of Beyer, Peacock No. 2817 showing the second injector, dual hand and steam braking, coal bunker and ornate chimney.

(A. Neale Collection)

A front three quarter view of Beyer, Peacock No. 2817 showing the smokebox door.

(A. Neale Collection)

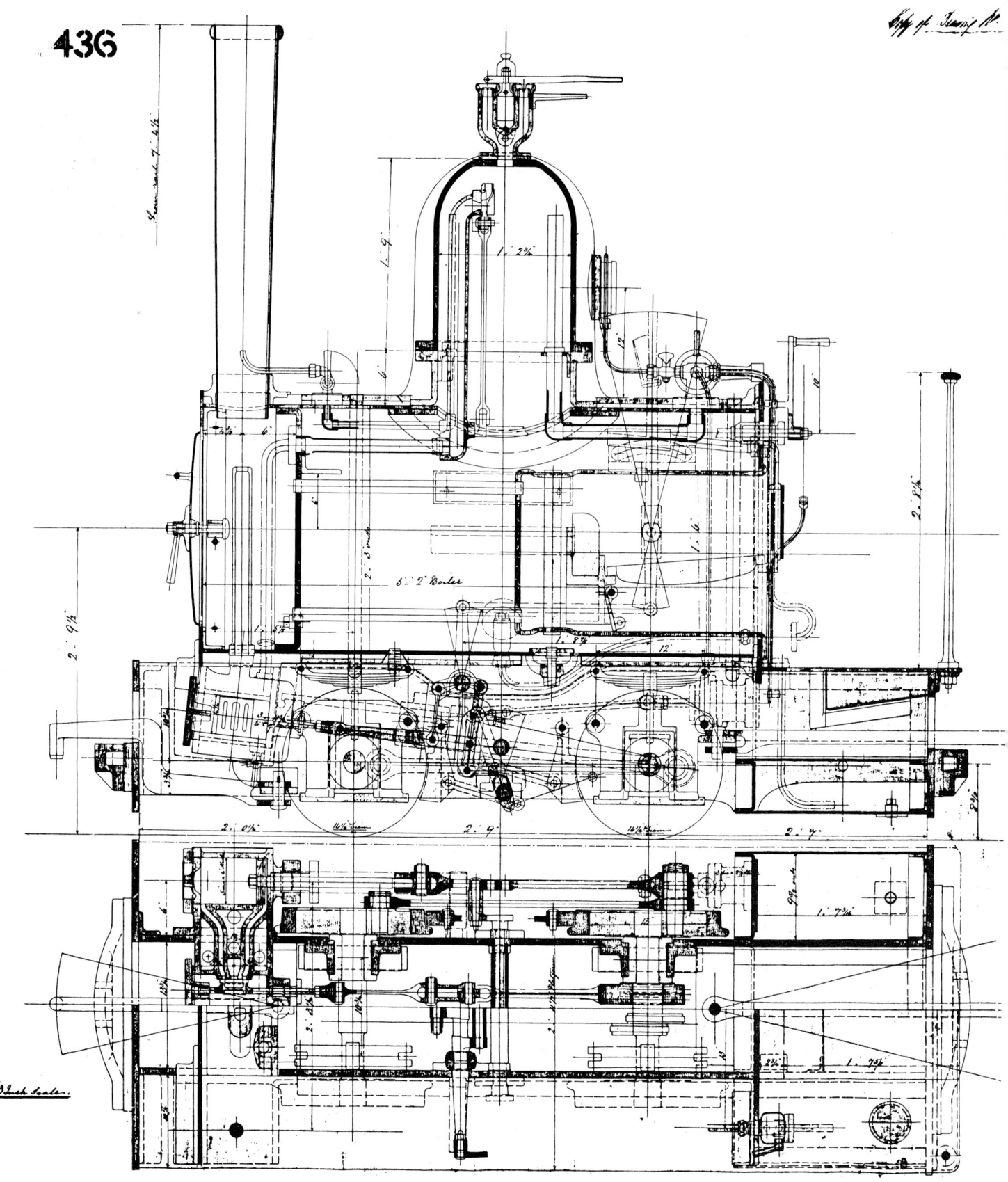

An official diagram of the Horwich 18 inch gauge locomotives in their original state before the addition of saddle tanks and auxiliary tenders. It is possible that the last three members of the class to be constructed carried saddle tanks as built.

(National Railway Museum, York)

tives were followed by another pair in 1899, *Mouse* and *Midget* and by the last representative of the class, *Bee* in 1901.

Operating experience had shown by this time that the major shortcomings of the design in its original form were that insufficient storage spaces were provided both from the point of view of water and coal. It was therefore decided to increase the water capacity from the original 26½ gallons by the fitting of an additional 50 gallon saddle tank. The design of saddle tank was arranged so as to cover the portion of the boiler/smokebox assembly forward of the steam manifold. The tank itself was made in a flat sided configuration so as to take full advantage of the maximum permitted width of 3ft. From surviving evidence, it is

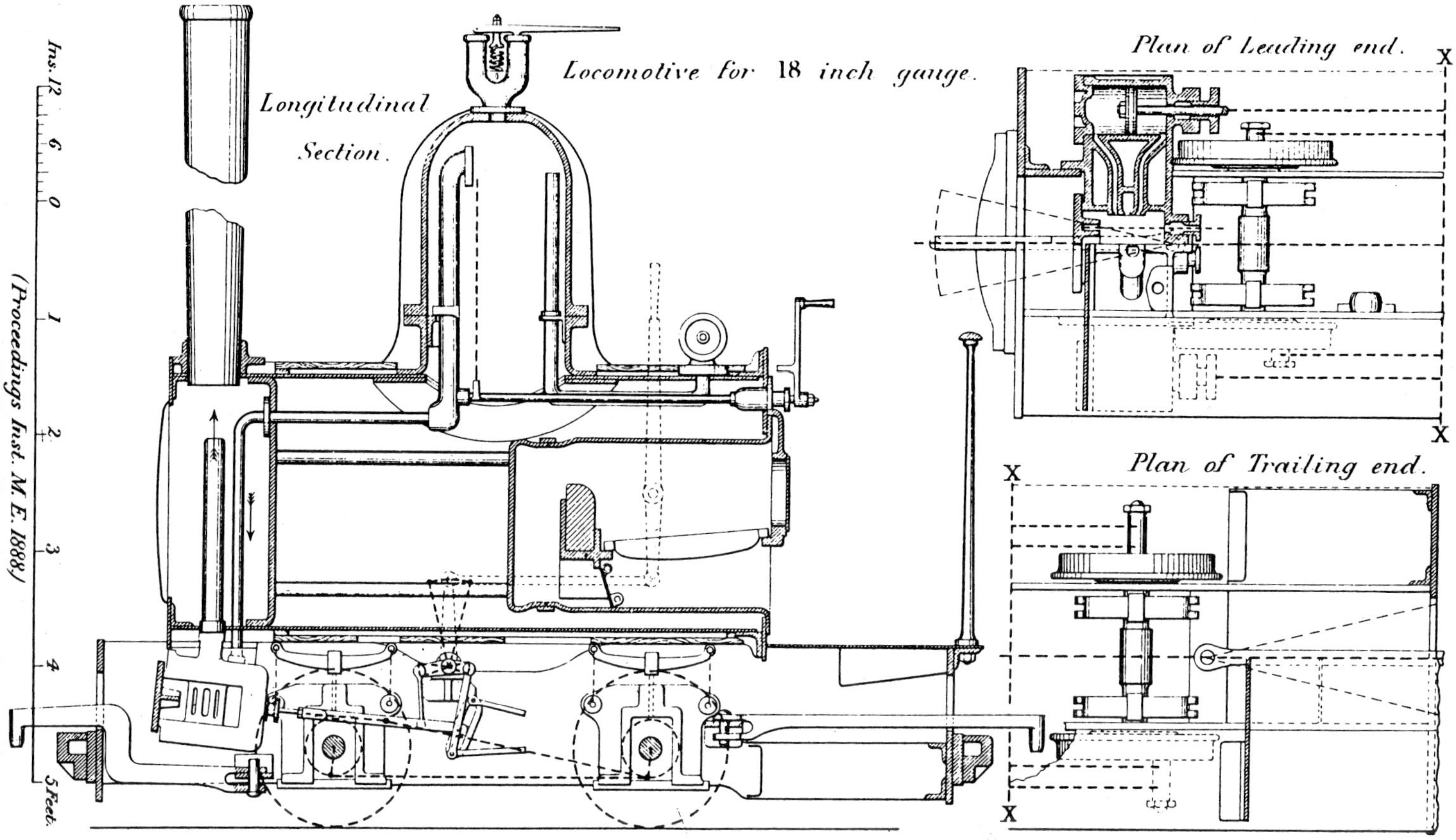

Longitudinal Section.

Locomotive for 18 inch gauge.

Plan of Leading end.

Plan of Trailing end.

The Horwich Works locomotives were discussed in a Paper prepared for the Institution of Mechanical Engineers in 1888. This set of drawings accompanied the Paper and they confirm the authenticity of those shown in the previous illustration as regards showing the condition of the engines as originally produced. The joint between the firebox wall and front tubeplate is of interest as this feature was later altered.

(The Institution of Mechanical Engineers)

Wasp, a Horwich built engine of 1891. Note the different design of lubricator from *Dot* and the motion shields level with the lower edge of the main frame.

(L&YR Society Courtesy J.B. Hodgson)

unclear whether the last three locomotives to be completed were actually built in the final form, but a very fine official diagram survives to show this state of modification. There does not appear to be any feature of this drawing by which its exact date can be ascertained, but it may be that the last three locomotives were constructed with saddle tanks. A modification necessitated by the fitting of these tanks was the blanking off of the filler caps on the original well tanks, which were at a lower level than the additional water space. The saddle and well tanks were linked by union pipes placed in rather prominent positions either side of the boiler. The left hand union pipe entered the upper front portion of the well tank on that side of the engine, as opposed to the forward top portion in the case of its right hand counterpart. This was effected so as to allow space for the mounting of the injector in its desired position. A notch was cut into the footplate on the left

hand side of the locomotive in order to allow space for the union pipe to pass through.

Before discussing the method by which the coal capacity was increased on the locomotives, it will be useful to consider the wagons used at Horwich in detail. These wagons appear to have attracted little attention from commentators over the years, largely owing to the fact that, with one exception, there are no known survivors. From the modeller's point of view, however, it is fortunate that drawings were prepared showing the different basic designs of wagon for the 1888 Institution of Mechanical Engineers Paper on the subject of the Guinness Brewery Tramway and other related topics. The first point to note when examining these drawings is that the influence of Crewe practice is very much in evidence, with the wagons being coupled by means of eyes and towbars. Throughout their existence, the steam locomotives were provided with rear drawbars to

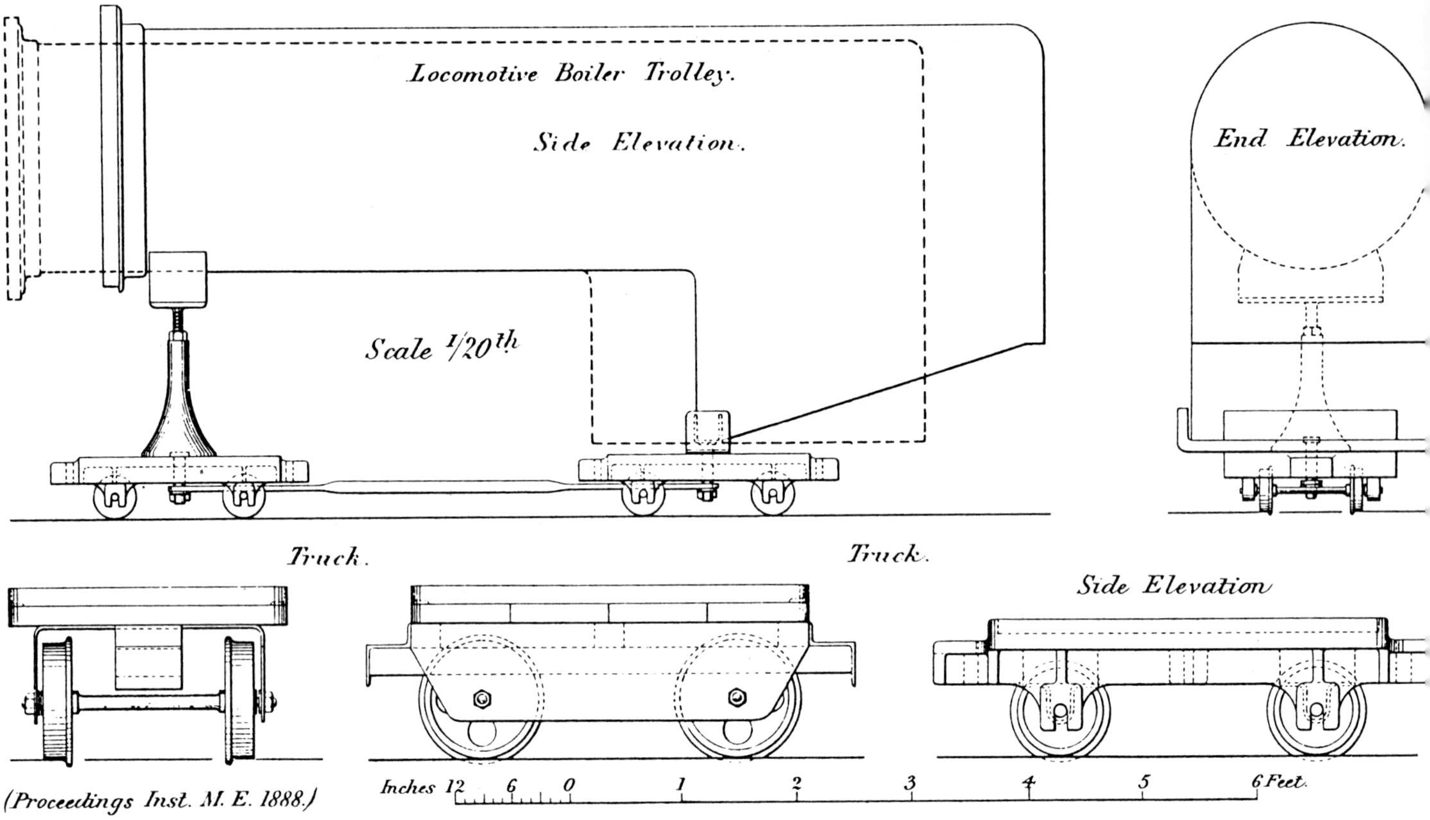

Locomotive Boiler Trolley.

Side Elevation.

End Elevation.

Scale ¹/20ᵗʰ

Truck.

Truck.

Side Elevation

(Proceedings Inst. M. E. 1888.)

Inches 12 6 0 1 2 3 4 5 6 Feet.

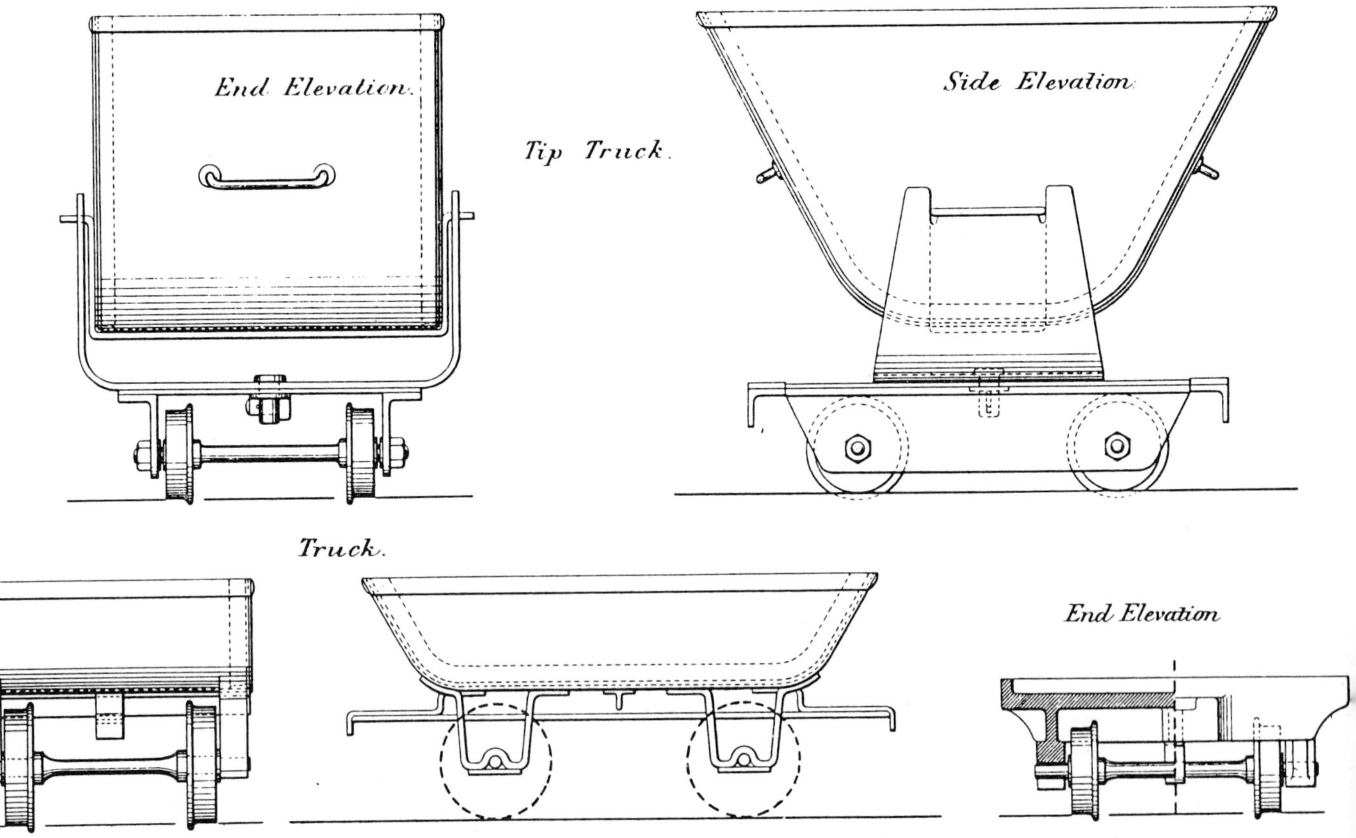

End Elevation.

Tip Truck.

Side Elevation.

(Proceedings Inst. M. E. 1888.)

Truck.

End Elevation

34

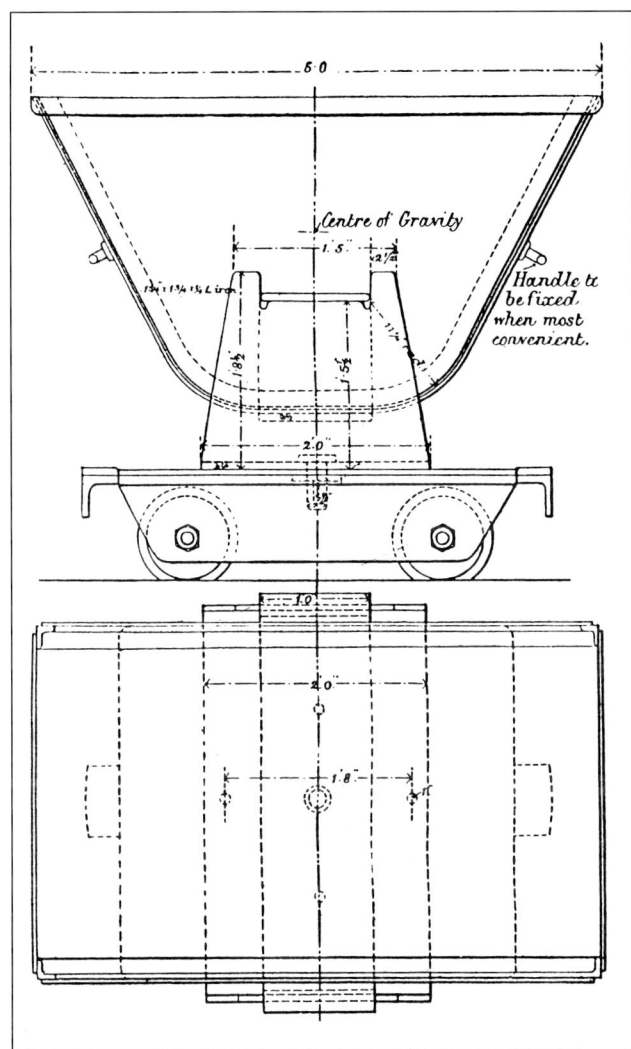

engage in the eyes on the wagons but the forward drawbars, present on official diagrams eventually gave way to eyes, as can be seen in the later photographs.

As with the system at Crewe, there were wagons produced in a form adaptable for the purpose of carrying standard gauge locomotive boilers, and these were illustrated in the 1888 Paper. It is a debatable point as to whether this practice was commonplace at either Crewe or Horwich: it was referred to in the Crewe context in *Engineering* in 1879 and illustrations exist showing wagons suitably equipped at both Crewe and Horwich. The practice could not, however, be described as conducive to safety in the workplace and it is unlikely to have been a part of normal working, merely being undertaken for demonstration purposes to show the potential of railways of this type. The Horwich wagons adapted to carry pedestals were of the cast iron variety.

Another type of flat wagon illustrated in the 1888 Paper had a sheet steel chassis with what appeared to be a platform and longitudinal rib, this latter being a load-bearing structure for the towbars which was made up from castings. This type of wagon had wheels of 1ft diameter as opposed to the diameter of approximately 8 inches used on the pedestal wagons.

The third type of wagon illustrated in the Institution's 1888 Paper was a tip wagon for coal or other mineral loads and a drawing of this wagon also appeared in *The Engineer* for 23rd September 1887. The construction of this type of vehicle was of the fabricated sheet steel variety and the skip cradle could be rotated to enable the skip to be tipped at an oblique angle from the wagon's longitudinal centre line. The skip merely rested in its cradle under its own weight, being restrained within its normal limit of travel by means of locating lugs. On occasions the skips on these wagons were removed altogether to enable loads such as timber baulks to be carried on the remaining por-

A faded view of *Dot*, one of the original Beyer, Peacock locomotives, in L&YR days, probably circa 1905. A saddle tank has now been fitted and the engine is towing an auxiliary tender. The tipper wagon and tender are of interest in that the basic designs for both were featured in the Institution of Mechanical Engineers Paper of 1888.

(L&YR Society Courtesy J.B. Hodgson)

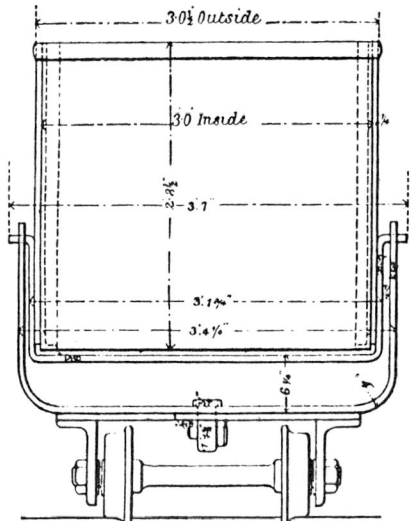

Above and left: Horwich narrow gauge wagons as illustrated in the Institution of Mechanical Engineers Paper on the subject of Brewery Tramways (and similar systems) in 1888.

(The Institution of Mechanical Engineers)

Another view of *Dot* in the early years of the present century, on this occasion the engine is seen hauling two wagons adapted to carry a standard gauge locomotive boiler. This was a special 'posed' photograph.

(L&YR Society Courtesy J.B. Hodgson)

Fly, a Horwich built locomotive of 1891 seen in L&YR days after the fitting of a saddle tank. The lined out livery and company crest can be seen, although the relatively poor state of turnout suggests a date during or immediately following the First World War.

(L&YR Society Courtesy J.B. Hodgson)

Right: Official frame plans of the Horwich Works locomotive design as represented by *Wasp* and *Fly* of 1891. These drawings contain useful details for modellers, particularly with regard to main frame configuration and the position of the cylinders. The short-lived valences underneath the motion are evident in these views.

(National Railway Museum, York)

Robin, one of the original Beyer, Peacock trio seen during LMS days. As with the Crewe Works 18 inch gauge locomotives, those at Horwich deteriorated dramatically in their state of turnout after the Grouping of 1923.

(L&YR Society Courtesy J.B. Hodgson)

tion. A photograph of *Midget* exists which also shows a tip wagon adapted in this manner.

The fourth basic type of wagon was a fabricated steel shallow open vehicle. Wagons of this type eventually proved their value by being adapted as tenders for the carriage of additional coal for the locomotives. In this form they appear on most of the photographs which show the locomotives in service or after withdrawal. When used as tenders, these wagons were equipped with 'treasure chest' style toolboxes and they often carried a supply of spare towbars.

As has been stated earlier, withdrawal dates for all except the last surviving steam locomotive on the narrow gauge system are difficult to ascertain, but *Wren* survived to be withdrawn from service by British Railways in 1962. Fortunately, the engine was not scrapped and its preservation will be dealt with in the appropriate section.

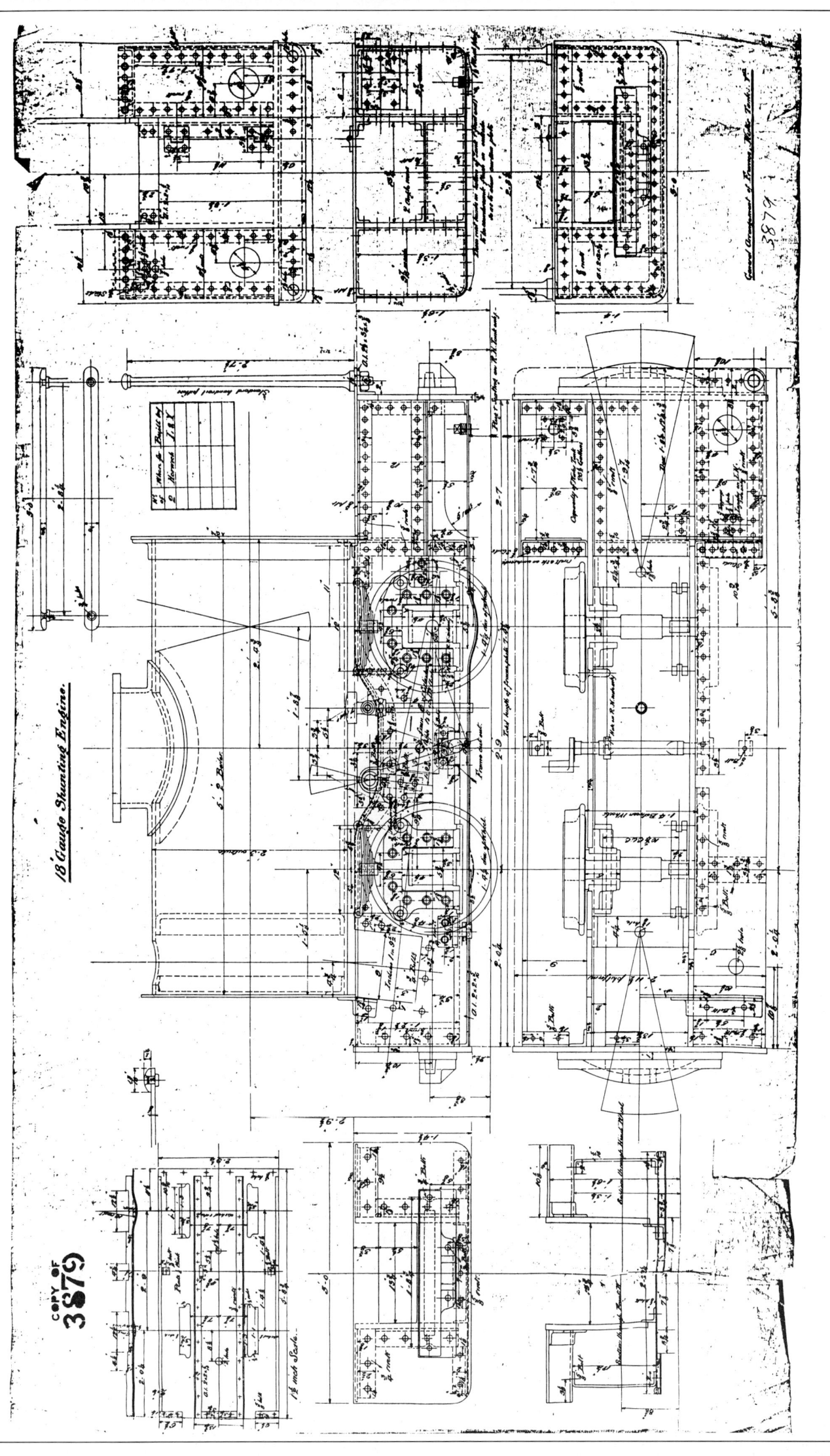

18" Gauge Shunting Engine.

General Arrangement of Locomotive, Fuller Tender.

3879.

COPY OF
3879

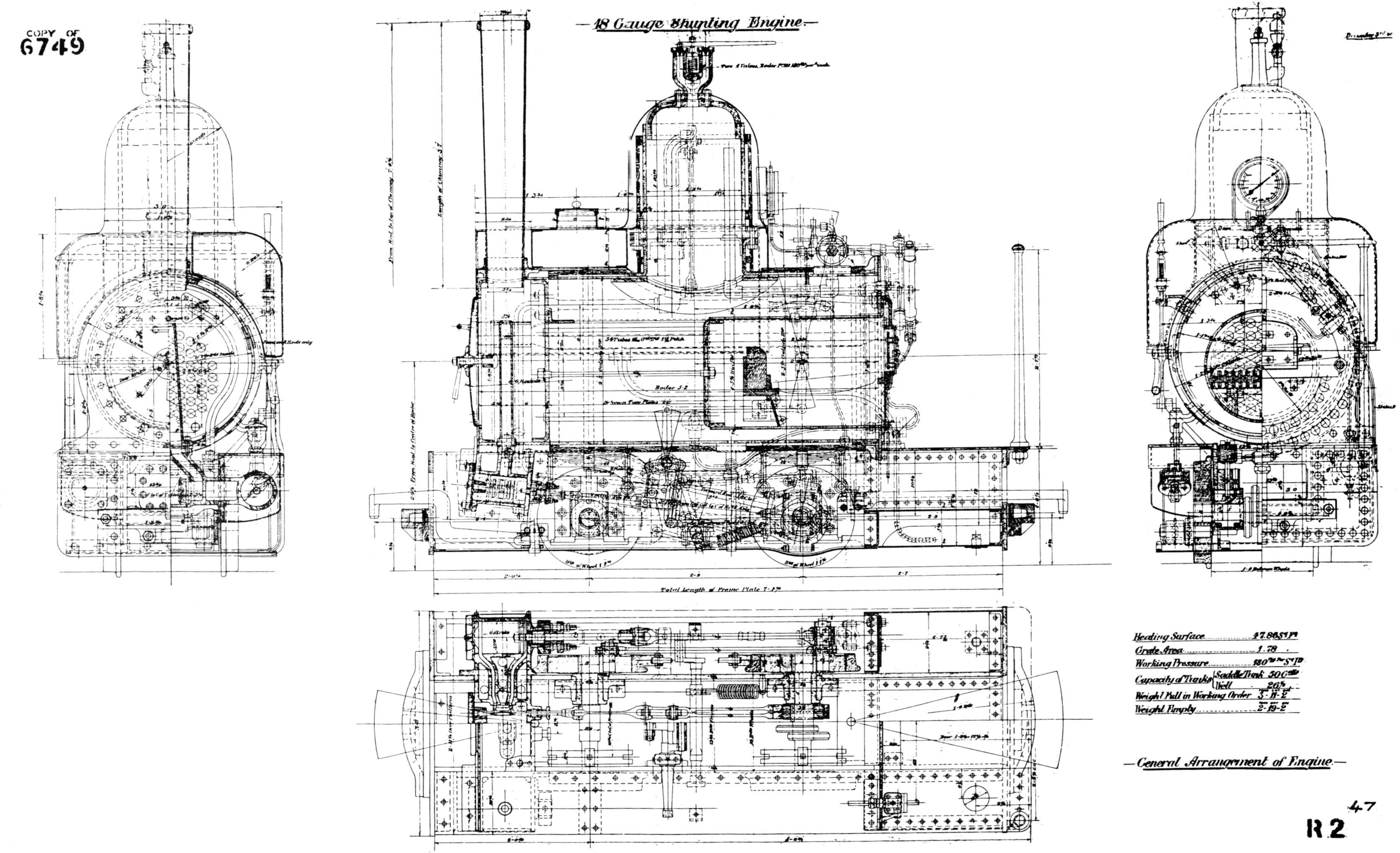

COPY OF
6749
—18 Gauge Shunting Engine.—
Heating Surface.........47.86 Sq Ft
Grate Area.........1.78 .
Working Pressure.........180 lbs per Sq In
Capacity of Tanks { Saddle Tank 50 Galls
Well . 26 .
Weight Full in Working Order 3-11-2
Weight Empty.........2-19-2
—General Arrangement of Engine.—
R2
47

Left: General arrangement drawings of the final form of the Horwich narrow gauge locomotive design. The motion shields are still shown in this diagram, although it is unlikely that they were ever fitted to the engines at this stage in their evolution.

(National Railway Museum)

A Comparative Table of Locomotive Dimensions

	LNWR *Tiny*	LNWR *Dickie*	L&YR *Dot*
Cylinders	4¼in bore 6in stroke	5½in bore 6in stroke	5in bore 6in stroke
Wheels	1ft 3¼in dia.	1ft 3in dia.	1ft 4¼in dia.
Wheelbase	3ft	3ft	2ft 9in
Working Boiler Pressure	90 psi (assumed)	90 psi	170 psi
Length Over Bufferplates	6ft 7½in	8ft 8in	7ft 4¼in
Overall Height	10ft ¼in (Orig.) 7ft 1¼in (Final)	7ft 5in	7ft 4½in
Weight in Working Order	2 ton 10 cwt	?	3 ton 11½ cwt
Water Capacity	28 gals	?	26½ gals (Orig.) 76½ gals (Final)

Midget in Horwich Works Yard circa 1933, not coupled to an auxiliary tender.

(L&YR Society Courtesy J.B. Hodgson)

Dot, one of the original 1887 locomotives awaiting scrapping during the 1930s. The casting incorporating the firehole door has been unbolted from the backhead and the safety valves removed. The tender is still attached and this view also shows the steam brake in front of the well tank.

(L&YR Society Courtesy J.B. Hodgson)

Wren seen in BR livery circa 1959, by then the only survivor of the Horwich narrow gauge steam locomotives. This locomotive is now preserved as part of the National Collection.

(L&YR Society Courtesy J.B. Hodgson)

2

The Military and Military Support Railways

The group of railways which saw the most widespread use of steam motive power in the United Kingdom during the pre-preservation era is the next to be considerated. This group comprised those 18 inch gauge lines constructed for military or military support usage. The first point to note in this context is that these lines have received comparatively little attention over the years in the railway media and visits to them by enthusiasts and historians were never actively encouraged. For this, reason, therefore, much information has had to be obtained from surviving internal records, from makers' drawings and other material.

Before discussion of these railways can be undertaken, a general consideration of small gauge locomotive evolution from 1862 to 1870 will be included so as to set the scene for a proper understanding of the pattern of 18 inch gauge locomotive development, particularly in relation to Woolwich Arsenal.

As we have seen, the steam locomotives used on the Works lines at Crewe and Horwich were of a configuration which combined a non-depending firebox with inside main frames continuous between buffer beams. This type of firebox and chassis layout was adequate for the intermittent pattern of work to be performed on the workshop lines, which allowed plenty of opportunity for 'blowing up' between turns on duty and made relatively light steam demands on the locomotives. In the year following the construction of *Tiny*, the introduction of steam locomotives onto the Festiniog Railway posed different problems for the locomotive designer. In applying the use of steam locomotives to a 'main line' between Portmadoc and Dinas of some 13¼ miles, with sustained gradients in the region of 1 in 80 over more than half of this length, it was a foregone conclusion that a conventional locomotive firebox, with its superior steam producing abilities and better ability to satisfy fluctuating steam demands, was a necessity. The major difficulty was the fact that the use of inside frames continuous between buffer beams on a narrow gauge locomotive with a depending firebox imposed two limitations. As the high pitched

boiler arrangement often used by the German manufacturers, where the firebox sits above the main frames, would not have found favour with British manufacturers of the period, the grate area would have been severely restricted. The other major limitation was that the sides of the outer firebox wrapper would have needed to be waisted in to allow the lower part of this wrapper to fit between the frames, as was the case with the Fletcher, Jennings locomotives for the Talyllyn Railway. The first six locomotives for the Festiniog Railway were therefore constructed with main frames extending rearward only to the front of the firebox, the rear buffer beam being attached to another pair of frames extending from the rear of the firebox. The two Manning, Wardle locomotives constructed in 1868 for the Festiniog & Blaenau Railway also possessed non-continuous main frames, with the rear portions actually flanking the firebox.

As early as 1861, however, a locomotive provided for use on a 2ft gauge line at Cross, Gidlow & Swanling Colliery in Wigan, was to be the British pioneer of another important trend in small gauge locomotive design. The locomotive concerned was constructed by Mr Isaac Watt Boulton of Ashton-under-Lyne and utilised cylinders of 5½in bore and 12in stroke, wheels of 2ft diameter and a 2:1 geared transmission. For present purposes, however, the significant feature of the design was the combined usage of a straight-sided depending firebox wrapper and main frames extending the full length of the locomotive between bufferbeams. These main frames were located outside the wheels in conjunction with flycranks. A larger locomotive built to the same gauge and layout appeared in 1864. Some

The engine supplied by Isaac Watt Boulton for use on a 2ft gauge line at Cross, Gidlow & Swanling Colliery, Wigan in 1861. This locomotive was allegedly a rebuild of an earlier standard gauge machine of 1856. The use of outside main frames extending the full length of the locomotive between bufferbeams is readily apparent.

(The Locomotive)

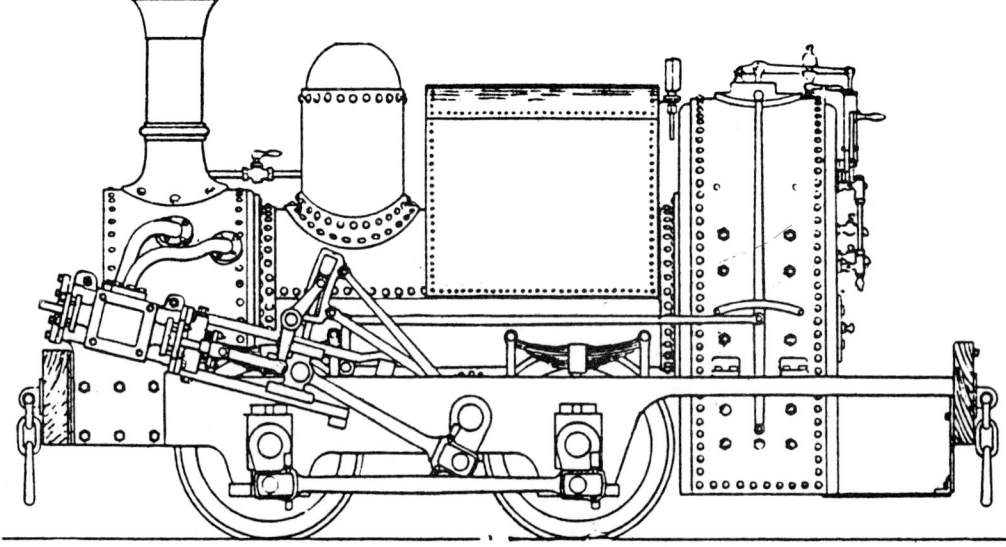

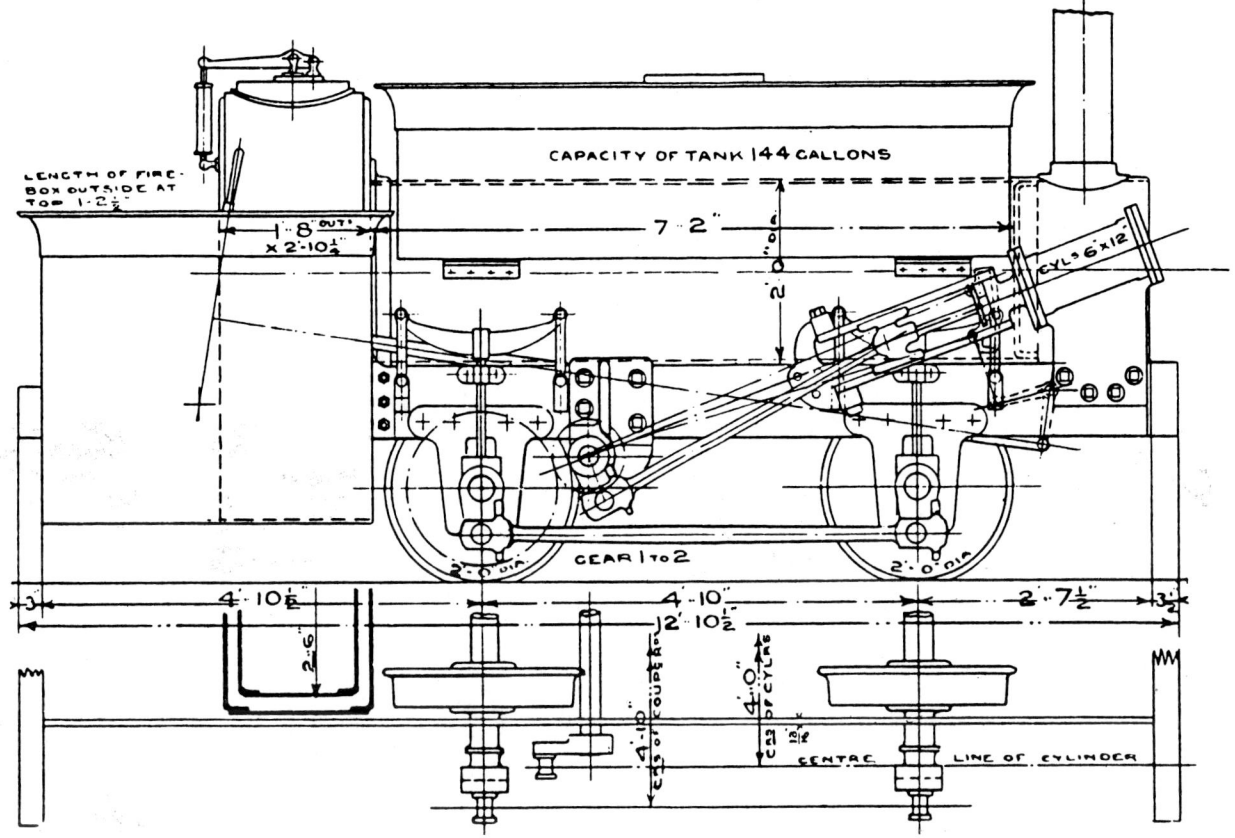

Lilliputian built by I.W. Boulton in 1864 as a later development of the locomotive in the previous drawing. This drawing shows the full-length outside main frames and the geared transmission.

(The Locomotive)

six years later a very important locomotive was constructed by Hunslet Engine Co. of Leeds for the Dinorwic Slate Quarries in North Wales. This engine, builder's No.51 of 1870, applied the principles of construction used by Boulton to a locomotive utilising direct, rather than geared drive. *Dinorwic*, as the engine was named, was destined to be the forerunner not only of the other 'Quarry Hunslets' but also of many other British built narrow gauge locomotives supplied for use by customers at home and overseas. The basic arrangement exemplified by *Dinorwic* was to have a profound influence upon the great majority of the steam locomotives used on the 18 inch gauge systems at Woolwich Arsenal, Chatham Dockyard and Deptford, as will be seen when these designs are considered.

Although the official date of opening of the narrow gauge system at Woolwich Arsenal was quoted in *The Locomotive* magazine for 15th October 1921 as 10th January 1873, it is certain from both *The Engineer* magazine and from records held by the Leeds Industrial Museum that the first narrow gauge steam locomotive arrived in 1871. The makers were Manning, Wardle & Co. Ltd, Hunslet's neighbours in Leeds, and rivals in the then buoyant market for industrial and contractors' locomotives. The engine was builder's No. 353 and it was ordered on behalf of the Secretary of State for War, being steam tested on 21st February 1871 and outshopped on 9th March that year.

The basic general arrangement of the locomotive was obviously influenced by that of *Dinorwic*, the Hunslet engine previously considered, but the locomotive's proportions were more appropriate to a gauge of 18 inches. The familiar domeless boiler with raised fire-box, handed down from the E.B. Wilson designs of the 1850s was present, along with an ornamental canopy similar to that used on a number of larger Manning, Wardle products of the period. The boiler barrel was 1ft 9in in diameter and 5ft 9in long, being joined to the smokebox tubeplate and firebox wrapper by flanging, as was the Maker's normal practice. The distance from the boiler centre line to the crown of the firebox wrapper was 1ft 11in and this outer wrapper was 1ft 6½in long and 2ft 4in wide. The boiler contained 20 brass tubes of 2in outside diameter (the old E.B. Wilson/Manning, Wardle standard) and the tank capacity was stated to be 90 gallons. The weight was recorded as 5 tons 6 cwt empty and 6 tons 12 cwt in working order. As with early standard gauge Manning, Wardles, one feedpump and one injector were fitted, the feedpump being driven from an eccentric mounted on the rearmost axle, as with certain standard gauge four-coupled locomotives, such as the engine which eventually became Wantage Tramway No.7. The wheels were 1ft 8in in diameter and the wheelbase was 3ft 3in The cylinders, although small by comparison with later steam locomotives used at Woolwich, were rather larger than those used on the Crewe and Horwich Works locomotives. The bore dimension was 6in whilst the stroke was 8in.

This first example of steam motive power on the narrow gauge line at Woolwich Arsenal proved to be so successful that twelve further Manning, Wardle locomotives, using the same leading dimensions, were constructed for use at Woolwich. A further six were also built for use on the narrow gauge line in Chatham Dockyard. As development of the design progressed, certain evolutionary trends could be discerned. The ungainly double buffer beam shown in the accompanying drawing was soon dispensed with on the prototype engine and the maker's records state that this locomotive was altered at Woolwich in conformity with No.477 of 1873, *Victoria*. The conventional pattern buffers gave way to the single iron-clad curvaceous oak

41

NARROW GAUGE LOCOMOTIVE.

THE HUNSLET ENGINE COMPANY, LEEDS, ENGINEERS.

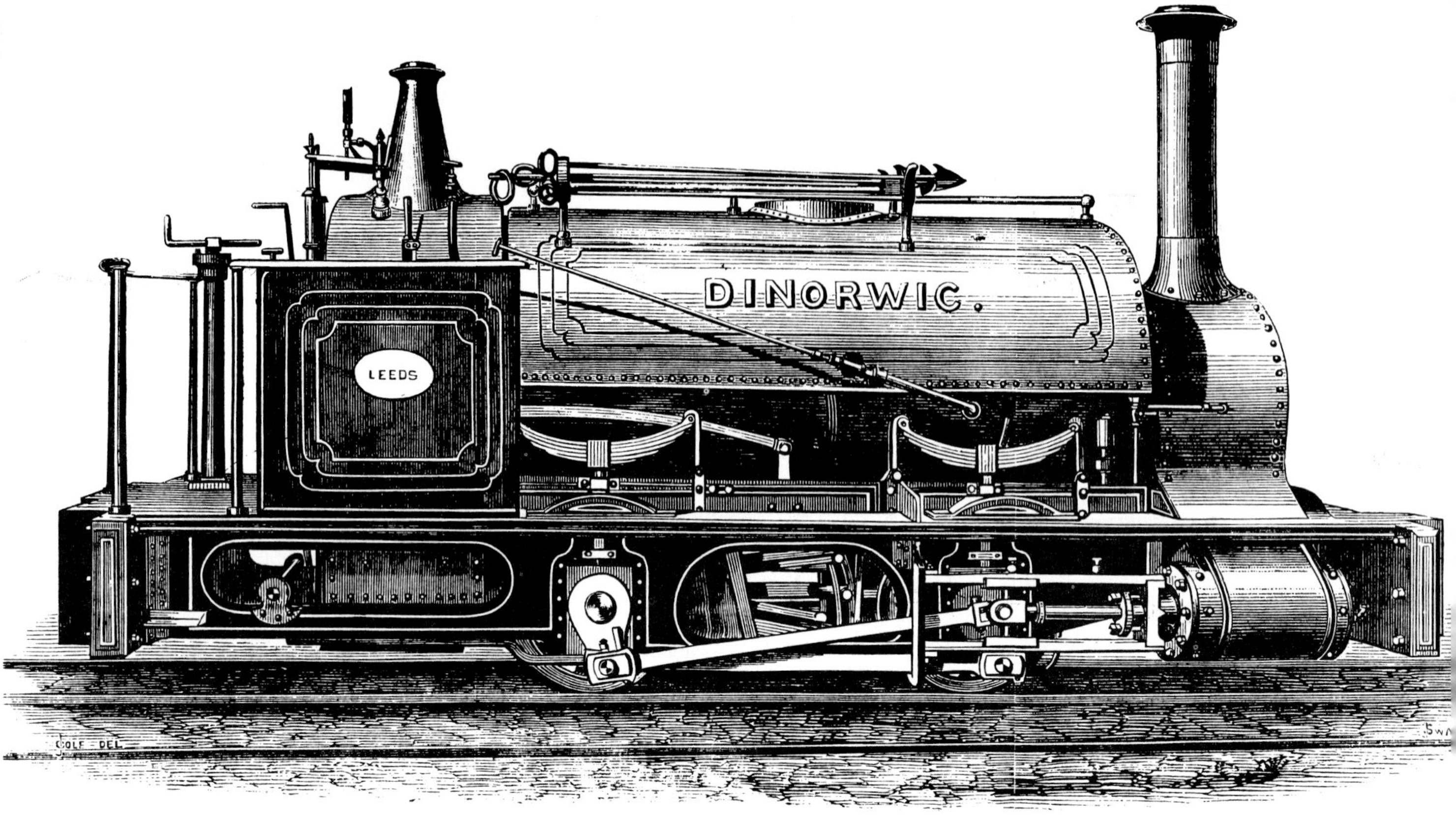

An engraving, taken from the maker's works photograph of Hunslet Engine Co. No. 51 of 1870. This locomotive, the first of the famous 'Quarry Hunslets' was constructed to a gauge of 1ft 10¾in for use at the Dinorwic Slate Quarries, Llanberis. The combination of a straight sided outer firebox wrapper, full length outside frames and direct drive to the rear wheels is evident.

(The Engineer)

NARROW GAUGE LOCOMOTIVE IN WOOLWICH ARSENAL.

MESSRS. MANNING, WARDLE, AND CO., ENGINEERS, BOYNE ENGINE WORKS, LEEDS.

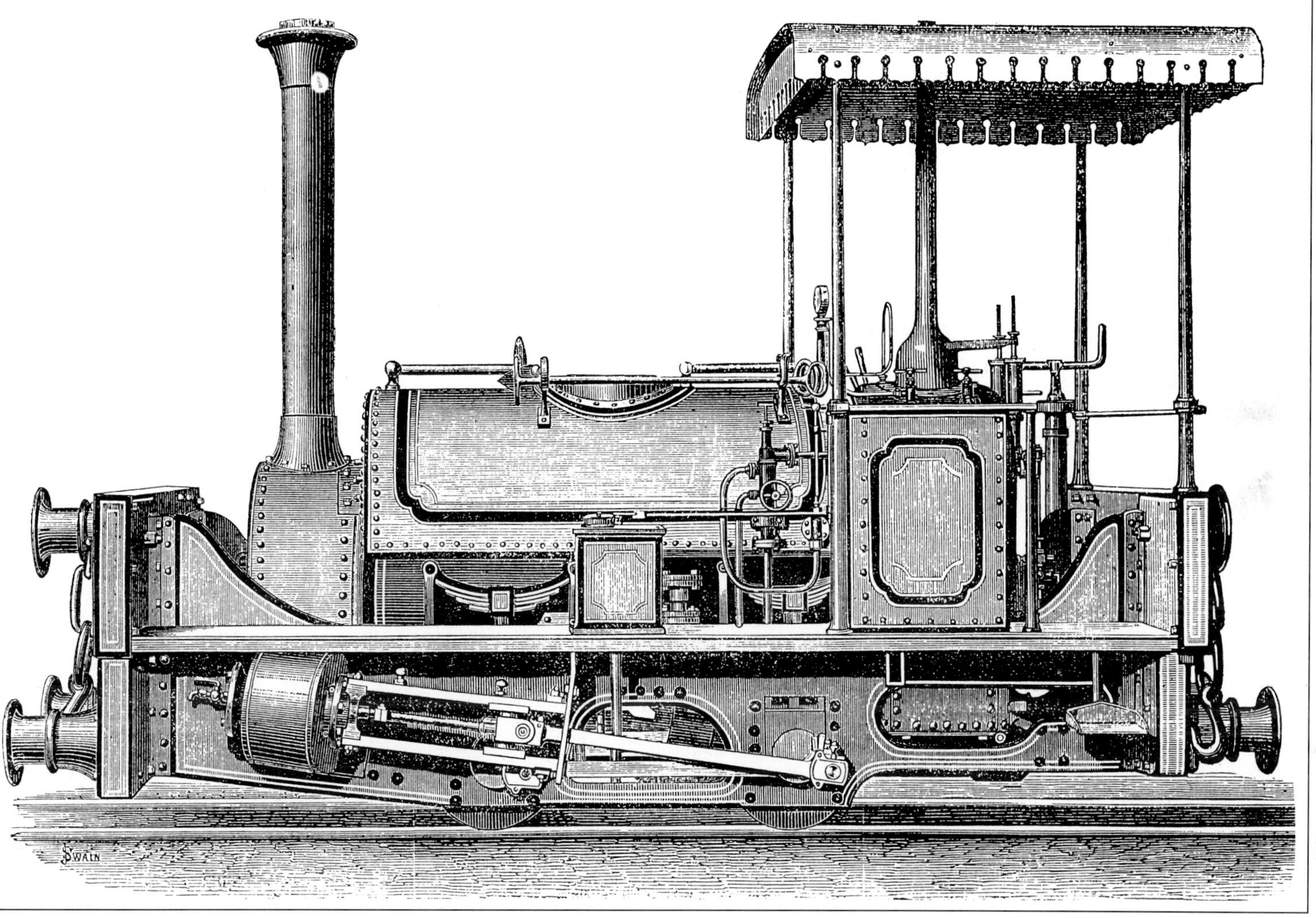

The first locomotive supplied for use on the 18 inch gauge system in Woolwich Arsenal. The engine was Manning, Wardle No. 353 of 1871 and it remained in use at Woolwich until shortly after the outbreak of World War One. Later 18 inch gauge developments of this locomotive saw service not only at Chatham and Woolwich but also in Russia and Argentina. The rear view shows the upper backhead detail and ornamental canopy along with the unsightly 'double' bufferbeam with which the engine was equipped when built.

(The Engineer)

Arquebus the last Manning, Wardle engine (1130 of 1889), built for the narrow gauge system at Woolwich Arsenal. Note the later pattern canopy with spectacle plate, the Beck's patent whistle, the cylindrical sandbox and the (almost invisible) bevel-geared handbrake.
(Maker's Official Photograph Courtesy R. Redman)

beams shown in the illustrations covering post-1873 examples of the general type.

All of these Manning, Wardles for Woolwich and Chatham carried names at some stage and the pioneer locomotive was named *Lord Raglan*. A basic difference in customer policy between Woolwich and Chatham was that whilst Woolwich Arsenal preferred main frames with their lower edges tapered upwards at both ends in conjunction with a long rear overhang, the engines built for use at Chatham had main frames whose lower edges were straight throughout their length.

The simple columnar handbrake found on No.353 as built did not find universal favour at Woolwich on narrow gauge steam locomotives supplied during the last three decades of the nineteenth century, and the remaining twelve Woolwich Manning, Wardles incorporated a handbrake with bevel gearing enabling a horizontal axis of turn for the handwheel. *Lord Raglan* was modified in line with the other classmates in this respect. At Chatham, on the other hand, the simple column was preferred and these were mounted on the left hand side of the locomotive, as opposed to the right hand side on the Woolwich examples. Initially, on both *Lord Raglan* and the early Chatham locomotives, the footplate was straight throughout its length and a cab step was provided on each side, but dropping of the footplate at the rear end became

Above: Lord Raglan seen during its final days of operation (circa 1915) at Woolwich Arsenal. The dropped rear footplate is visible as is the bevel geared handbrake (close examination reveals the handwheel to have five spokes). The canopy has been removed and the original pattern sandboxes replaced by examples of the cylindrical pattern used on all subsequent narrow gauge Manning, Wardles built for use within the Arsenal. Further examination of this photograph reveals that the feedpump vacuum relief valve body was located on the right hand side of the tank just in front of the firebox. A single buffer, possibly of a composite pattern, is fitted at each end but its design is non-standard when compared with other Woolwich 18 inch gauge locomotives. A towbar is being used to haul timber baulks on two four-wheeled wagons adapted for this purpose.

(Courtesy J. Townsend)

Right: A staff photograph taken outside the Locomotive Repair Shop at Woolwich Arsenal in 1906. One of the narrow gauge Manning, Wardles can be seen on the right. The lower smokebox door handle has been obscured by some removable (to enable the doors to be opened) footplate sheeting added in front of the smokebox and replacement chimney cap has been fitted. The combination of snap headed tank rivets and spectacle plates, allied to an original pattern cab roof profile, suggest that the engine is *Coehorn* (Manning, Wardle No. 696 of 1878), although this cannot be stated for certain. The mounting of a lamp on the chimney was standard RAR practice of the period.

(Courtesy A. Turner)

This view is of considerable historical importance as it shows the third narrow gauge steam locomotive supplied to Woolwich Arsenal, (Manning, Wardle 482 of 1873), *Albert Edward*, at work in March 1918 in the Sawmill area. A large all-over cab has been fitted together with the Neath pattern spark arrester usually associated with the 'Culverin' class Hudswell, Clarke locomotives. The smokebox has been modified to enable the front to hinge downwards as one unit, thereby allowing a larger access aperture. The lined out livery can clearly be seen, as can the cylindrical sandbox, of a type found on some 'Quarry Hunslets'. Although not visible in this view, the injector body was located in a horizontal plane, in contrast to the type with which the locomotive was originally fitted. When replacement firebars were supplied by the makers to a subsequent unknown user of this engine in 1920, they were found not to fit, indicating a relatively late reboilering carried out within the Arsenal.

(Imperial War Museum)

standard from 1873 onwards and the steps were dispensed with.

An important feature possessed by the 6in by 8in cylindered Manning, Wardles at both Woolwich and Chatham was the peculiar design of smokebox door. The door was of the 'double' variety with two hinges and two handles. These latter components were placed one above the other on the left hand door and located slightly offset to the left of the engine's vertical centre line. Rather unusually for a Manning, Wardle design the upper portion of the tank cross-section consisted of a simple semi-circle on these 6in by 8in cylindered locomotives. A flatter topped tank would have been more in keeping with the Maker's standard practice, but it should be remembered that the semi-circular cross-section could be found on the tanks of a few early Manning, Wardle products, the best-known probably being *Disraeli* (No.268 of 1869) for the Mawddwy Railway in Wales.

Apparently, in direct competition with their Leeds neighbours, Hunslet Engine Co. produced a 0-4-0ST specification with 5in by 8in cylinders during the 1870s. No locomotive of this design was ever constructed to 18in gauge, however, and the best known example was probably *Louisa* (Hunslet No. 195 of 1877) supplied to the Dinorwic slate quarries. This Hunslet specification greatly resembled its rivals' contemporaries in most respects, but despite being built to wider gauges it was slightly smaller than the 6in by 8in Manning, Wardles.

The Woolwich 18 inch gauge Manning, Wardles were all scrapped or sold by the Arsenal by 1919 and information about their disposal can be found in Appendix 1.

The early success of steam locomotive haulage at Woolwich Arsenal led to a demand there in the latter part of the 1870s for locomotives with a greater power output than the little Manning, Wardles could sustain. There was also an element of political pressure placed upon the War Office to order locomotives from other builders and accordingly in 1878, when the first Woolwich locomotive to use enlarged cylinder dimensions was constructed, it was built by Vulcan Foundry Ltd of Newton-le-Willows. The locomotive in question was the builders' No. 838 of 1878 and it was delivered to the Royal Carriage Department of Woolwich Arsenal, carrying the numberplates R.C.D No.3. As can be seen from the accompanying maker's photograph, the design of the engine closely followed that of its Manning, Wardle precursors in the use of full length outside framing, outside cylinders, a domeless boiler with raised firebox, a bevel-geared handbrake and an ornamental canopy. The practice of using one feed-pump and one injector was continued, with the injector body being mounted in the vertical position as built.

In comparison with the cylinder dimensions of the

46

The destruction of many of the photographic archives of Chatham Dockyard resulted in the loss of much material that would have been of use to railway and dockyard modellers and historians. This photograph, which appeared in *Navy and Army Illustrated* for 5th April 1902, is of considerable historic interest in spite of its indifferent quality. It shows the locomotive *Khartum* "leaving the storehouse by Dockyard Railway". The injector (horizontal bodied) and nameplate, complete with mis-spelling, are visible.

On 30th May 1908, *Khartum*, whilst hauling an open workmens' 'knifeboard' bogie carriage and the enclosed officers' car, collided with the standard gauge locomotive *Newcastle* (Hawthorn, Leslie 2450 of 1899) on the sharp curve near to the Smithery opposite No.3 Slip. The crash took place at one o'clock on a Saturday afternoon when a nearby signal box was unmanned. At least thirteen employees were injured and both locomotives sustained damage, the bulk of which was to *Khartum's* front end, the front buffer assembly was apparently broken off in the accident. At the time of writing, the only known survivor amongst the railway stock involved in the accident is *Newcastle* which, as *Commander B.*, can be seen at the Hollycombe Steam Collection near Liphook.

The Maker's official photograph of Vulcan Foundry No. 838 of 1878 *R.C.D No.3*. The initials R.C.D. convinced a number of observers over the years that this locomotive was constructed for use at Chatham (on the presumption that they stood for Royal Chatham Dockyard) but they actually stood for Royal Carriage Department, one of the three departments of the Royal Arsenal at Woolwich at this time. The locomotive was renamed *Iron Duke* after the unification of the Arsenal's railway system in 1890/1 and it is officially recorded as being broken up for scrap in 1914.

(Courtesy F. Jones)

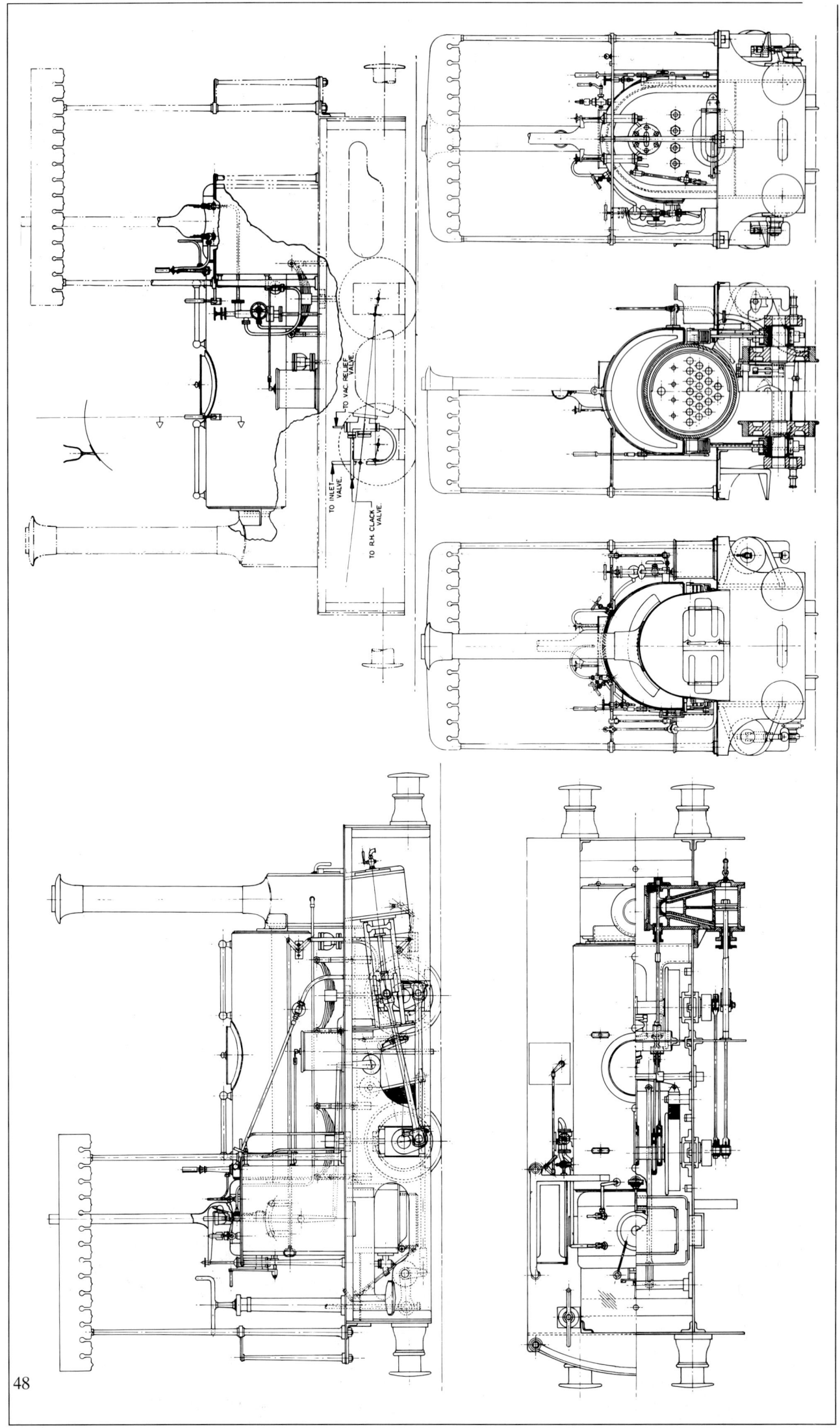

TO VAC. RELIEF
VALVE.

TO INLET
VALVE.

TO R.H. CLACK
VALVE.

Manning, Wardle No. 424 *Busy Bee* (See page 52 for Caption)

48

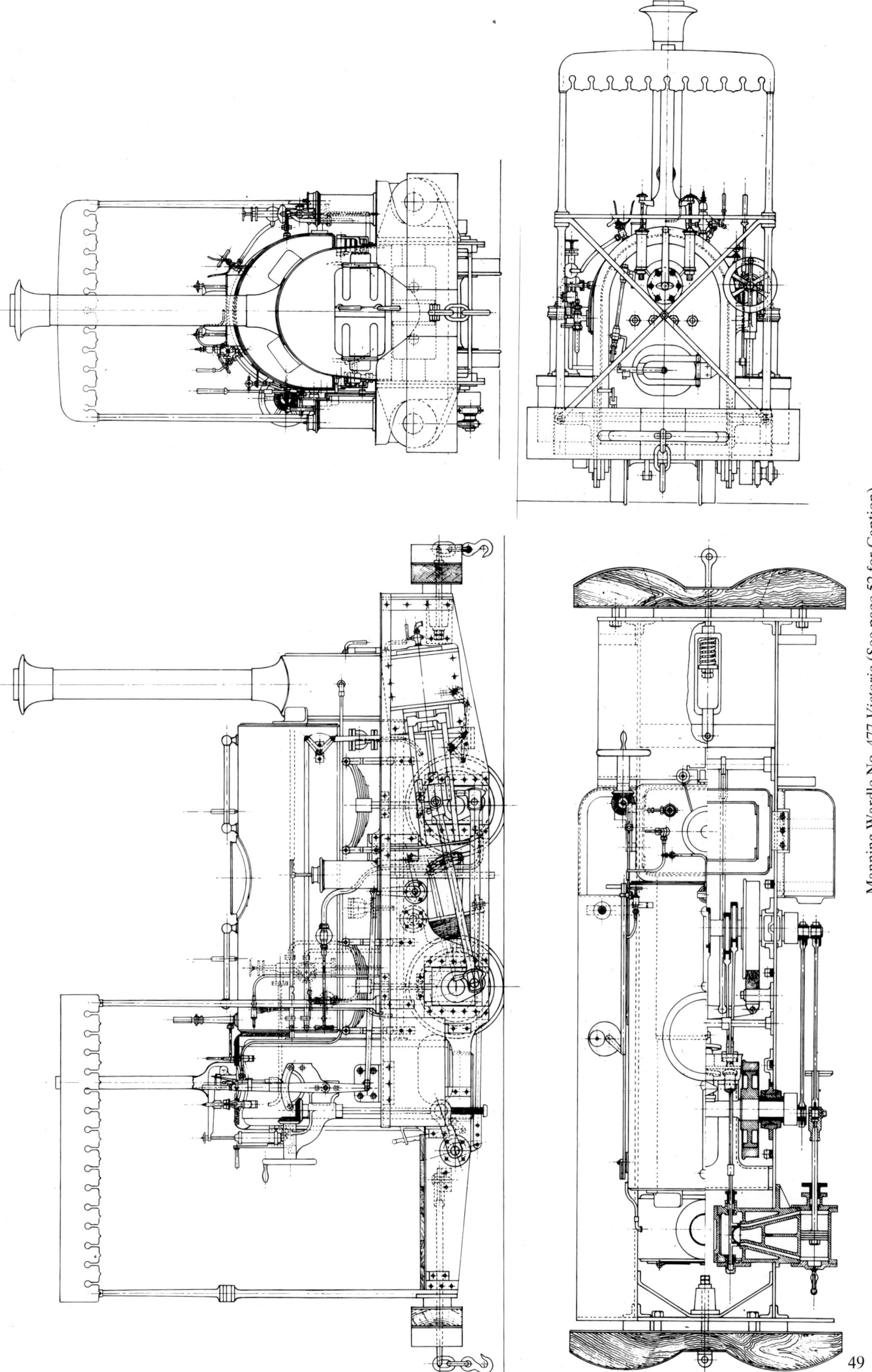

Manning Wardle No. 477 *Victoria* (See page 52 for Caption)

49

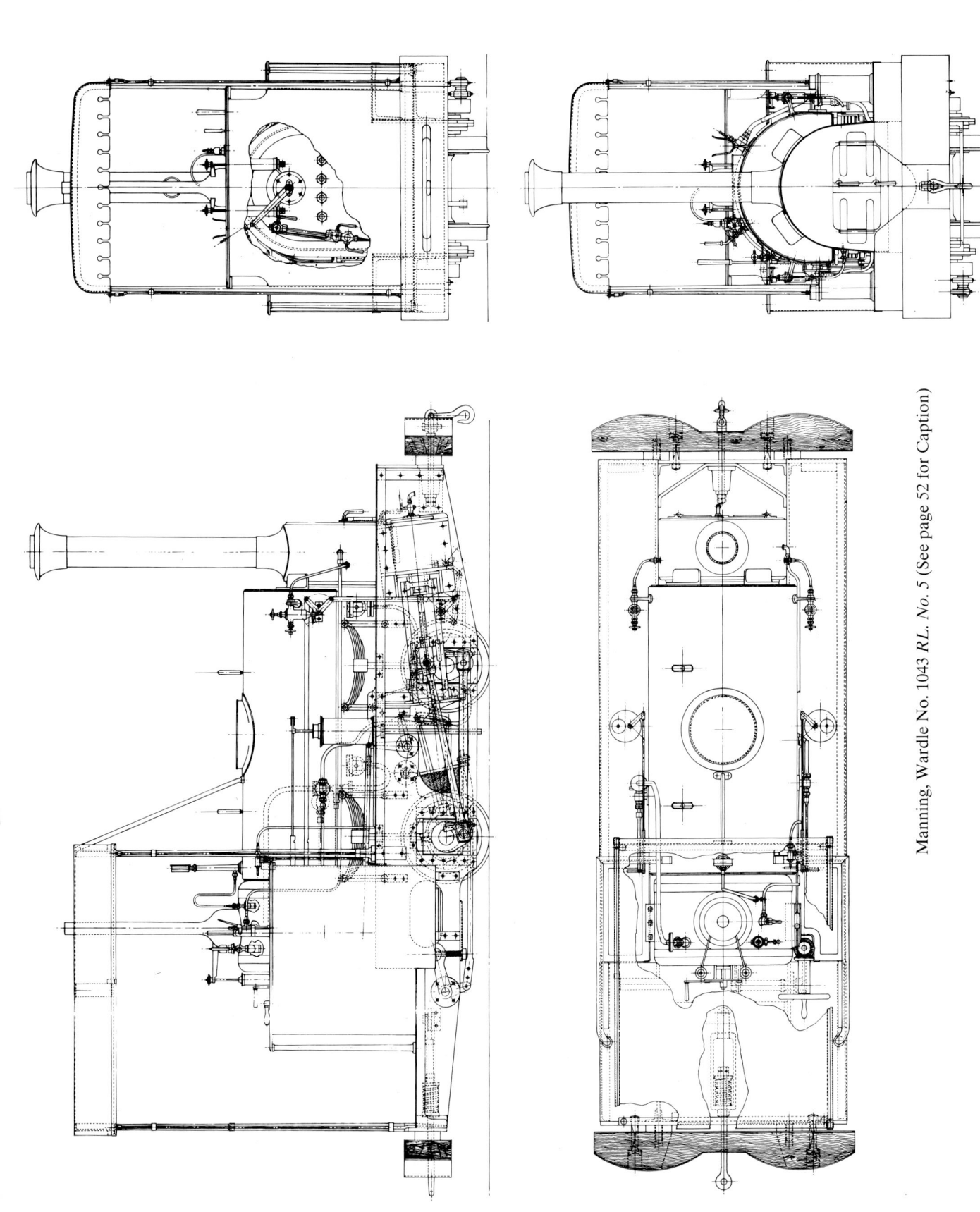

Manning, Wardle No. 1043 *RL. No. 5* (See page 52 for Caption)

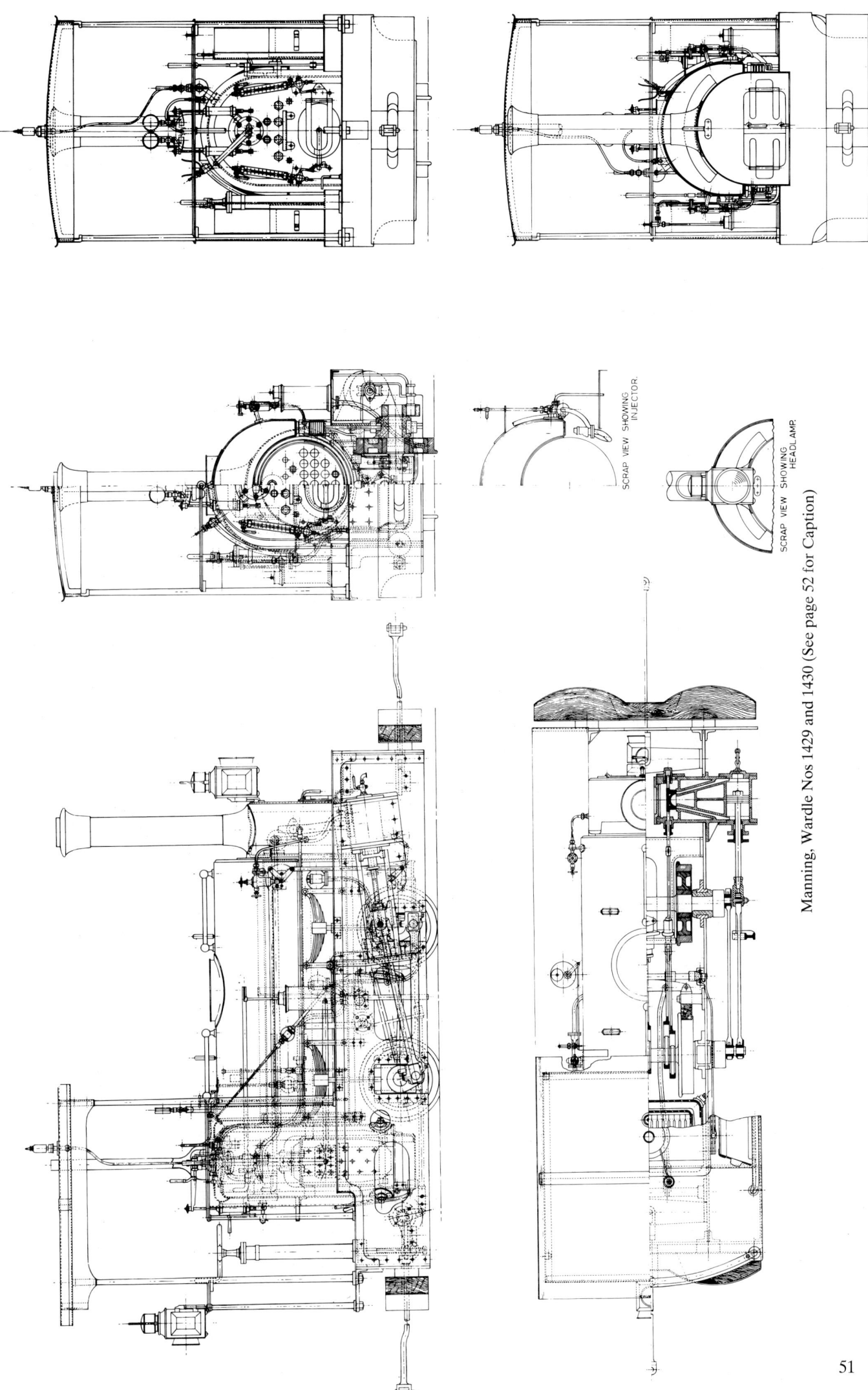

SCRAP VIEW SHOWING INJECTOR.

SCRAP VIEW SHOWING HEADLAMP.

Manning, Wardle Nos 1429 and 1430 (See page 52 for Caption)

51

Arrangement drawings page 48: Reconstructed general arrangement drawings of Manning, Wardle No. 424 of 1872 *Busy Bee*, a locomotive supplied to the Admiralty for use in Chatham Dockyard. The simpler pattern of main frame when compared to the design used on No. 353 can be observed. The feedpump vacuum relief valve and control bar for the water inlet (which could not turn a full 360 degrees) can be seen in these drawings. The single full width iron-clad oak buffer had yet to appear at this stage. *Burgoyne* (448 of 1873) supplied to the School of Military Engineering was similar but it would have been fitted with drawhooks rather than the towbars used in the Dockyard. *Burgoyne* was purchased (per RE Committee Minutes 1052 and 1070 of 1873) for use at the SME in connection with four purposes: (1) instruction in driving locomotives; (2) testing tramways and bridges; (3) for conveying material to different parts of Field Works, and (4) for experimental purposes. No drawgear is shown in these views.

(The Late R. Smithers)

Arrangement drawings page 49: Reconstructed general arrangement drawings of Manning, Wardle No. 477 of 1873, an engine delivered to the Woolwich Arsenal as *Victoria* and given the name *Boxer* after the death of Queen Victoria in 1901. The dropped rear footplate (comprised of timber planking on a sheet iron base), absence of cab side-sheets and bevel-gears on the handbrake column are all features of interest to modellers. The familiar iron-clad oak buffers have now made their appearance and the rear drawbar is sprung. The position of the vacuum relief valve on this locomotive as built is difficult to ascertain, the most likely alternative being that it was secured to the rear right hand side of the tank by means of a special bracket, as with the locomotive in the next drawing. The end view of the injector reveals that it was of the vertical body pattern, similar to that fitted to *Lord Raglan* as built but with the control for the water inlet mounted close to the cock itself, rather than on a shaft extending above the side sheets originally fitted to that engine.

(The Late R. Smithers)

Manning, Wardle engines of 6in bore and 8in stroke, those of the Vulcan engine were 7in bore and 9in stroke. The firebox heating surface was 14 sq ft and that of the boiler tubes was 86 sq ft giving a total of 100 sq ft. The comparative figures for the Manning, Wardle class were respectively 63½ sq ft, 11½ sq ft and 75 sq ft, although these latter figures were revised on later Manning, Wardle drawings. The grate area on *R.C.D No.3* was 2½ sq ft as opposed to the figure of 1.8 sq ft quoted for *Victoria*. The coupled wheels were 1ft 9in diameter and the overall weight of the engine in working order was 6 tons 14 cwt, which allowed for the tank capacity of 100 gallons of water and 4 cubic feet of coke carried on the footplate. Although this locomotive enjoyed a life span of the order attained by its Woolwich contemporaries, the only one of its class. It latterly bore the name *Iron Duke*.

As will be discussed in detail in a subsequent section, the preferred specification of locomotives held in reserve for use on 18⁶inch gauge trench supply railways during the period from 1885-1889, was a 0-4-2 tank configuration with 7½in by 12in cylinders and an approximate weight in working order of 10 tons. As a direct consequence of the abortive Suakin campaign of 1885, twelve locomotives of this basic type became surplus to immediate direct military requirements. These were therefore delivered to the Royal Arsenal. Seven examples came from John Fowler & Co. of Leeds, whilst a further five were supplied by W.G. Bagnall Ltd of Stafford. The original reason for ordering these

Arrangement drawings page 50: Reconstructed general arrangement drawings of a later Woolwich Arsenal Manning, Wardle, No. 1043 of 1887. This engine was originally supplied to the Royal Laboratory as *RL. No.5*, being renamed *Torpedo* after the unification of the Royal Arsenal Railways network in 1890/1. An entry in the Maker's records concerning the previous engine (No. 939) supplied to the Royal Laboratory states that the points on the canopy fringe were to be dispensed with on future R.L. locomotives, although the Maker's plans of No. 1043 only show this process as being carried out in relation to the front and rear fringes, as the others were dispensed with altogether. The firebox cladding is shown cut away to reveal the steam feeds for the whistle and pressure gauge and the canopy is also shown cut away for clarity purposes. Although Maker's records and photographic evidence suggest that Nos 1043 and 1130 left Boyne Engine Works without fire iron brackets, it is thought that both were soon fitted with these components and consequently they appear in this illustration. From the modeller's point of view it is unfortunate that precise details of the nameplates of the Woolwich Manning, Wardles do not survive.

(The Late R. Smithers)

Arrangement drawings page 51: Reconstructed general arrangement drawings of Manning, Wardle Nos 1429 and 1430 of 1899. These locomotives, named respectively *Khartum* and *Prompt* were supplied to the Admiralty for use in Chatham Dockyard. The upper part of the main frame is now dropped at the rear end (in lieu of a cab step) but the general pattern of evolution from No. 424 is evident. The injector is now of the horizontal body pattern. The original Maker's drawings show an additional handrail of a type similar to the one fitted to the Fell locomotive *Ariel* at Aldershot, but in view of the photographic evidence and a lack of reference to such a fitting in the Maker's records this is unlikely ever to have been fitted. The rear portion of the cab floor overhanging the main frames was a feature apparently liked by the Admiralty but not by Woolwich Arsenal. The cab footplate was of the chequer plate variety and the assumed full length of the towbars is shown in the front part of the sectional plan view. As with other reconstructed general arrangement drawings in this volume, certain components are shown in cutaway form to assist with clarity. The nameplates on these locomotives, and also on the earlier *Comet* (No. 910 of 1884) were brass plates with 2½in block letters, but the livery of the locomotives is unrecorded.

(The Late R. Smithers)

locomotives was revealed in *The Engineer* for 6th March 1885:

"Mr W.G. Bagnall, Castle Engine Works, Stafford, has obtained a considerable contract from Government for portable railway plant and small locomotives for the Soudan (sic). This railway, it is understood, will be used as a feeder for the wider gauge permanent railway to be laid down by Messrs Lucas & Aird, conveying the materials for its construction and running alongside of it. As the order has to be completed within a limited time, it is intended to at once enlarge Mr Bagnall's works."

From surviving records it appears that the Fowler locomotives were designed by Major Thomas English and that their cylinders, wheel and wheelbase dimensions were similar, if not identical to his Vulcan Foundry 0-4-2T locomotives (to be described). All were fitted with domed boilers, long side tanks, stove pipe chimneys and, almost certainly, the English patent trailing truck control. The first five (builder's Nos 5058-5062 of June 1885) had the locus of drive of the big end offset forward and upward from the rear coupled crankpin by means of a bearing contained in a housing attached to the coupling rod (an underhung offset arrangement was, as we shall see, found on the Fell locomotive *Ariel* supplied for use at Aldershot). The purpose of the manufacturers using this arrangement was to raise the level of the cylinders above potential ground level obstructions in a manner similar to that accomplished by use of the Greig & Beadon patent jackshaft drive system patented in 1880. The last two members of this group, Nos 5063 and 5064 of December 1885, were built to a 'new design'. Outside Joy's valve gear was fitted and the cylinders were set rather lower than on Nos 5058-5062 with the drive being direct to the crankpin.

In a view showing the Locomotive Shed at Woolwich circa 1905, two of these narrow gauge Fowlers are visible on the extreme right of the picture. It is interesting to notice that both had by this stage been fitted with cabs and that the leading engine, at least, of the two had been fitted with the standard type of Woolwich bufferbeam whose front profile was concave in the centre rather than convex as had been the case when the engine was built.

In contrast with most other early RAR locomotives, *Flamingo* (No. 5062 of 1885) never carried a cab throughout its entire working lifetime and whether this engine actually worked within the Arsenal after 1889 is debatable. Paragraph 44 of the 1889 Manual of Military Railways suggests that three locomotives were stored for potential immediate siege train 'call-up'. These would certainly have included the Vulcan engines *Mars* and *Venus* and it is suggested that

The locomotive shed at Woolwich Arsenal circa 1905. The two narrow gauge locomotives shown on the extreme right of the picture are Fowler 0-4-2T locomotives fitted with cabs by the Arsenal's repair shop. The front bufferbeam on the leading locomotive has clearly been replaced by one of a more typical Woolwich pattern whilst the height of the cylinder end covers suggests that the engine is of the offset drive variety. The front weatherboard fitted to the trailing engine of the two appears to be made of wood.

(Courtesy A. Turner)

Flamingo was the third member of this group, at least during the period after 1889 and before 1896. In the event all three passed in 1905 to Longmoor for construction work on the new standard gauge railway there. The other six Fowler locomotives of this basic type all survived the First World War at Woolwich and were probably scrapped following sale attempts in 1920-1.

The five Bagnall locomotives of this wheel arrangement carried the works Nos 710-714 of 1885 and were supplied to the Royal Arsenal at a cost of £565 each. The cylinder and driving wheel dimensions were the same as those of the Vulcan Foundry locomotives (the trailing wheel diameter apparently goes unrecorded) but the tank capacity was somewhat less at only 120 gallons. The weight in working order was approximately 10½ tons and inside Stephenson/Howe link motion was adopted, driving externally-mounted slide valves through rocker shafts in a manner similar to that later adopted by the Stoke-on-Trent firm of Kerr, Stuart. As with the Vulcan and Fowler locomotives, a domed boiler was utilised in company with a plain stovepipe chimney, but unlike the other two 0-4-2T classes, a cab roof was fitted and this was supported on four pillars.

Although the majority of the 0-4-2T Military Specification locomotives lasted until at least 1919 at Woolwich they do not appear to have been as popular in service as the locomotives specifically designed for use on the RAR. Leslie S. Robertson in *Narrow Gauge Railways Two Feet and Under* referred only to the Bagnall locomotives. He stated that the design of the trailing truck on these locomotives was unsatisfactory and that they were apt to de-rail in service. Be that as it may, four of the five Bagnall 0-4-2 wing tank locomotives survived World War One and these were sold to J.F. Wake of Darlington by 1920.

The next design of locomotive to be considered was constructed specifically for use at the Arsenal and the order for these engines was placed with yet another different firm. The design was in many respects an

An engraving of *Serapis* (Bagnall No. 711 of 1885). Five of these 0-4-2 wing tank locomotives were originally constructed for shipment to Suakin (as per *The Engineer* for 6th March 1885). So far as is known, however, all five spent their entire working life at the Royal Arsenal. The engine illustrated was the first of the class to be withdrawn from service and it was scrapped in 1912. The remaining four locomotives all survived to be sold after the end of World War One, passing to J.F. Wake of Geneva Works, Darlington.

enlargement of the Manning, Wardle class with which it shared a number of common characteristics. Amongst these were the domeless boiler with raised firebox, the wheel arrangement and outside frames, the use of one feedpump and one injector and the adoption of the saddle tank configuration. Significant differences were the shape of the tank and cab, the use of a conventional pattern smokebox door, the entry of the valve rods through the fronts of the steam chests and the fact that most members of the class did not possess a split-level footplate. The resemblance in general arrangement to the Manning, Wardles was not surprising as the builder of the new design was Hudswell,

The first of the Hudswell, Clarke narrow gauge locomotives for the Royal Arsenal Railways, *Carronade* (builder's No. 268 of 1884). The class was known, rather strangely, by the name of the second locomotive of the series, *Culverin* (No. 269).

(Courtesy R. Redman)

Clarke & Co. Ltd, another Leeds concern. The locomotives possessed cylinders of 7in bore and 12in stroke and wheels of 2ft 1in diameter and their weight in working order was approximately 8.6 tons.

Some fourteen locomotives of this general design were turned out between 1884 and 1915 but it must be remembered that there were a number of differences in detail between individual members of the class. At the time of Leslie S. Robertson's Paper in 1898, this design appears to have been the most popular one for 'Main Line' work with the Manning, Wardles at that stage being preferred for Shop work. By 1921, a feature in *The Locomotive* magazine stated that the 'Culverin' class, as these locomotives had become known, were mostly used for Shop work, presumably having been displaced from the Main Line by newer designs of locomotive constructed firstly by Kerr, Stuart and later by Avonside.

Owing to the use of the 'Culverin' class in later years for Shop work, the need arose to prevent the emission

Another locomotive of the basic 'Culverin' type, RL. No.6 supplied to the Royal Laboratory in 1887 (Hudswell, Clarke No. 295). There are a number of differences from the locomotive shown in the previous illustration, the most obvious being the main frame shape and the dropped footplate. After the unification of the RAR system in 1890/1, the engine was named *Grenade*.

(Courtesy R. Redman)

Contemporary engraving of Royal Arsenal 'Culverin' class locomotive *Hector* (Hudswell, Clarke No. 274 of 1885).

(Engineering)

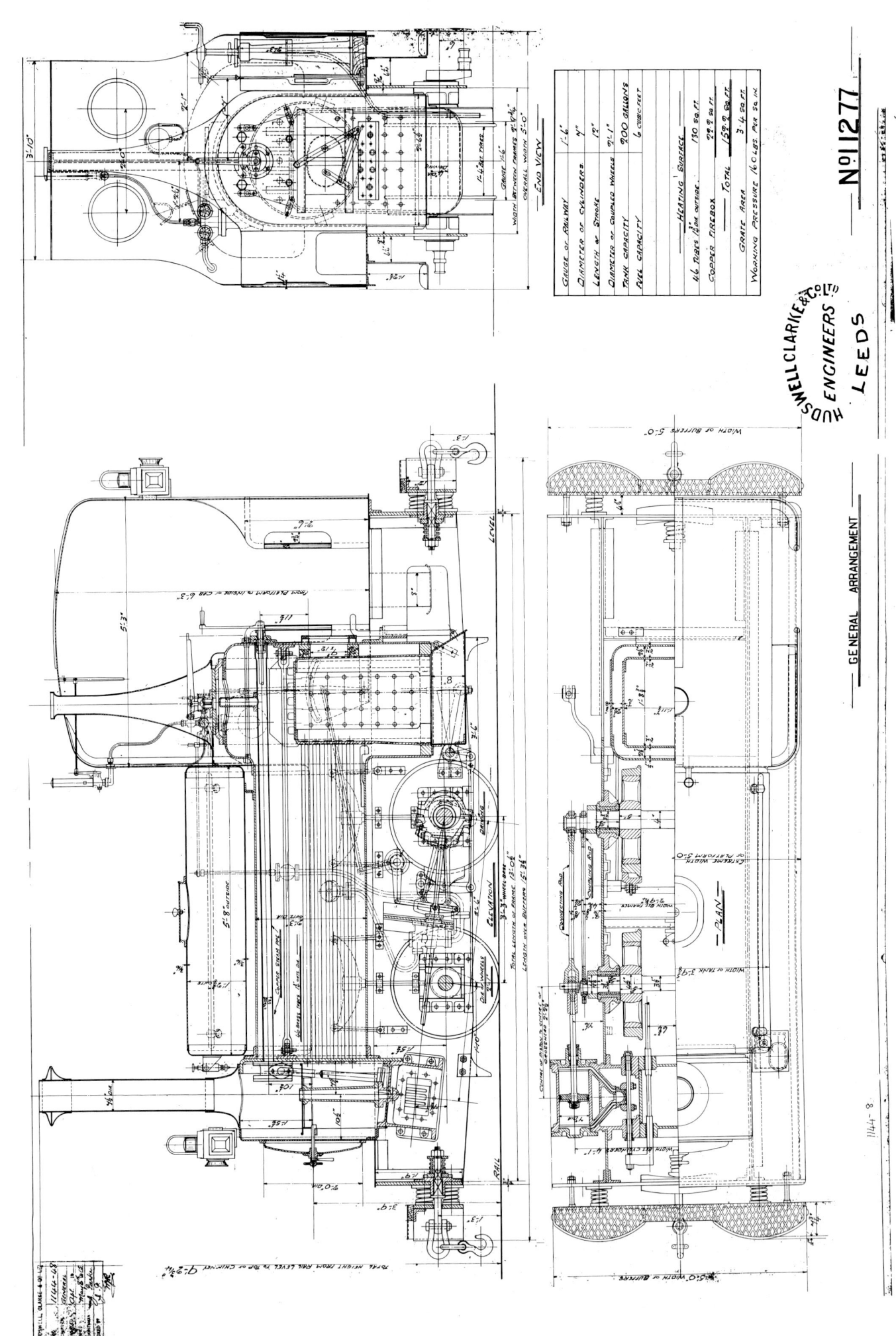

END VIEW

GAUGE OF RAILWAY	1'-6"
DIAMETER OF CYLINDERS	7"
LENGTH OF STROKE	12"
DIAMETER OF COUPLED WHEELS	2'-1"
TANK CAPACITY	200 GALLONS
FUEL CAPACITY	6 CUBIC FEET

HEATING SURFACE	
46 TUBES 1¾" DIAM OUTSIDE	130 SQ FT
COPPER FIREBOX	22·9 SQ FT
TOTAL	152·9 SQ FT
GRATE AREA	3·4 SQ FT
WORKING PRESSURE	160 LBS PER SQ IN

Nº 11277

HUDSWELL CLARKE & CO LTD
ENGINEERS LEEDS

GENERAL ARRANGEMENT

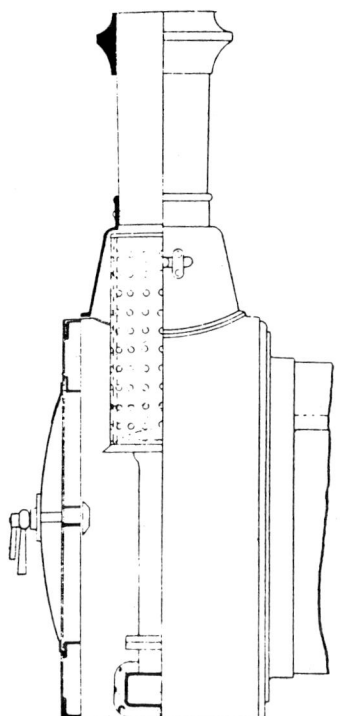

A partly sectional side elevation drawing showing the basic design of the Neath pattern spark arrester, which was eventually fitted to the 'Culverin' class locomotives of the Royal Arsenal Railways. The device consisted of a large multi-perforated cylindrical petticoat pipe with its upper portion accommodated within a tapered 'bubble' extension to the smokebox. The fitting of this appendage necessitated a shorter chimney.

(The Locomotive)

of potentially dangerous sparks, particularly where explosives were present. The fitting of internally mounted spark arresters had actually commenced with the Manning, Wardle, *Arquebus* and, as will be seen, five internal combustion locomotives were supplied between 1896 and 1904 in an attempt to reduce spark emissions in areas close to 'Danger Buildings'. The problem was aggravated subsequently as a result of the more intensive working necessary in the years preceding and during World War One. A special spark arrester was therefore patented by Mr Neath, the Foreman of the Locomotive Department and this was fitted to the 'Culverin' class as they were brought into the Repair Shop for overhaul. The 'Neath' spark arrester was also fitted to some members of the earlier Manning, Wardle locomotives during their final years at Woolwich.

Despite the apparent popularity of the 'Culverin' class, none were retained after the sharp reduction in narrow gauge operations after World War One, and all of the class were sold during 1921-22.

The 1880s saw much experimentation at the Royal Arsenal in the field of novel forms of railway motive power. Shortly before this period Colonel Frederick E. Beaumont RE had built an 18inch gauge compressed air locomotive. This locomotive proved to be deficient

This engraving was featured in *The Engineer* for 26th January 1894 in conjunction with a caption which described an engine lately designed for special work on 18 in gauge by Messrs Bagnall of Castle Engine Works, Stafford. The basic design shows obvious affinities with an earlier Bagnall product, No.1424 of 1893, a 3ft 6in gauge inside framed locomotive supplied to London County Council in 1893. Although fitted with a feedpump and outside Baguley valve gear, it is plain to see that this design formed the basis of the RAR locomotive *Ajax* completed during the following year. This fact is further exemplified by the quoted dimensions for the proposed design of 7in by 12in cylinders and a weight in working order of over 8 tons.

NARROW GAUGE TANK LOCOMOTIVE
MESSRS. W. G. BAGNALL, STAFFORD, ENGINEERS

An unidentified 'Culverin' (believed to be *Scipio*) at work on a munitions train in March 1918. In spite of the engine's allocation to this task, the Neath pattern spark arrester has not been fitted. The large toolbox, oil cans and duty board indicating the train's purpose are of interest.

(Imperial War Museum)

in power and on occasions had to be towed back to its shed. Colonel Beaumont appeared to be undeterred by the difficulties with this engine and, according to accounts in the Journal of the Society of Arts and the Proceedings of the Institution of Mechanical Engineers (both in 1881), a six-cylinder (actually a double 'triplex' compound) compressed air locomotive underwent 3-4 months of trials within the Arsenal. This four-coupled standard gauge locomotive was constructed by

'Culverin' class locomotive, *Hannibal* (Hudswell, Clarke No. 281 of 1885) seen at Woolwich Arsenal circa 1920. The Neath pattern spark arrester is evident but otherwise the engine is in substantially original condition. The battered side panel is an indication of the hard usage which these locomotives endured during World War One. The water inlet valve for the feedpump can also be seen, as can the body of the feedpump vacuum relief valve (immediately in front of the feedpump clack valve).

(The Locomotive)

58

Another view of *Culverin*, this time seen on what is probably an empty freight stock working. This engine was reboilered (along with *Militades*) in 1918-19 and the enclosed upper side portions of the cab appear to have been of pure RAR origin as Maker's drawings for the last five 'Culverins' to be constructed (Hudswell, Clarke Nos 1144-1148 of 1915) show the original pattern of 'wrap over' open-sided weatherboard cab.
(The Locomotive)

Manning, Wardle (No. 761) in 1880 and a contemporary engraving illustrated this locomotive hauling an 18 inch gauge open bogie 'knifeboard' carriage.

During 1886 and 1887 it is known that an experimental 18 inch gauge steam locomotive ran within the Arsenal. This locomotive was described by Thomas Crampton in the Proceedings of the Institution of Mechanical Engineers (1886) as: "a narrow gauge locomotive with four adhesion wheels running on regular work, having two equal cylinders on each side, of 6 inches diameter and 7 inches stroke, which worked on cranks opposite to each other, or 180 degrees apart; the two cranks were close together driving on the outside of the same wheel, one being an overhung or return crank". This engine had clearly been produced as a test bed for a (probably abortive) standard gauge 2-2-2-2T design which appeared in *Iron* magazine and in which the pairs of cylinders were placed diagonally opposite one another in relation to the uncoupled driven axles in order to obtain the ultimate balanced locomotive. The 18 inch gauge locomotive was a con-

Bagnall 0-4-0 tank locomotive No. 1442 of 1895 *Ajax* supplied to the War Office in 1895 for use at Woolwich Arsenal. A substantially similar engine, *Rameses* (No. 1452 of 1896) was shipped to Trinkitat in the Sudan for use on a line of 18 inch gauge linking that port to some water wells at El Teb. This engine's mechanical components were generally standard with those of metre gauge Bagnalls Nos 1447-1451 and 1467-1474 of 1895-6.
(Courtesy F. Jones)

version of an engine which, it was claimed, originally possessed 7in by 14in cylinders and a boiler pressure of 145 psi.

This description does not match any 18 inch gauge locomotive built purposely for the Arsenal or military use, but the two Vulcan Foundry locomotives used at Suakin may have returned to England for use in the Crampton experiments. This suggestion is given weight by the passage in the Proceedings which reads: "and on testing each (locomotive) by itself without a train, to ascertain the friction, the altered engine was found to start with 30 per cent less power than the unaltered. Further exhaustive experiments were being carried out". The unaltered locomotive may have still been extant in 1889, but was probably scrapped before 1896.

Following the 1880's wave of construction of locomotives for military requirements, fewer new locomotives were supplied for use on the narrow gauge network during the ensuing decade. Those which were supplied were not without interest, however, and in 1895 Bagnalls supplied a further engine of a different design to those which they had built previously. This locomotive was of the 0-4-0 wheel arrangement and it was equipped with the peculiar design of inverted saddle tank with which some locomotives constructed by this builder were fitted. The driving wheels of this locomotive were 2ft 1in diameter and the cylinders were 7in bore and 12in stroke. The engine was makers' No. 1442 of 1895 and bore the name *Ajax*. As with four of its other Bagnall stablemates, it survived the First World War to be advertised for sale.

Narrow Gauge Railways Two Feet and Under records that the RAR had 36 18inch gauge steam locomotives in use in 1898. Documentary evidence would suggest that this total comprised 13 Manning, Wardles; *Iron Duke*; nine 'Culverins', six Fowler 0-4-2Ts (*Flamingo* being in store), five Bagnall 0-4-2Ts, a Bagnall 0-4-0T and an odd converted *Handyside* (described in a subsequent section).

In 1896, as has already been mentioned, the Royal Arsenal took delivery of its first internal combustion locomotive. This engine was constructed by Richard Hornsby & Sons Ltd of Grantham as their No. 1705. It was powered by a single-cylindered Hornsby-Akroyd oil engine rated at 9½hp employing geared and jackshaft transmission. The wheels were 1ft 8in diameter with a 3ft 6in wheelbase. The cooling water ran in a coiled pipe passing through a column at the front, through which cold air was drawn. The draught of air through these pipes was created by the exhaust gases from the cylinder. This locomotive was named *Lachesis* and three further locomotives of a similar type *Clotho* (No. 4535 of 1900), *Atropos* (No. 5242 of 1901) and *Hecate* (No. 5883 of 1902) were supplied to the Royal Arsenal. These last three differed in having a front pony truck increasing the total wheelbase to 8ft 6in and a fully enclosed cab. In 1904, a Hornsby-Akroyd locomotive employing a larger 15hp opposed-piston engine was constructed (builder's No. 7226). This engine also found its way to Woolwich, bearing the name *Alecto*, but it was originally supplied to the Inspector of Iron Structures, Chatham (possibly in error). For the reason

The Hornsby-Akroyd oil-engined 0-4-0 locomotive *Lachesis* supplied to Woolwich Arsenal in 1896. Four further compression-ignition locomotives constructed by this builder during the ensuing eight years saw service on the Royal Arsenal Railways system, but all were disposed of from the Arsenal by 1920.

(The Engineer)

Hornsby oil-engined locomotive *Lachesis* seen in a rear three-quarter view when new in 1896.
(Courtesy J. Townsend)

already stated, the Royal Arsenal authorities would certainly have wished to make further use of internal combustion locomotives at this stage but the Hornsby-Akroyd locomotives proved to have insufficient tractive effort to gain greater popularity there than they achieved. Some years later, just two months into the Great War, Baguley-McEwan Pratt Ltd of Burton-on-Trent supplied a petrol-engined rail tractor derived in design from rail tractors supplied by a predecessor firm (McEwan Pratt Ltd of Wickford) for overseas plantation work. This locomotive was builder's No. 630 and named *Megaera* . Its appearance could be distinguished by a large centre cab with radiators mounted on the front and rear and coupling of the axles by means of

W.G. Bagnall No.1452 of 1896 after being dug from the sand, circa 1922, following over a decade of dereliction. It is seen here mounted on a 600 mm gauge War Department Light Railways 'D' class bogie wagon chassis. The engine was scrapped shortly afterwards at Atbara (Sudan Railways) workshops.

(Courtesy D. Ellis)

chains and sprockets. As with the oil-engined Hornsby-Akroyd locomotives, *Megaera* did not survive the 1918-22 wave of narrow gauge locomotive sales at Woolwich, being sold in the auction of 15th November 1921.

After the 1896 introduction of internal combustion power, the next major development in the locomotive practice of the narrow gauge portion of the Royal Arsenal Railways was the construction of the 'Pompey' class. These locomotives were built by Kerr, Stuart & Co. Ltd of Stoke-on-Trent between 1901 and 1914. In its general styling, the design followed the classes constructed by this maker for gauges of 1ft 11½in and above, with its straight sided smokebox, boiler barrel devoid of dome, cab reminiscent of the Skylark class, concentric saddle tank and outside slide valves actuated by inside valve motion. The wheelbase was 3ft 3in and the wheels were 2ft diameter. As with the 'Culverin' class, the 'Pompey' class locomotives were fitted with cylinders of 7in bore and 12in stroke but they were slightly heavier at 9.1 tons in working order. The boiler pressure was 150 psi.

Pompey (Kerr, Stuart No. 1267 of 1912) hauling an open bogie wagon. Despite being the eighth member of the class in works number order, the class was known by the name of this locomotive. The cab design has been lengthened to meet the rear of the saddle tank, thereby dispensing with the gap between the cab and the tank present on Nos 761-763 of 1901.

(The Locomotive)

largest and most modern design of steam locomotive to see service on the 18 inch gauge RAR lines, the choice of builder fell on the Bristol concern of Avonside Engine Co. Ltd. In 1915-6 a series of 16 locomotives of the 'Charlton' class, as these locomotives were known, were supplied. In the use of the 0-4-0 outside framed

configuration and a 3ft 3in wheelbase, these engines certainly followed earlier practice. However but the use of a saddle tank, which had hitherto been the order of the day for most of the narrow gauge steam locomotives constructed specifically for use at the Arsenal (as opposed to being designed for possible trench supply

Right: Maker's general arrangement drawing of oil-fired 'Charlton' class Avonside locomotives (Nos 1715-1718 of 1915 and 1747-1748 of 1916). The oil burner and preheating coil are visible in these views. The use of the side tank configuration in this design was contrary to the normal practice for 18 inch gauge 0-4-0 steam locomotives supplied to the Royal Arsenal Railways.

(Leeds Industrial Museum via G. Horsman)

A Maker's photograph of *Bristol* (Avonside Engine Co. No. 1715 of 1915).

(Courtesy F. Jones)

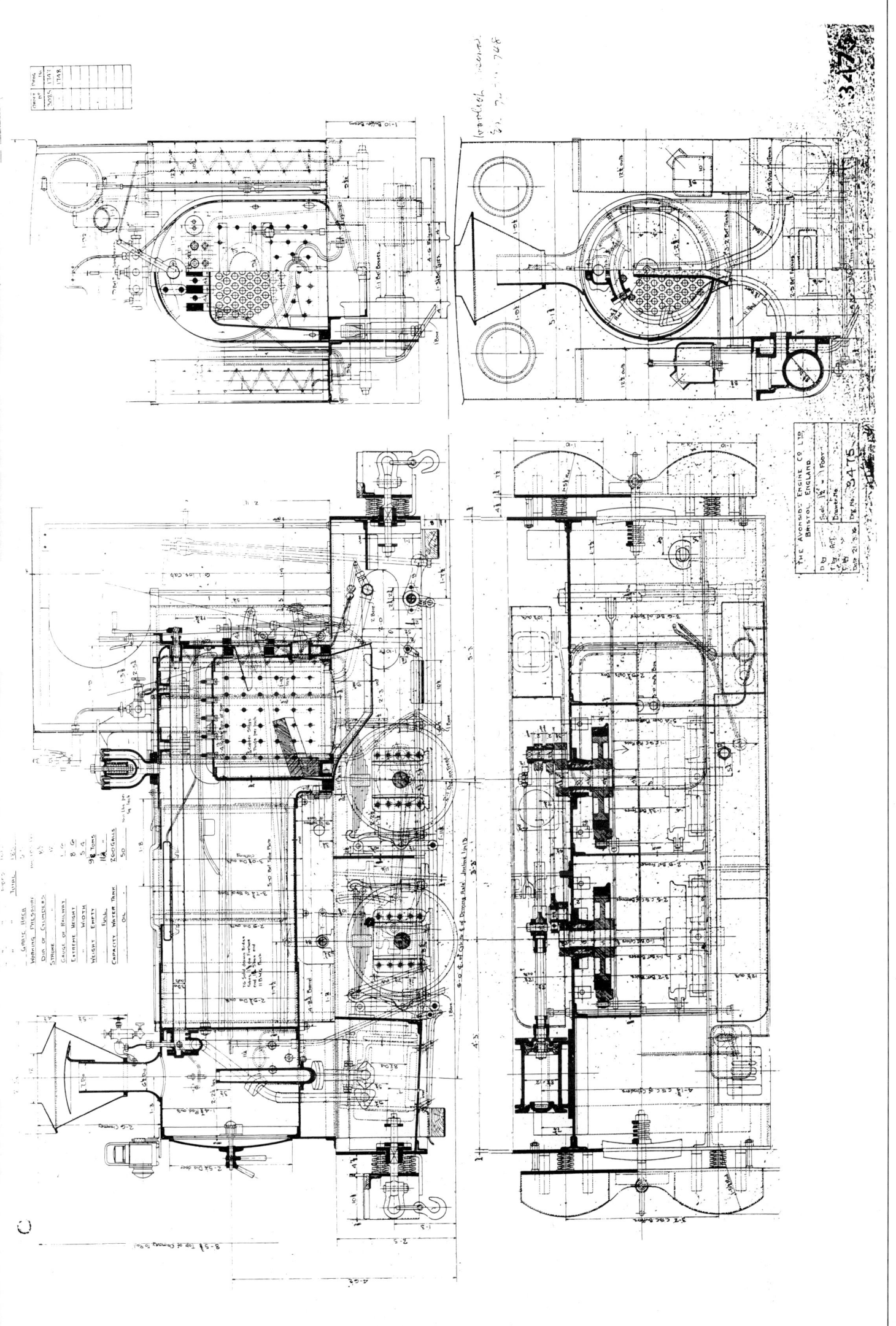

Derby (Avonside No. 1747 of 1916) seen with a Superintendent Saloon. This latter vehicle had certain minor differences from the one shown with *Culverin*, including a third (droplight) window in one end.

(*The Locomotive*)

Avonside 0-4-0T *Charlton* (No. 1752 of 1916) at the Arsenal circa 1919. Unlike *Bristol* and *Derby* this engine was coal fired, a fact indicated by the lack of an oil pipe leading from the rear portion of the tank into the frame aperture beneath the cab.

(*The Locomotive*)

use) was rejected on the 'Charlton' class, in favour of the side tank configuration, accompanied by a firebox which sat above the main frames rather than between them.

The design of these locomotives bore a great resemblance to some of the Maker's products for use on wider gauges. The cylinders were 8½in bore and 12in stroke with outside slide valves actuated by outside Walschaerts valve gear. The wheels were 2ft 1in in diameter and the working pressure was 160 psi. The side tanks held 260 gallons of water and, for the oil-fired members of the class, there was an additional

Coal-fired Avonside 0-4-0T *Sheffield* on a passenger working, probably in 1919. The two compartment closed bogie carriages were constructed within the Royal Arsenal during the 1890s whilst the toast-rack vehicles were Bristol Carriage & Wagon Co. products of 1917 vintage. At least three of these vehicles were fitted with handbrakes after delivery, although 18 inch gauge passenger trains were never equipped for continuous braking. In addition to the Fowler and Woolwich built examples, four open Thirds are known to have been built by Bristol.

(The Locomotive)

capacity for 50 gallons of fuel oil. The weight empty was 9½ tons and in working order, this was increased to 11¼ tons. A balloon pattern spark arrester was fitted to all members of this class, whether coal or oil-fired.

The 'Charlton' class proved to be popular in service, particularly on the Arsenal's internal passenger services from which they largely displaced the 'Culverin' and 'Pompey' classes. An old archive film of the Arsenal, shot in March 1918 and now in the possession of the Imperial War Museum, shows two members of the class engaged on such duty. Six members of the class (Nos 1715-1718, 1747 and 1748) were, however, equipped for oil burning and were allocated to Danger Building work when originally delivered. The burners were of the Kermode variety and the fuel oil was pre-heated by means of a helical coil supplied with steam from a manifold located above the firebox. The spark arresters were still necessary on these locomotives, however, as lighting up and steam raising to a pressure of 20 psi could only be accomplished by using solid fuel in the form of wood. As soon as the requisite pressure was attained, the burner would operate and oil firing could commence.

The popularity of the 'Charltons' was reflected by the fact that they were the most numerous single class of locomotive to operate on the RAR narrow gauge system. All 16 locomotives remained in use at the time of compilation of the feature on the subject of the Royal Arsenal Railways in *The Locomotive* in 1921, but the inevitable disposal of most of the class took

Manchester 0-4-0T, (Avonside No. 1754 of 1916). The practice of displaying a headboard denoting a route allocation or duty is demonstrated to advantage in this view.

(Courtesy F. Jones)

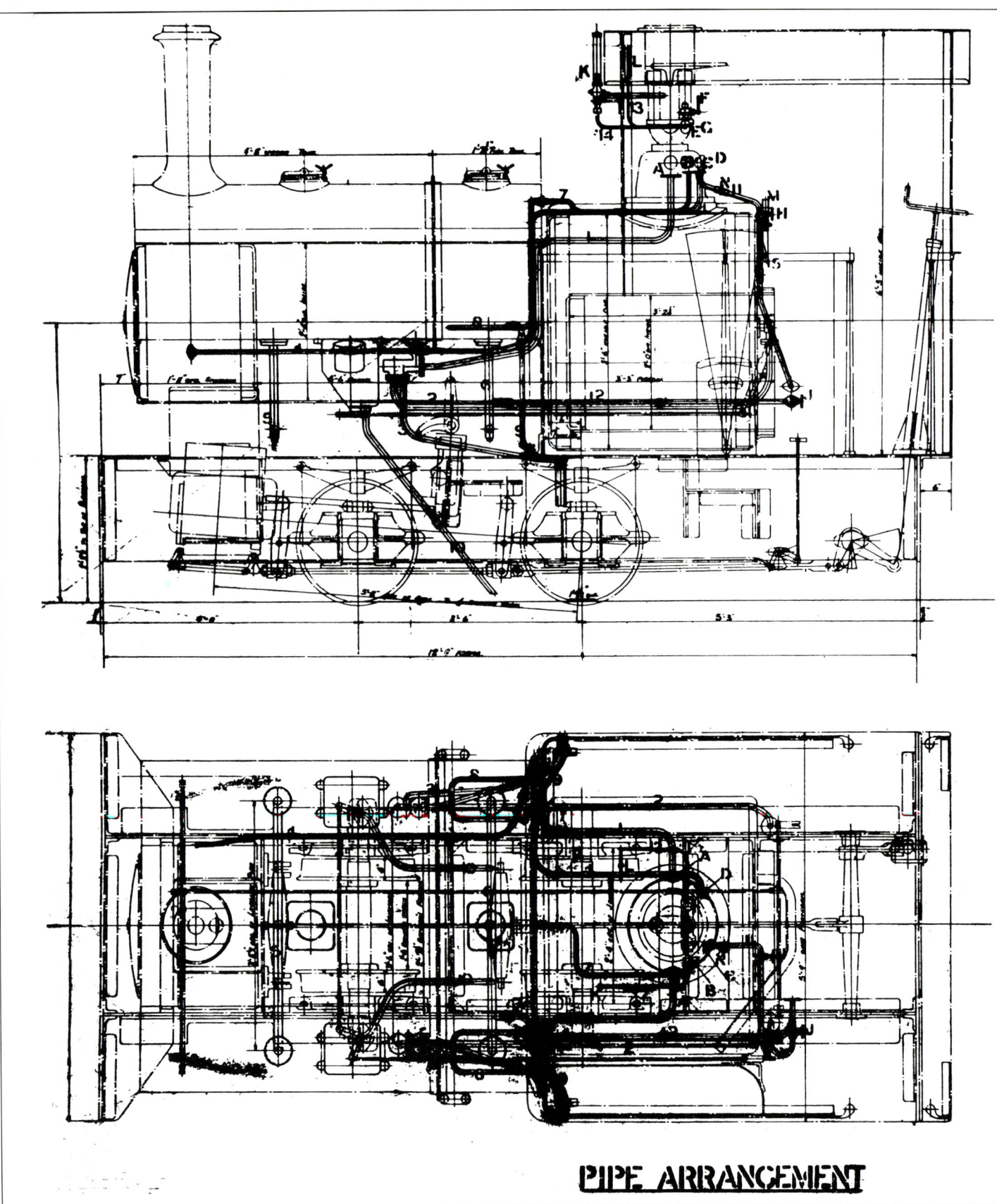

PIPE ARRANGEMENT

place during the years 1922-33. Four of these locomotives, however, survived the post-Armistice rundown of the 18 inch gauge system within the Arsenal and the last survivor in service was, appropriately, *Woolwich* itself, which was not ultimately disposed of until 1959-60. Fortunately, this locomotive was not scrapped but was sold to a dealer based away from the Arsenal and it remains in existence, maintained in operational condition, to the present day at Bicton Park in East Devon. Further details of the engine's career there and

of that line itself will be found in the appropriate chapter.

The sale of this locomotive by the Arsenal ended nearly nine decades of steam locomotive usage on the narrow gauge system, although diesel locomotives of this gauge continued to be present there until the after the cessation of ordnance manufacture in 1967. The 'Charlton' class was not the last 18 inch gauge design of steam locomotive proposed for the Royal Arsenal Railways however, as in May 1940 an oil-fired 0-4-0ST

Left and right: A pipe arrangement drawing of the abortive Royal Arsenal Railways Bagnall 0-4-0ST (No. 2636) ordered and cancelled in 1940.

(Courtesy A. Civil)

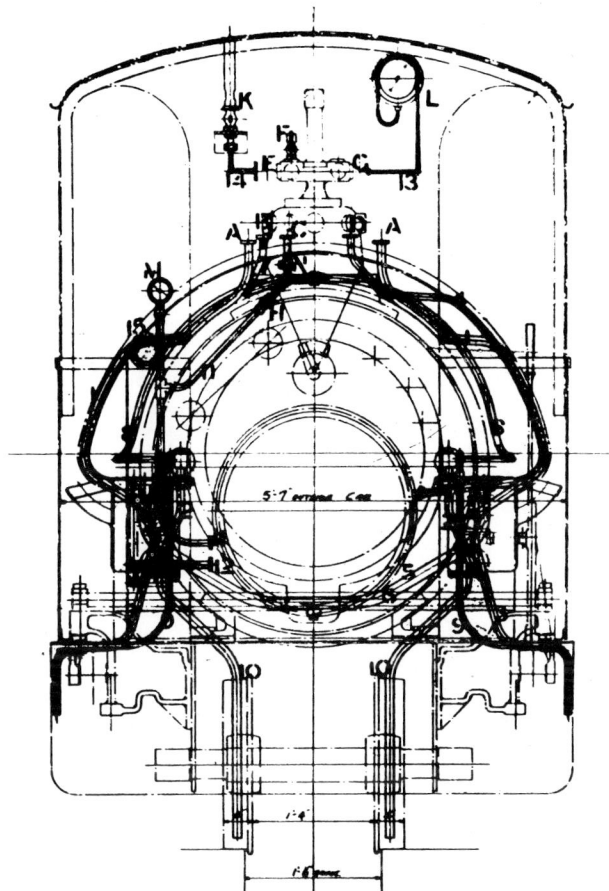

was ordered from Bagnalls. The proposed locomotive was described as having 7in by 12in cylinders, outside frames and a full length saddle tank, but otherwise it was basically the same type as the Maker's No. 2081. The locomotive would have had 1ft 9½in diameter wheels and a wheelbase of 3ft 6in. The firebox would have been of the Bagnall standard cylindrical pattern. The builder's number allocated for the engine was 2636 but the order was cancelled in November 1940 and the completed parts were finally incorporated into a 600 mm gauge locomotive for UNNRA.

Table of Leading Dimensions for Selected RA. Locomotive Classes

Class	'Victoria'	'Iron Duke'	'Culverin'	'Pompey'	'Charlton'
Builder	Manning, Wardle	Vulcan Foundry	Hudswell, Clarke	Kerr, Stuart	Avonside
Cylinders	6in x 8in	7in x 9in	7in x 12in	7in x 12in	8½in x 12in
Wheel Dia.	1ft 8in	1ft 9in	2ft 1in	2ft 0in	2ft 1in
Boiler Pressure	140 psi	?	160 psi	150 psi	160 psi
Coupled Wheelbase	3ft 3in	3ft 9in	3ft 3in	3ft 3in	3ft 3in
Heating Surface	75 sq ft	100 sq ft	152 sq ft	149 sq ft	185 sq ft
Grate Area	1.8 sq ft	2½ sq ft	3.4 sq ft	3.9 sq ft	5½ sq ft
Length over Buffers	14ft 5in	14ft 11in	15ft 3½in	15ft 11in	15ft 1in
Overall Width	5ft	5ft	5ft	5ft 4½in	5ft 4in
Overall Height	8ft 10½in	8ft 5in	9ft 3in	8ft 3in	8ft 5½in
Weight in Working Order	6 ton 12 cwt	7 ton 11 cwt	8 ton 12 cwt	9 ton 2cwt	11 ton 5 cwt

NB All linear dimensions quoted to nearest half inch.

Rolling Stock at Woolwich Arsenal

The details of rolling stock in use during the lifetime of the 18 inch gauge railway system at Woolwich Arsenal are rather sketchy, and the situation is not helped by the apparent dearth of surviving manufacturers' drawings. The disparity in dates between the delivery of the first narrow gauge steam locomotive to the Woolwich Arsenal system (1871) and the official opening of the narrow gauge line in January 1873 has already been mentioned, and it appears that the locomotive in question (Manning, Wardle No. 353 of 1871) probably spent some of its career during the intervening period shunting standard gauge wagons. There are two factors in

particular which appear to support this assertion. The first of these is that the engraving of Manning, Wardle No.353 reproduced in *The Engineer* showed mixed gauge track, in addition to the 'double' buffers on the locomotive. The second factor is inherent in the statement in *Engineering* magazine and the Vignes Technical Study that an experimental stretch of 18 inch gauge cast iron plateway was in use at Chatham Dockyard by 1870 and it is likely that at the time of ordering the first narrow gauge locomotive for use at Woolwich the War Office was still undecided about the suitability of a locomotive-worked 18 inch gauge line

A view showing the cross member supporting the bogie pivot on an ex-Royal Arsenal Railways ammunition van chassis. The forked end to the cross member, embracing the leaf spring assembly, is visible on the far side and the helical spring for the drawgear can also be seen. This photograph was taken at Bicton, Devon in June 1990.

(Author)

for use within the Arsenal complex. The process of moving standard gauge wagons would have provided an adequate test of the capabilities of the Manning, Wardle engine. No details of the earliest narrow gauge rolling stock used at Woolwich appear to be available but it would seem that, particularly where passenger vehicles were concerned, there was a fair degree of similarity with the vehicles used at Chatham Dockyard.

The early Third class 'knifeboard' carriages used at Woolwich, with their single longitudinal seat on each side, were clearly descended from their Chatham counterparts illustrated in *Engineering*, but they differed from the latter in possessing outside-framed bogies and standard RAR buffer and drawgear components. One

This RAR bogie was latterly converted into a four-wheeled wagon chassis by the removal of the drawgear and the fitting of additional bearing surfaces above the axleboxes to take a body. The pivot and drawgear mounting still survive, however. The last significant modification made to this basic design of bogie was the introduction of a strengthened version in 1916. Photographed at Bicton in June 1990.

(Author)

variant of the design was constructed by John Fowler & Co. around 1885 but an example photographed about 1920 appears to have been constructed within the Arsenal, having standard RAR pattern cast bogies.

An early First class closed bogie carriage design was distinguishable by its diagonally planked body panelling and barred windows on the doors. As running at Woolwich these carriages appear to have had three compartments for passenger accommodation, with attendant lamps and roof ventilators. Their date of construction would appear to have been the early 1890s. At least one of these vehicles was still extant at the time of filming in March 1918.

One of the distinctive vehicles which saw service on the RAR was the Superintendent Saloon. This design of carriage dated from the period of expansion of the narrow gauge network which saw the route length rise to approximately 55 miles by 1898. The body was unusual by RAR standards in the fact that no roof ventilators were provided and the roof was of a design clearly inspired by the Spooner 'curly roof' luggage vans of the Festiniog Railway. The ventilators were actually placed over the windows in the doors, which were centrally positioned along the carriage body. In addition to the windows in the doors, six further windows were provided on each side of the body and four on each end, giving a total of eighteen. The body sides, waisted in at the solebars, and ends were also embellished with panelling. The length of the body was approximately 15ft. The solebars were of composite construction being of timber faced with iron or steel overhanging the body at each end. No details apparently survive of the seating arrangements or the bogies, but it is likely that the former were arranged so as to face inwards from the inside faces of the body, so as to adopt a 'conference-orientated' formation, and that the latter were mechanically of the same type as those shown on the wagon drawing in the 1898 Institution of Mechanical Engineers Paper *Narrow Gauge Railways Two Feet and Under*.

It seems certain that at least two vehicles of this basic design existed as the views of them accompanying the locomotives *Culverin* and *Derby* show similar car-

A Woolwich view dating from 1899 showing Manning, Wardle 0-4-0ST *Arquebus* (No. 1130 of 1889) with one of the early First class vehicles. The other vehicle is an early knifeboard Third class vehicle.

(The Navy & Army Illustrated)

One of the early Third class carriages on the 18 inch gauge RAR system seen circa 1920. This example is fitted with standard RAR pattern cast iron bogie frames. The general design is very simple, being composed largely of timber planking sawn to the appropriate lengths, strengthened with irons. These carriages were unbraked and apparently unsprung. As with the sprung bogie vehicles, it was necessary to provide retaining irons to prevent the body from parting company with the bogies in the event of a derailment and one of these is visible in front of the bogie in the foreground. Also visible is a lamp-iron on the end bulkhead.

(The Locomotive)

riages but differing in that one was equipped with an additional window of the droplight pattern at one end. The second window from each end on the sides of the body was also a droplight on the coach seen with *Derby* and it is likely that this was also the case with the one shown with *Culverin*. These carriages were constructed by the RAR workshops, probably about 1895.

At the turn of the century, as a result of further expansion within the Arsenal, the decision was taken to augment the supply of enclosed carriages with vehicles of greater capacity and a design was evolved which would seat 32 passengers. These bogie carriages were 24ft long over headstocks and 6ft wide. The roof, in contrast to the Superintendent Saloon, was of a conventional shape and four torpedo roof ventilators were fitted. As with the earlier First class carriages, oil lighting was provided and the position of the lamps can be discerned from examination of the photographs. Two doors were provided on each side of the carriage body, with two windows being located between these doors. Between one end of the body and its nearest door there were three square windows, on each side and between the other end and its nearest door there were a further two similar windows on each side. The body appears to have been divided into two compartments with the partition being located equidistant between the opposite pairs of doors. As with the Superintendent Saloon, there were two windows in each end and the total number of windows, inclusive of those fitted to the doors, was 22. Additional ventilation was provided by louvres located above all of the windows.

As had been the case with the Superintendent Saloon design, panelling was incorporated into the bodywork of the carriage, although in this case, of a simplified design. The body was waisted in at the solebars and the door hinges were arranged so as to face inwards towards each other. The solebars were of channel section steel construction and the width dimension of 6ft quoted earlier would appear to apply to the chassis. When compared with the channel framed bogie wagons in use on the RAR the solebars on these carriages appeared to be rather lower in relation to rail level and also that the bogie wheels were rather smaller, probably about 9 inch diameter, than those found on the standard wagons. It is a possibility that the bearing irons for the springs were allowed to protrude above the upper level of the solebars in order to reduce the overall height. This modification would have been possible on a passenger vehicle as the upper portions of the springs could have been enclosed by the structure of the seats. It was almost certain that these fine vehicles were First/Second class Composites and that this was the reason for the body partitions. They remained in use until the cessation of narrow gauge passenger working.

With the increased intensity of activity at Woolwich during World War One the need arose for some additional Third class carriages. Unlike the vehicles just described, which were built within the Arsenal, an external supplier was relied upon once more, in this case the Bristol Carriage & Wagon Co. The old 'knifeboard' open carriage design was considered outdated, even for Third class use by this time, and so the seven new vehicles were constructed during the year ended 31st March 1917 to a 'toast-rack' configuration, without windows or doors but with a roof and protective curtains for use in inclement weather. The dimensions of these vehicles were similar to the two compartment coaches already described but the passenger capacity was rather greater as each of these carriages could hold fifty passengers. As with the two-compartment carriages, the 'toast racks' remained in use until 1922–3.

From surviving Woolwich Arsenal records it does not appear possible to ascertain the total number of passenger vehicles in use at any one time, although it is likely that during World War One the number exceeded twenty. When one considers the propensity for survival exhibited by railway carriage bodies as garden sheds, henhouses, bungalow extensions and other similar capacities, it is rather surprising that the Woolwich vehicles seem to have disappeared without trace. There was not even the slightest amount of interest shown by the dealers in Government Surplus equipment made available by the cessation of hostilities at the end of the 1914-1918 War.

The earliest reliable records relating to narrow gauge wagons in use on the RAR system date from the pre-unification period during the 1880s. A surviving John Fowler works photograph of 1885 showing the 0-4-2T locomotive *Cormorant* also illustrates three bogie vehicles. The nearest of these to the locomotive is identifiable as one of the early open Third class carriages already described, whilst the two-plank open

Cormorant, a locomotive constructed by John Fowler & Co. of Leeds in 1885 to the War Office 0-4-2 tank specification of the period. Unlike the Vulcan Foundry design, these locomotives were fitted with round topped firebox wrappers. The offset drive and outside link motion are features of interest, as is the design of buffer.

(University of Reading)

wagon immediately behind it is of similar dimensions and uses the same standard Fowler plate framed bogies. The last vehicle is of fully open configuration with end fences, plate-framed bogies and a chassis slightly shorter in length than that of the two-plank

This Maker's photograph shows J. Fowler & Co. No. 5064 of 1885, ultimately named either *Owl* or *Pelican* (it cannot now be ascertained which of these two names this locomotive carried). All of the Fowler 0-4-2 tanks eventually used at the Royal Arsenal were named after birds. Nos 5063 and 5064 possessed several detail differences from *Cormorant*, the most important being lower set cylinders with direct drive to the crank and outside Joy's valve gear. These locomotives were an afterthought design completed when the prospect of usage at Suakin had passed, although certain other Fowler narrow gauge designs were developed from them.

(University of Reading)

open wagon. One of the vehicles visible in an early photograph appears to be a Fowler wagon chassis of this period, although the illustration is not sufficiently clear to prove this beyond doubt.

At the time of the preparation of Leslie S. Robertson's Paper *Narrow Gauge Railways Two Feet and Under* there were approximately 700 narrow gauge carriages and wagons in use on the RAR system, and with the unification of the system, came the evolution of standardised under frame designs. By 1898 the familiar channel section steel-framed bogie chassis which was to be associated with the remainder of the life of the narrow gauge system had come into being. The wagon depicted in Robertson's paper combined this type of chassis with a five-plank pitch pine body surmounted by a canvas covered zinc roof, which was intended to isolate the dangerously inflammable cargo

A set of drawings originally produced for the 1898 Institution of Mechanical Engineers Paper *Narrow Gauge Railways Two Feet and Under* showing a covered ammunition van of the period. The channel framed steel chassis became standard for bogie wagons constructed for RAR narrow gauge use from the late 1890s onwards, (although its basic design dated back to the 1870s), as did the peculiar form of suspension in which the spring buckles were gripped by the opposite ends of the cross-member housing the bogie pivot.

(Institution of Mechanical Engineers)

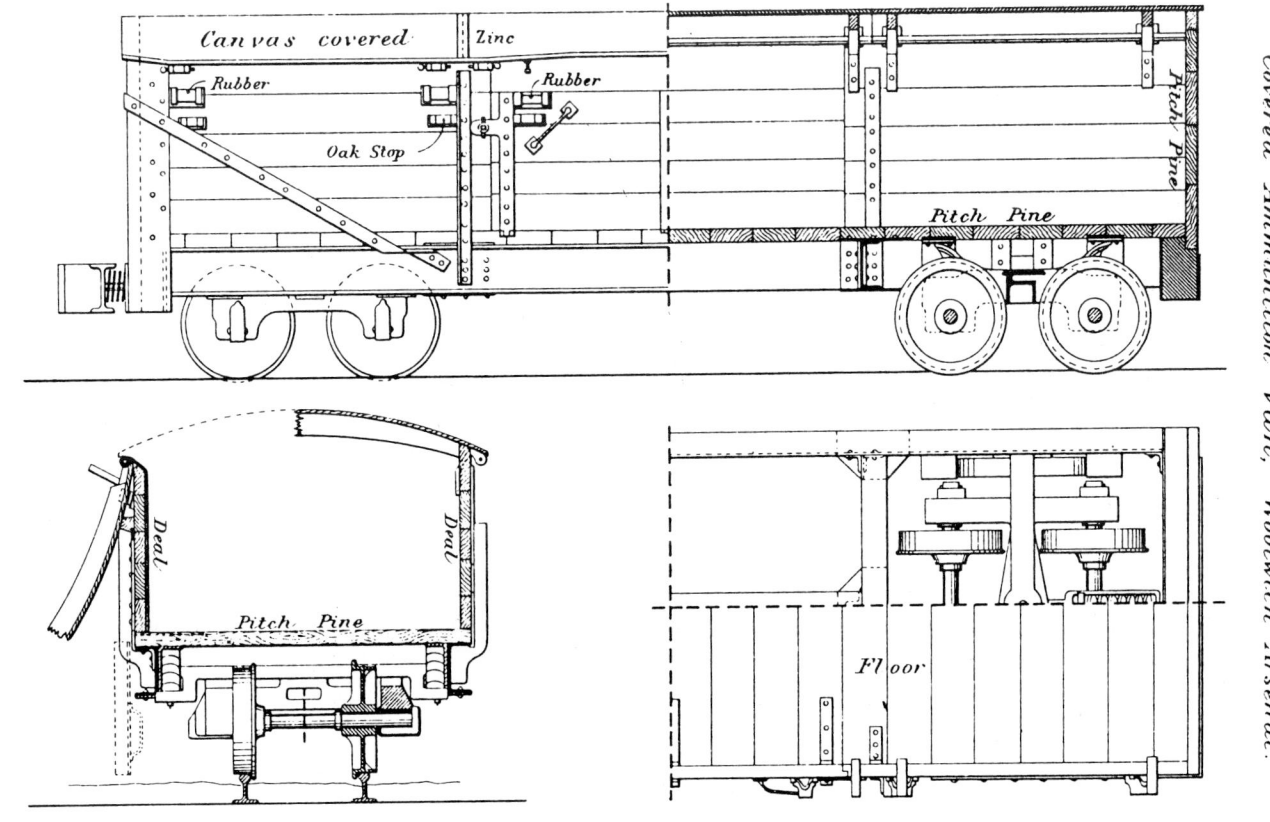

A four-wheeled standard covered ammunition wagon of P.W. Maclellan parentage, purchased for preservation from the Royal Arsenal in 1970 and currently (1992) displayed in the Conwy Valley Railway Museum alongside a John Knowles clay 'tub'.

(Courtesy D. Brewer)

The Woolwich Arsenal System and Operational Methods

As early as the 1820s, a primitive tramway for the movement of stores between various buildings within the Royal Arsenal complex had been authorised. Details of the early history of this system are sketchy but a fortunate survival from the historian's point of view is an Ordnance Survey map of the Arsenal surveyed in 1864 and drawn in 1866. This map indicates that by this time, the tramway had become a railway in its own right with a connection to the South Eastern Railway's North Kent main line. The connection was some distance to the east of Woolwich Arsenal station, with the approach being made facing the Plumstead side. This standard gauge railway passed through the Arsenal's boundary wall at the latter's south-easterly corner and its 'main line' was continued so as to curve round (initially in a north-easterly and finally a south-westerly direction) to reach the shipping sheds, just to the north of the Military Store Department. The line then continued round to run to the north of the Carriage Department in a south-easterly direction before swinging north-easterly to make a junction with itself just to the north-east of the Gun Factory Department.

Within the loop of the internal 'main line', there were branches serving many of the individual buildings comprising the Military Stores Department and the Gun Factory. There were also other branches outside of the main line loop serving, amongst others, buildings of the Laboratory and the Carriage Department. From the north-easterly part of the main line, two branches served the Proof Butts. Unfortunately, no details appear to survive concerning the extent to which (if at all) SER locomotives would have been allowed to enter the Arsenal complex at this early stage, or whether the track was of a nature so as to allow this to be possible. Internal traffic at this time was purely horse-worked and no standard gauge locomotives were purchased for use by the Arsenal until 1875.

The main 1864-66 plan illustrated all too well, however, why the use of a railway line of 18 inch gauge was implemented at Woolwich Arsenal. Access to many of the lines serving individual buildings could only be obtained by small wagon turntables, owing to the severely restricted space available in some areas. Another difficulty was that some buildings did not process sufficient materials to justify the capacity available in a standard gauge wagon and therefore parts of the system were under-utilised. Additional pressure for the use of an 18 inch gauge system was brought about in the late 1860s by the fact that the Admiralty had experienced similar difficulties with a standard gauge tramway in Portsmouth Dockyard, and as a result

Right: Part of an Ordnance Survey map of 1878 showing the railway system associated with the Royal Gun Factory, the Royal Laboratory and the Royal Carriage Department sections of the Arsenal.

(Public Record Office Ref. WO78/3008)

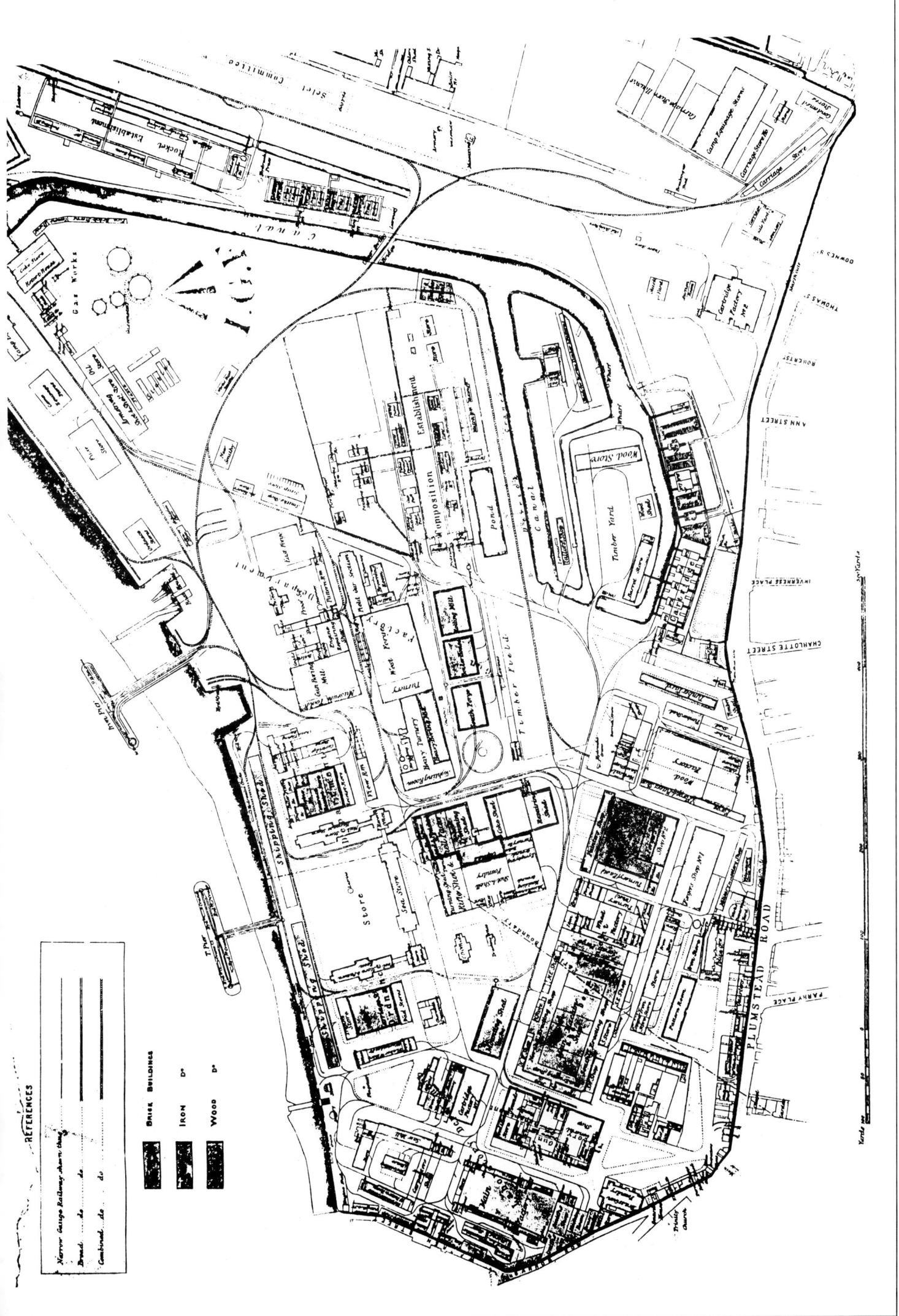

desired to utilise some 18 inch gauge permanent way in Chatham Dockyard, then undergoing reconstruction and extension under the direction of Colonel Pasley RE.

It was decided therefore to experiment with 18 inch gauge railway systems at both Woolwich and Chatham in the late 1860s, with the Chatham line at least being horse-worked during its first few years. As has already been noted, the official opening date quoted in *The Locomotive* magazine for the 18 inch gauge system at Woolwich Arsenal as 10th January 1873 is not easy to reconcile with the Manning, Wardle records which show the first locomotive, *Lord Raglan*, as having been delivered to the Arsenal in March 1871. It is suggested that in the meantime the engine may have been used in the pursuance of construction work on the narrow gauge system. The practice of narrow gauge steam locomotives hauling standard gauge wagons (another possibility), did not become standard practice after 1873 on the Arsenal's Railways, although it should also be noted, however, that *The Locomotive* in 1921 recorded that the Hornsby-Akroyd locomotives had been used to shunt standard gauge trucks over parts of the RAR system where the fire risk was exceptionally acute. This was accomplished by means of the use of special 'divider' trucks which were obsolete by this time.

According to the feature in *The Locomotive*, the first section of narrow gauge track to be opened for normal service ran between the West Wharf and the rear of the Shell Foundry. If a close examination of the 1878 Ordnance Survey map is undertaken, it can be seen that there is a pure narrow gauge line branching off from the mixed gauge trackwork situated to the north of, and at the western end of, the Shipping Sheds. This line passed to the west of the Ordnance Stores and then swung round through 90 degrees to pass to the north of the Carriage Erecting Shop before following a course to the north of, and finally into, the Shell Foundry.

During the first 25 years of narrow gauge operation there was considerable enlargement of the Royal Arsenal Railways network and the 1893 Ordnance Survey map is representative of this early period of consolidation. Unfortunately, the extreme western tip of the Arsenal Complex (actually part of the Royal Laboratory area) has emerged on the reproduced map in a rather dark contrast, but this is as a result of the condition of the original. The area of the Complex to the west of the East Wharf housed the three departments responsible for the operation of the RAR system prior to the end of 1890, namely the Royal Laboratory, the Royal Carriage Department and the Royal Gun Factory.

With effect from 1st January 1891 the decision was taken to unify the railway system and for the ensuing three decades it was placed under military control. The first Traffic Manager of the unified RAR system was Lt E.P.C. Girouard of the Royal Engineers and he arranged for the Arsenal's railway to be used for the purpose of training Royal Engineers personnel in the skills necessary for the operation of railways. By 1898, the date of Leslie S. Robertson's Paper *Narrow Gauge Railways Two Feet and Under*, the Royal Arsenal Railway network was said to comprise 30 miles of narrow gauge track and 25 miles of mixed gauge permanent way. In the 1893 map, the pure narrow gauge lines are those denoted by a thin line, whereas the mixed gauge trackwork is indicated

Right: An Ordnance Survey map showing the Woolwich Arsenal site in 1893 and its railway system. The narrow gauge trackwork is indicated by the thin line and the mixed gauge by the broader shaded line. The ring configuration of narrow and standard gauge main lines is clearly visible and the Locomotive Shed can be seen to the south of the Gas Works. A much later set of maps, which are too complex for reproduction in this volume, show the extent of the RAR system at its most extensive, just after the conclusion of World War One. By this time, the 18 inch gauge metals extended to Erith Marshes (some distance to the east of the 1893 map) and the narrow gauge passenger service ran between Dial Square, near the Main Gate at the west of the Arsenal, and 'Berber Railway Station', on the edge of Erith Marshes.
(Public Record Office Ref. WO78/3008)

for the most part by the broader line. Although not mentioned in Leslie Robertson's Paper, there was a small amount of purely standard gauge track at this stage. This was located principally in the vicinity of the Proof Butts.

A virtue of the narrow gauge part of the RAR system, which was mentioned in the Robertson Paper, was the fact that the main line was in the form of a ring, rather akin to London's 'Inner Circle'. In actual fact it was possible for a narrow gauge train to traverse a ring main line in more than one possible configuration, a fact well illustrated in accompanying plans. The advantage of a main line in the form of a ring was that a narrow gauge wagon could be loaded in a particular shop, moved to the nearest junction with the main line and then taken round the appropriate portion of the ring to the most convenient junction in relation to its ultimate destination. Such a mode of operation ensured the minimum of inconvenience in the form of locomotive or train reversals. The RAR system was at this time divided into six operational sections, linked by telephone and it was estimated that, in 1898, an average of 400 wagons (or 2,000 train tons inclusive of tare weight) passed over the narrow gauge main line daily. In addition, there were special coal workings and passenger trains, these latter workings being principally for the use of the Arsenal's workforce. Passenger trains were run at this stage at 30-minute intervals with stops being made approximately $\frac{1}{4}$ mile apart. It was estimated that each day a total of 3,200 passenger-miles were worked at an annual cost of £200.

A feature of interest about the operational methods employed on the Royal Arsenal Railways is that semaphore signalling does not appear to have been widely used. Photographs taken during the first two decades of the twentieth century do not show signalling of this type and those of the 1918-20 era show that most trains carried indicator duty boards displaying their functions. The operational rules as at 1943, covering narrow and standard gauge working have fortunately survived and these will be discussed in the following Section.

After the conclusion of the South African War in 1902 there was a relaxation of activities at the Arsenal for a few years, and the decision was taken at this time to place the responsibility for the upkeep of the permanent way in the hands of a civilian railway engineer in the form of Mr N.W.J. Gibson. Captain Girouard (as he had by then become) was succeeded as Traffic Manager by Captain D. Miller RE, who was to remain in charge of operations during the period leading up to the outbreak of World War One.

The period from 1914-21 proved to be an eventful one for the RAR as Captain Miller was required for duties elsewhere and he was succeeded in turn by sev-

ROYAL ARSENAL
WOOLWICH
GENERAL PLAN

RIVER THAMES

War Department Property
NORTH WOOLWICH.

eral other Royal Engineers officers with railway operating experience in civilian life. The vastly increased demand for munitions resulted in further enlargement of the RAR system and by the end of the war, the standard gauge extended to a distance of 120 miles, most of which was also equipped for narrow gauge working by means of a third rail. There was also for a short period a stretch of 2ft gauge line in use. By this time, the Arsenal site extended to an area of 1,300 acres, with a maximum length of over three miles and a maximum width of over one mile. The river frontage extended to nearly four miles and much of the railway system, including a station utilising materials salvaged from the abortive Suakin-Berber Railway, and known as 'Berber Junction', lay within an area to the east of that shown in the 1893 Ordnance Survey map.

As a measure of the intensity of operations on the railway system during World War One, it was estimated that over a million standard gauge wagons were exchanged with the South Eastern & Chatham Railway during the course of the War, with approximately 7,000 being exchanged in a single week. This compared with a maximum weekly figure of 1,085 during the South African War. The increased traffic intensity necessitated the construction of a new 16-road standard gauge marshalling yard at the eastern end of the Arsenal for dealing with the wagon exchanges.

As an indication of the demands placed upon the operating staff during the First World War, it interesting to note that the total RAR shed staff rose in number from 134 in August 1914 to 433 in September 1918, with the number of drivers during the same period rising from 55 to a little under 200. These figures comprise personnel responsible for both narrow and standard gauge facilities. Although the activities of the First World War resulted in there being 62 18 inch gauge steam locomotives in use at one time, the expansion of the standard gauge network during the same period, and the corresponding modernisation of facilities which this entailed, it was realised that when the Armistice came there would be little further need for a

narrow gauge main line. By the end of 1922, all except ten of the narrow gauge steam locomotives which had operated on the RAR system had been sold and the workers' passenger service (which had operated so intensively from Dial Square to the eastern end of the Arsenal during the period of hostilities) with its First, Second and Third class accommodation had been discontinued in favour of an all-Third class standard gauge service. Narrow gauge operations were thereafter confined to the serving of magazines. The portions which remained were to prove their worth subsequently during World War Two, although certain technical and historical observations must be made before considering this period.

In 1921 the decision was taken to bring control of the RAR system under civilian influence and at the time of the feature in *The Locomotive* ultimate responsibility rested with G.H. Roberts CBE, M.Inst. C.E., M.Inst. Mech.E. who acted as Superintendent of Electrical, Mechanical and Civil Engineering at the Royal Arsenal. In the same year, the post of Permanent Way Engineer was abolished, with Mr Gibson leaving his residence in Dial Square, at the western end of the Arsenal in consequence, and Mr F.W. Turner, a former Great Eastern Railway employee, took over as Traffic Manager. The RAR system remained under civilian control for the remainder of its existence.

One of the aspects of the RAR which enhanced its distinctive character, but not its ease of operation, was the requirement for mixed-gauge turnouts. The arrangements for these are shown in an accompanying plan. The basic principle behind these turnouts was

The mixed gauge switches, point levers and turnouts used on the Royal Arsenal Railways at Woolwich. The turnouts shown are all of the single-switch variety but the handles labelled 'Fig.3' controlled a turnout of the three-switch variety. The operating practices in use at Woolwich enabled the use of partially self-acting pointwork.

(The Locomotive)

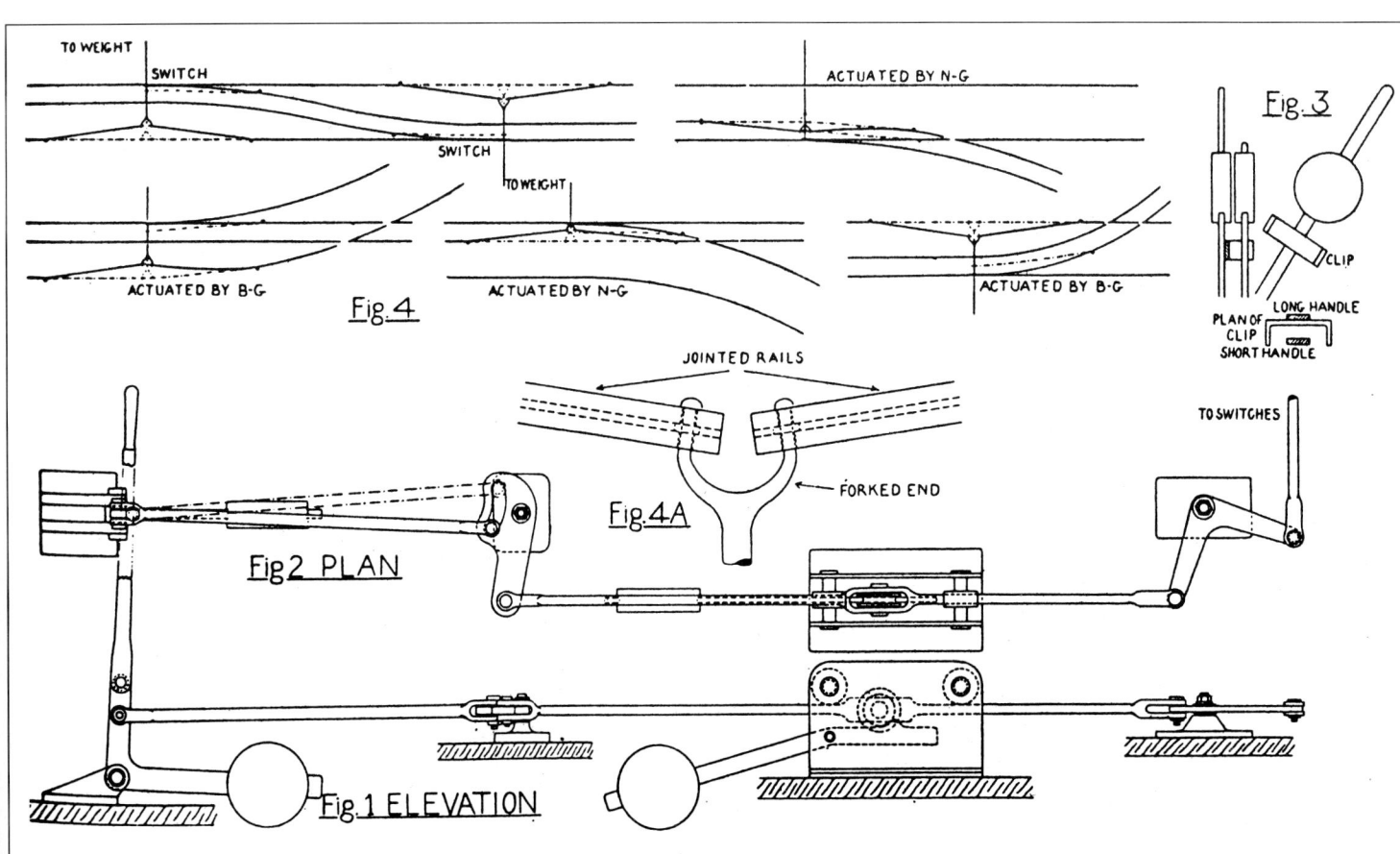

that the two rails opposite the rail being switched (in the standard or narrow gauge sense depending upon which gauge actuated the turnout) were jointed with the open ends being connected to a fork mounted on the end of the switch rod. The weight on the switch held the ends of the jointed rails in an open rest position, thereby setting the normal route in accordance with standard operational procedures. It was possible, however for a train coming from the trailing direction to bear against the jointed rails, which rested in a position so as to be 4in tight to gauge, so as to reverse the switch. The weight would then reset the switch to its normal rest position as soon as the train had passed. The jointed rails were each approximately 10ft long, so as to prevent the switch from resetting itself when a train was in progress over it (the distance between adjacent axles in a train being less than 20ft).

The type of three-switch turnout control illustrated in the plan exhibited a more complex structure. In this instance one switch was common to both gauges, whilst one switch was purely standard gauge and the other was purely narrow gauge. Points of this kind were controlled by two levers, the longer of which was linked to the exclusively standard gauge switch, whilst the shorter lever was linked to the exclusively narrow gauge switch and the switch common to both gauges. A clip was fitted to the longer lever in such a manner as to embrace the shorter one. The rationale behind this mechanical contrivance was that narrow gauge trains approaching from the trailing side were often unable to move both the combined and standard gauge switches under their own weight. By means of a certain amount of play between the clip and the shorter lever, narrow gauge trains approaching from the 'blocked' trailing side were only required to actuate two switches (ie the one for the purely narrow gauge line and the common switch). If the longer lever was moved, either manually or by means of a standard gauge train approaching

from the 'blocked' trailing side, then the adjacent face of the clip on the longer lever would cause the shorter lever to move so as to adjust the common switch to the correct position for the desired direction of travel for the standard gauge train.

One of the problems faced at Woolwich Arsenal in laying out the railway system was inherent in the large number of road crossings. This difficulty is readily apparent from an examination of railway remains at the Arsenal today. In some instances, therefore, it was necessary to site point lever and weight assemblies below ground level, thereby incurring the penalty of further complication during construction.

Much of the early permanent way for purely narrow gauge lines on the RAR system consisted of cast iron tram-plates of standard sizes with grooves which had outer faces the requisite 18 inches apart. This type of permanent way will be described more fully in connection with the narrow gauge trackwork at Chatham, but it was of interest in the Woolwich context in the fact that plates of this type were actually cast within the Arsenal itself. A photograph of the interior of one of the Royal Carriage Department buildings shows this type of permanent way in place. Although it was highly praised in *Engineering* in 1875, this type of trackwork did not find long term favour with the Woolwich authorities as it was claimed, over two decades later, that it damaged the wheel treads of both locomotives and rolling stock. It must also be remembered that such track was not suitable for mixed gauge pointwork and that it would also have been of little use in military railway experimentation. By the end of the nineteenth

Ruston & Hornsby diesel locomotive No. 213840 of 1942 seen shortly before its 1971 departure from the Arsenal. Today this engine still survives, on the private Great Bush Railway in East Sussex, having been regauged to 2 ft.

(Courtesy D. Brewer)

century, therefore, it was standard RAR practice to use 41 lb/yd flat-bottomed rail for purely narrow gauge lines, 56 lb/yd flat-bottomed rail for mixed gauge lines and 105 lb/yd for heavy standard gauge gun roads where vehicle weights were eventually to reach 170 tons. By 1921 British Standard flat-bottomed rail of 75 lb/yd. was the norm for mixed gauge lines whilst the 56 lb/yd. rail, which had formerly been used for this purpose, was now standard for the pure narrow gauge lines.

Although the role of the 18 inch gauge railway in the Royal Arsenal was very much diminished after 1922, it was still of sufficient importance to warrant the purchase of five diesel-mechanical locomotives, including the pioneering double-bogie Hunslet locomotive, *Albert*, builder's No. 1722 of 1934, and the proposal for the construction of a new steam locomotive. Some remaining portions of the old narrow gauge system remained active right up until the 1960s, although there was comparatively little usage of the RAR system after the Suez crisis of 1956. The manufacture of munitions at Woolwich finally ceased in 1967.

The 1943 RAR Standing Orders Book

Although surviving documentation of RAR operational procedures is rare, one particularly interesting survival is the 1943 Standing Orders Book. Most of the RAR system was standard gauge by this time but the principles of operation would not have been greatly altered from the First World War period. The General Orders (Nos 1-13) dealt with routine matters such as punctuality, overtime, the duties placed upon drivers to train stokers in relation to locomotive care and Traffic Section requirements, the care of stores such as overalls and shunting poles and the economical use of locomotive coal.

The Shed Orders (Nos 14-30) covered several important points. Drivers were required to stable their engines as directed by the Traffic Foreman, and to assist in the coaling and watering of them whilst on shed. Each driver was also required to obtain a log sheet before leaving the shed and to hand it to the Train Despatcher for the relevant Section (or other responsible person), to have the time of arrival for the job inserted and initialled. The log sheet had to be collected before returning to the shed and deposited at the Clocking Station at the end of a shift. There were miscellaneous provisions relating to the reduction of fire risks from locomotive ashpans and to the supply of softened and unsoftened varieties of locomotive water from particular hydrants. The prompt recording of engine defects in a 'Repair' book kept at the Locomotive Sheds was required and one provision in particular obliged the proper care and testing of fittings such as water gauges, injectors and sanding gear. This provision went on to read: "Where engines are fitted with two injectors or with pump and injector, both must be used frequently to prevent either becoming unworkable". The reference to a pump and injector was certainly redundant from the narrow gauge point of view by 1943 as the last such locomotives so fitted had been sold in 1922!

Drivers and stokers were obliged to take every care in ensuring that locomotive boilers were fired in such a manner as to prevent the emission of smoke, particularly when near offices and inside shops. On coal-fired locomotives frequent firing in small quantities and the judicious use of the firehole door, blower and damper were urged in order to minimise smoke emission. Stoking was prohibited altogether in the vicinity of Danger Building enclosures, as was the standing of coal-fired locomotives in these areas. Interference by drivers with the proper working of spark arresters was also prohibited, as were additions to cabs which impaired either the look-out which was obtainable or the prompt access to any of the engine's controls.

Special instructions (Orders 60-72) were issued to drivers of oil-fired locomotives. It was recognised that a steam pressure of between 10 and 25 psi was necessary to activate the ejector supplying oil to the burner, this being raised by means of solid fuel. No oil was to be admitted until it could be carried well into the firebox which was sufficiently hot for ignition to take place. The procedure to be used when starting the oil burner was first to turn on the main blower, to create a forward draught, and then the ejector. The oil supply would then be turned on and only left on if prompt ignition resulted. Finally the steam blower would be turned off once the oil was burning satisfactorily. In order to shut down the oil burning process, the oil tank cocks would be turned off and steam would be allowed to blow through the burner nozzle for a few minutes to ensure clearance of the oil pipes to the burner. The valves on these pipes would then be shut off, followed by the steam supply to the ejector. There were assorted orders in this section relating to the prevention of excess smoke emission, the cleaning out of the Avonside 'balloon' spark arresters and the elimination of fire risks from oil spillage associated with tanks, burners and ashpans.

From the operational point of view, much detail is revealed by the Running Orders (Nos 31-59). The first of these orders prohibited the movement under steam of any engine by any person other than drivers, stokers or other authorised individuals. Locomotives at rest were required to be put in mid-gear and the brakes put on at the end of a shift. Stokers were not to assume complete control of an engine except in very exceptional circumstances. Locomotives working in sections or on the 'main line' were not permitted to leave their work without reference to the Train Despatcher for the section in question who was obliged to dispose of any trucks for that section before releasing the engine. Whilst in a particular section the locomotive driver was obliged to obey the instructions of the Train Despatcher with regards to all train movements. As early as 1898, it is recorded that the sections were linked by telephonic communication. When locomotives were working in a department, rather than on the 'main line', the Departmental Foreman exercised the functions of a Train Despatcher.

By 1943 the frequent passenger narrow gauge service which had existed at the time of World War One had given way to a Third class standard gauge service on which speeds were restricted to 12 miles per hour inside and 15 miles per hour outside the East Gate Wall. It seems likely that speed restrictions for the narrow gauge passenger workings were similar. In foggy weather train speeds could be restricted to 3 miles per hour.

Head and tail lamps were to be lit under all circumstances at the same time as street lamps and in foggy weather or during falling snow. Shunting and goods locomotives were obliged to carry a red light at each end, one at the base of the chimney and one at the centre of the cab. Passenger locomotives were required to carry a lamp over the left buffer and one at the base of the chimney when working smokebox first, and a lamp in the centre of the cab and one over the left buffer when working cab first, a tail lamp being carried by the rearmost carriage in both circumstances. The fastening of doors on passenger carriages before departure was the responsibility of the Shunter Guard.

Engines were required to carry a duty board at each end which had to be changed by the driver with each change of duty. These appear on several of the extant photographs of the narrow gauge locomotives, although contravention of this provision is much in evidence.

As there were few semaphore signals, drivers were obliged to approach all crossings and turnouts at reduced speed and weighted points were to be reset after traversing, if necessary, in favour of the 'main line' in most instances.

In general railway traffic had right of way priority over road traffic but this rule had been reversed by 1943 as regards ambulances and fire tenders.

Locomotive Development at Chatham Dockyard

As has already been noted, the mainstay of early 18 inch gauge operations at Chatham Dockyard was a class of Manning, Wardle locomotives of similar basic specification to those used at Woolwich Arsenal. There were, as has also been stated, a number of detail differences between the basic design of the Chatham locomotives and their Woolwich contemporaries, particularly with regard to the configuration of the main frames and the handbrake arrangements.

In all, six locomotives of the basic type were supplied to Chatham Dockyard and they are listed here with their delivery dates: No.386 *Trafalgar* (6/12/1871), No.424 *Busy Bee* (4/12/1872), No.506 *Fidget* (13/4/1874), No.910 *Comet* (11/9/1883), No.1429 *Khartum* (2/2/1899) and No.1430 *Prompt* (2/2/1899).

From Maker's records it can be discerned that the basic design was altered somewhat during the period 1871-1899. No.424 is recorded as being slightly reduced in overall length and width when compared with No.386 (a fact also referred to in *Engineering* in 1875). No.506 was the first of the Dockyard locomotives to have the RAR pattern composite buffer and the ornate canopy shown on the Maker's drawings of No.424 had given way to a more austere pattern by the time of the construction of Nos 1429 and 1430.

Unlike their RAR counterparts, there is comparatively little information about the disposal of the small Chatham Manning, Wardles, although an advertisement in *Surplus* for 15th August 1921 lists *Trafalgar* and *Prompt* as being for sale. The precise scrapping dates of these locomotives are unknown.

Although strictly speaking beyond the scope of this volume, it should be noted that four Manning, Wardle locomotives of similar dimensions were supplied for export, with three going to Argentina. The last of these (No. 2039) was not completed until 1924, thereby resulting in a total period of construction for the basic type of 53 years.

After the turn of the century heavier loads encountered on the 18 inch gauge railway system at Chatham Dockyard dictated the need for more powerful locomotives than those hitherto used. Unlike events at Woolwich more than two decades earlier, however, there was no policy change in terms of the manufacturer to be selected and the first of the larger locomotives was supplied by Manning, Wardle in 1903 as their No. 1614. The new locomotive was named *Sunbeam* and its general style of turnout was rather more appropriate to its period of construction than the style of the last two examples of the smaller design which preceded it. The skimpy pillar cab gave way to the enclosed variety of the characteristic outline that was to be associated with the Makers during their last three decades of production. The double smokebox doors were dispensed with in favour of the conventional pattern door complete with the Maker's standard wheel fastener. An American style 'balloon stack' with spark arrester was fitted and the saddle tank was of a pattern whereby the large upper radius was concentric with the longitudinal centre line of the boiler.

Although larger in most details than its forerunners, the design of *Sunbeam* was of interest in that the wheelbase was not enlarged and remained at 3ft 3in The forward section of the main frame was 3ft 11 in long as against 3ft 9in for *Khartum* whilst the rear section measured 5ft 6in long as against 4ft 0 in for the latter. The cylinders on this design were 9in bore and 12in stroke and the driving wheels were 2ft in diameter. The boiler pressure was 160 psi and the heating surface was 140 sq ft made up of 117 sq ft for the tubes and 23 sq ft for the firebox. The grate area was 4 sq ft. As with the earlier 18 inch gauge Manning, Wardles for Chatham and Woolwich, the layout of one feedpump and one injector was adhered to and the relief valve and test cock assembly was located, as with the earlier counterparts, on the right hand side of the locomotive immediately ahead of the cab space. The buffers were of the same pattern as employed on *Khartum* and the drawgear consisted of long towbars which were coupled to the rolling stock by means of pins engaging in knuckle joints. A photograph of *Khartum* shows that this locomotive had been equipped with such towbars soon after its delivery to Chatham. The handbrake column was positioned at an angle to the vertical in rather similar fashion to the configuration adopted on the three 6-inch locomotives exported by the Makers to Argentina. It was also located, contrary to earlier Chatham practice, on the right hand side of the locomotive.

MANNING.WARDLE & Cº Lᴼ ENGINEERS.LEEDS Nº 1818

A Maker's photograph of Manning, Wardle No. 1818 of 1913 supplied to an updated version of the design used for No. 1201 of 1890 and also for use in Argentina. A sister engine, (No. 2039) was supplied to the same South American customer as late as 1924. The buffers and drawgear were fitted to all three locomotives after arrival in Buenos Aires.

(Leeds Industrial Museum Courtesy G. Horsman)

Sunbeam must have proved to be satisfactory in service for in the following year the Admiralty took delivery of a similar engine from the same source. This was named *Shamrock* and was the Maker's No. 1636 of 1904. In 1913 a further locomotive of the same class was constructed and this was named *Ready*. The engine in question was No.1808 of 1913. In 1912, however, the Admiralty took the decision for the first and only time to order an 18 inch gauge steam locomotive from another supplier for use at Chatham Dockyard. Comparatively little information is known about this locomotive, apart from the fact that it was constructed by the Kilmarnock concern of Dick, Kerr & Co. Ltd. Named *Thistle*, the engine in question was fitted, according to surviving Chatham Dockyard records, with cylinders of 9in bore and 12in stroke, whilst the boiler barrel was quoted as being 2ft 3in diameter and 5ft 6in long. The grate area was 4 sq ft. It is interesting to note that all of these quoted dimensions were identical to those of *Sunbeam* but the heating surface was given as 165 sq ft. The heating surface for *Ready's* boiler is recorded as being identical to that of its sister, *Sunbeam*, yet the Dockyard records give the boiler barrel length for this locomotive as being 6ft 6in which is clearly erroneous. The suggestion

which can be made is that the Dockyard records had the boiler barrel lengths for *Thistle* and *Ready* transposed, bearing in mind the difference in quoted heating surfaces for these locomotives and the fact that Dick, Kerr are unlikely to have constructed an exact replica of the Manning, Wardle design. Unfortunately, it has not been possible at the time of writing this volume to find Maker's drawings or a photograph of *Thistle*.

As happened at Woolwich, there was a steady run down of the narrow gauge locomotive fleet after the cessation of hostilities in 1918 and the smaller 6-inch Manning, Wardles were disposed of by the end of the 1920s. It may be that *Shamrock* was also disposed of during the 1920s as this locomotive apparently goes unmentioned in surviving Dockyard records. The other three 9-inch locomotives were a little more fortunate, however, and *Sunbeam* was even photographed at work in 1934. By this time the rather large apertures in the cab sides had been partially enclosed as a measure to provide better protection for the driver, but otherwise the locomotive had been little altered.

Some accounts suggest that attempts were made to sell the three remaining narrow gauge Chatham Dockyard locomotives in 1937 but any such sale, if con-

Right: Maker's general arrangement drawings of *Sunbeam* (Manning, Wardle No.1614 of 1903). This class exhibited much more modern appearance than the smaller locomotives of the type represented by *Khartum*. The American style spark arrester is a distinctive feature, rather reminiscent of the 'Charlton' class at Woolwich Arsenal.

(Leeds Industrial Museum Courtesy G. Horsman)

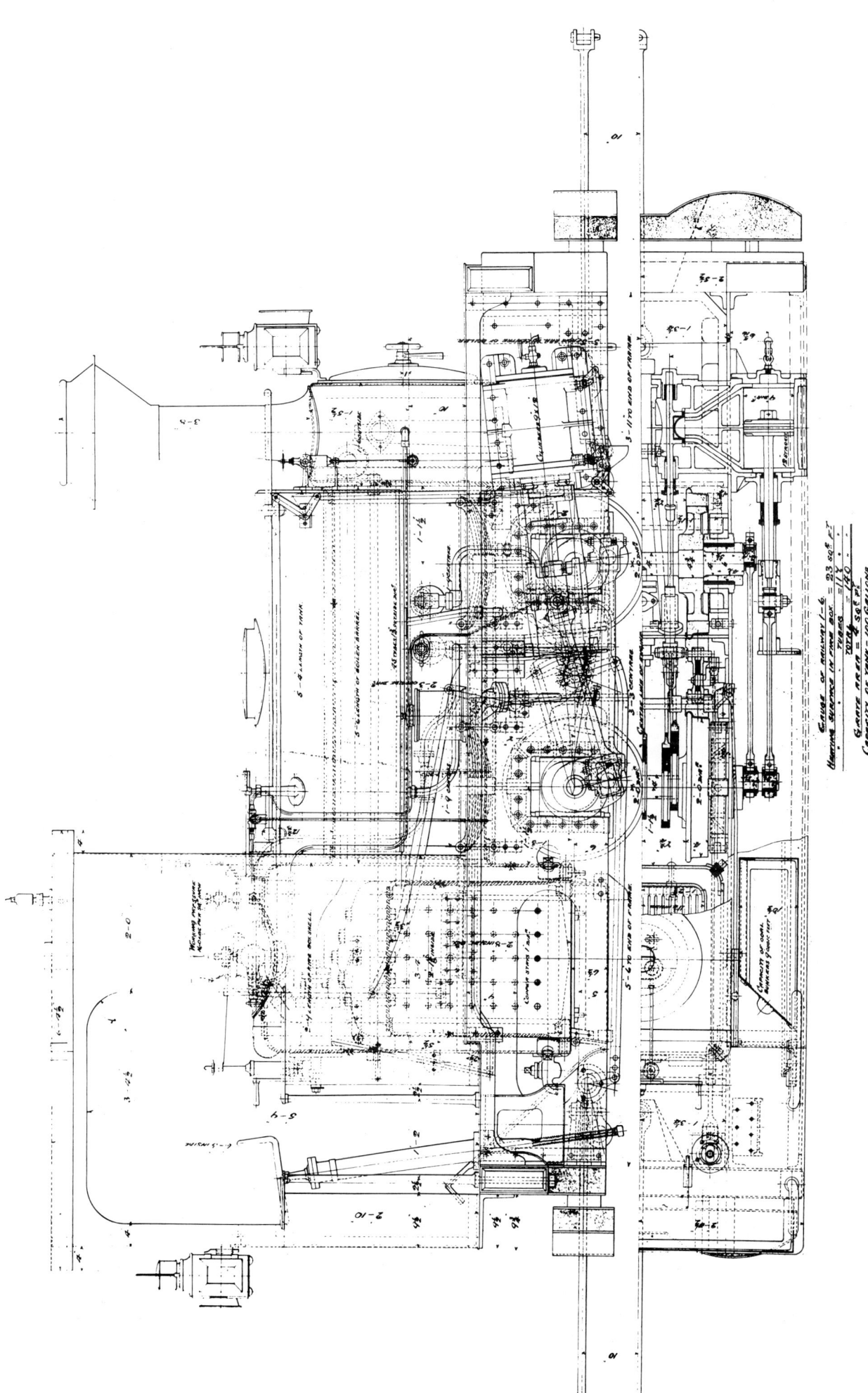

MANNING WARDLE & C?.
BOYNE ENGINE WORKS
LEEDS.

ORDER N? 53700 ENGINE N? 1614

Maker's photograph of *Sunbeam* showing the pipework for the blower and for the feedpump vacuum relief valve, together with the control for the feedpump water inlet (mounted on a column on the saddle tank). The original picture from which this plate was taken was a crumpled illustration from the Maker's catalogue. The nameplates used on *Sunbeam*, *Shamrock* and *Ready* were all brass with 3 in block lettering whilst the first two of these locomotives carried brass plates with 3½in letters and figures on the rear of their cabs. These bore the respective legends *No.18 – 1903* and *No.19 – 1904*. *Thistle*, the Dick, Kerr engine of 1912, is known to have been allocated the number 26 by 1949 although its original number was 20. *Ready* originally carried a plate proclaiming it to be *Yard No.3* although it had been allocated the number 16 by 1949.

(Courtesy R. Redman)

Sunbeam at work on the Chatham Dockyard narrow gauge system on 10th August 1934. The cab cutout has been partially sheeted in to give greater protection from the elements and there is also some additional sheeting fitted around the smokebox. The control lever and column for the water inlet to the injector is also visible, as is the recess in the middle of the front bufferbeam.

(R.G. Pratt)

templated, was not proceeded with. From a surviving portion of a Fixed Asset Register which details assets held by the General Services Section in 1949, it can be seen that the three locomotives were still officially extant at this time. It was standard accounting practice from the Dockyard's point of view to regard each locomotive as two separate assets, namely a boiler, which was depreciated over twenty years, and a chassis, which was depreciated over forty years. Rather surprisingly, therefore, *Sunbeam*, which originally cost £720 and which would have been 46 years old by this time, is shown as still having a written down value, albeit only £49. *Thistle* (original cost £800) was shown as having a written down value of £162 and *Ready* (original cost £750) was shown as having a written down value of £182.

The final disposal date of these engines is not recorded in the Register but in the light of the disposal of some standard gauge steam locomotives from Chatham shortly after the date of the Register, it is suggested that the three narrow gauge locomotives did not last much longer. It is probable that they were out of service by the time of compilation of the Register and that such 18 inch gauge operation as existed at this time was confined to hand propulsion.

Rolling Stock Used at Chatham Dockyard

From the point of view of the consideration of rolling stock, it has been decided to deal with the items used at Chatham Dockyard separately from those used at other military and military service establishments. The reason for this course of action is that drawings of the early Chatham rolling stock appeared in *Engineering* magazine during 1875 and these illustrations form a convenient starting point for discussing the evolution of the rolling stock that was used on the lines considered in this chapter. The drawings in *Engineering* were also considered to be of sufficient significance for inclusion by Vignes during the compilation of his Technical Study some two years after their original publication. They are reproduced here in an accompanying illustration.

The first wagon shown here is a cast iron four-wheeler of a design probably derived from its Crewe counterpart. The dimensions of this type of wagon were also very similar to the Crewe cast iron examples with the overall length being 4ft 3in, the wheelbase being 2ft 6in and the wheel diameter 1ft 1in The main body of the wagon was a one piece casting dropped onto the axles and secured by bolts beneath the latter. The main difference between this design of wagon and the Crewe examples was that a new refinement was introduced in order to facilitate the carriage of loads sufficiently long as to warrant the use of two wagons. The upper part of the Chatham wagon's platform incorporated a circular groove 2ft 7in diameter, 4in wide and 1¾in deep. Into this groove could be dropped balls of 2½in cast iron shot which formed the bearing surface for a similar groove (but only ¾in deep) in the underside of a removable turntable. This latter component could act as the support for a bolster as both turntable and truck proper incorporated a central pivot hole of 1½in diameter. Exclusive of the chequer reliefs on the truck platform and upper part of the turntable, which were about ¾in deep, the general metal thickness of both truck and turntable was approximately 1in As with the Crewe cast iron wagons, those at Chatham could carry relatively heavy loads and as another indication of Crewe influence, the wheels used on them were originally only 9in diameter in order to keep the centre of gravity as low as possible. One wheel was able to run loose on each axle and this was arranged so that these wheels were diagonally opposite one another. This arrangement facilitated the use of cylindrical rather than coned treads as it dispensed with the need to mitigate the effect of the differential in distances travelled on a curve between the wheels at each end of an axle.

An important feature to notice about these early Chatham wagons is that the drawgear arrangements were copied directly from those in use at Crewe. Wagons were coupled by means of towbars rather than conventional link couplings. Although the standard design of towbar was to undergo alteration during the first two decades of operation of the Chatham Dockyard tramway, their use was to remain the norm throughout the period of locomotive haulage, so much so that the larger Manning, Wardles were shown as being fitted with them on the Maker's plans. The bars engaged, as with the Crewe wagons, in suitable eyes on the wagons, these being integrally cast in the cast iron vehicles.

The wooden four-wheeled wagon shown in *Engineering* was used for the carriage of light stores. The wheels, as with the cast iron wagon, had flanges with a width of 1¼in. The wheelbase was 2ft 6in and diagonally opposite wheels were loose on their axles, which, as with the cast iron wagon, were allowed 0.625in lateral play. The wheels were cast with six T-section spokes and their nominal diameter was 17½in. The axles were 1¾in diameter on the central shank and this was reduced to 1.625in through the wheel boss and 1½in at the journals which were supported by cast iron plain bearings. The chassis was 5ft 2in long and the oak main frames were 3in wide and 4in deep, with the same material being used for the end cross-members. The main frames were strengthened by the use of additional side members 2½in wide and 3in deep through which four cross-tie bolts passed, these being 0.625in diameter at their extreme ends.

Rather strangely, there do not appear to have been any iron hoops surrounding the buffer ends of the main frames for strengthening purposes and this suggests that these wagons saw less locomotive haulage than the cast iron variety, although they were fitted with eyes for towbars. The superstructure consisted of a teak platform of 1in thickness and side and end pieces of 1in thick red pine with the end components being, rather strangely, of ogival configuration. The side and end pieces were strengthened by vertical stiffening irons 11in high, 1.125in wide and ¼in deep, secured by bolts ¼in diameter at their outer extreme ends. The tare weight of this design of truck was 560 lbs. A simpler wooden framed truck designed purely for hand propulsion had similar side and cross framing but wheels of only 9in diameter and a platform of spruce boarding with a thickness of 1½in and a side overhang of 6in beyond each main frame. The tare weight of this wagon was 504 lbs. The tare weight of the cast iron wagon, by means of comparison, was approximately 1,568 lbs and that of its turntable was 441 lbs inclusive of the shot.

There was another variation on the wooden framed four-wheeled wagon theme which possessed the same wheels, axles and axleboxes as the larger type just described but the structure of this general purpose wagon was rather more complex in its nature. The chassis assembly had no less than five longitudinal oak members. The outermost pair were 6ft 1½in long, 2in wide and 3in deep. The innermost pair (upon which the lower platform was mounted, and to the underside of which, the axleboxes were secured by means of bolts of 0.625in shank diameter) were of 3in square cross-section. The centre member was 4½in square in cross-section and the same length as the outermost pair, these all terminating at the inner ends of the cross members. The inner pair of longitudinal members were extended to form the buffers and it is presumed that the cross-members were 'halved-in' to the inner pair of longitudinal members. The cross members appear to have been of the same section as the outer pair of longitudinal main frames and they would have been of such a width as to give an overall chassis width of 3ft 6in.

Overleaf: A selection of four-wheeled and bogie vehicles in use on the 18 inch gauge tramway at Chatham Dockyard in 1875.

(Engineering)

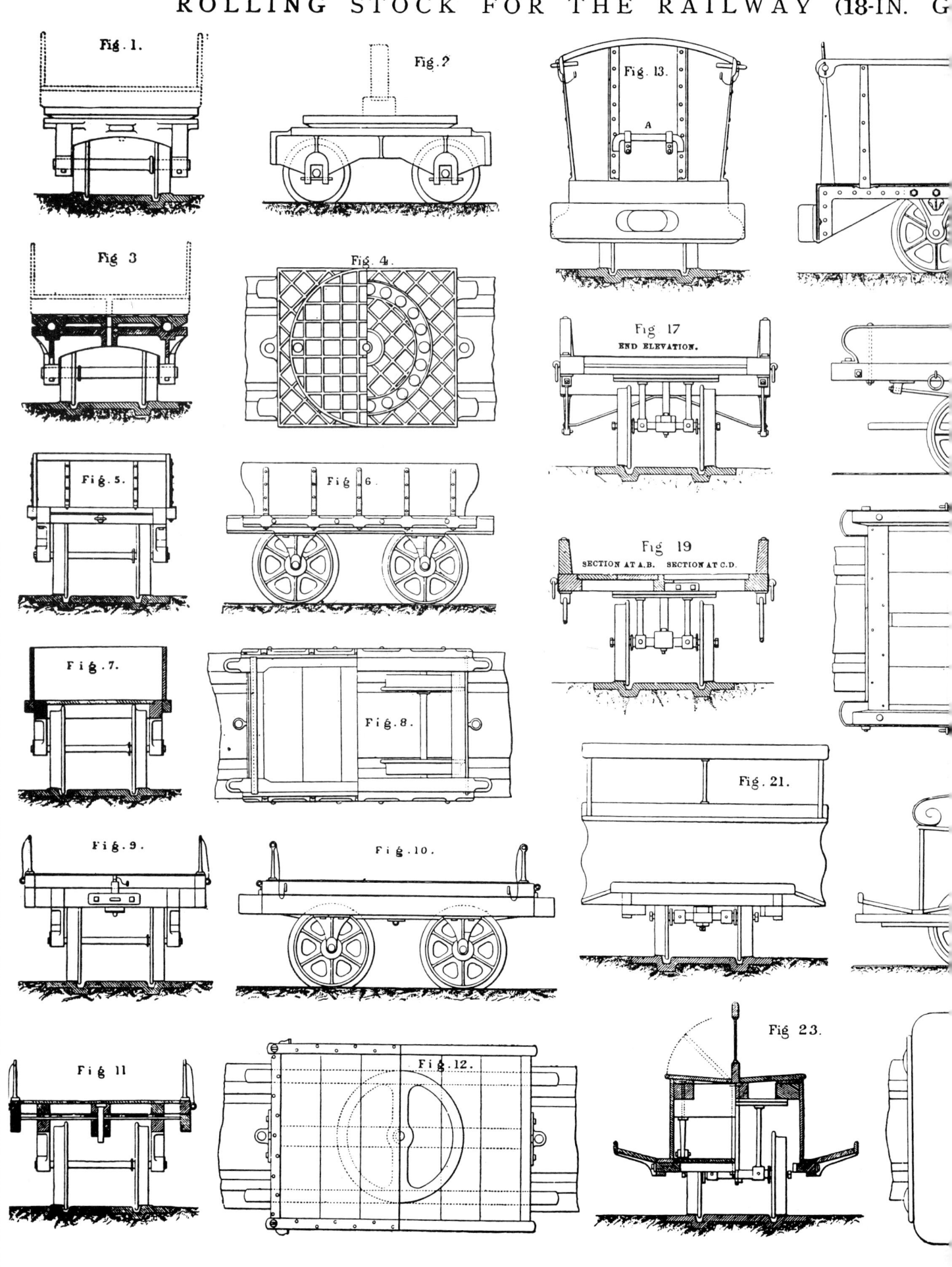

Fig. 1.

Fig. 2

Fig. 13.

A

Fig 3

Fig. 4.

Fig 17
END ELEVATION.

Fig. 5.

Fig. 6

Fig.7.

Fig. 8.

Fig 19
SECTION AT A.B.   SECTION AT C.D.

Fig. 21.

Fig. 9.

Fig. 10.

Fig 11

Fig. 12.

Fig 23.

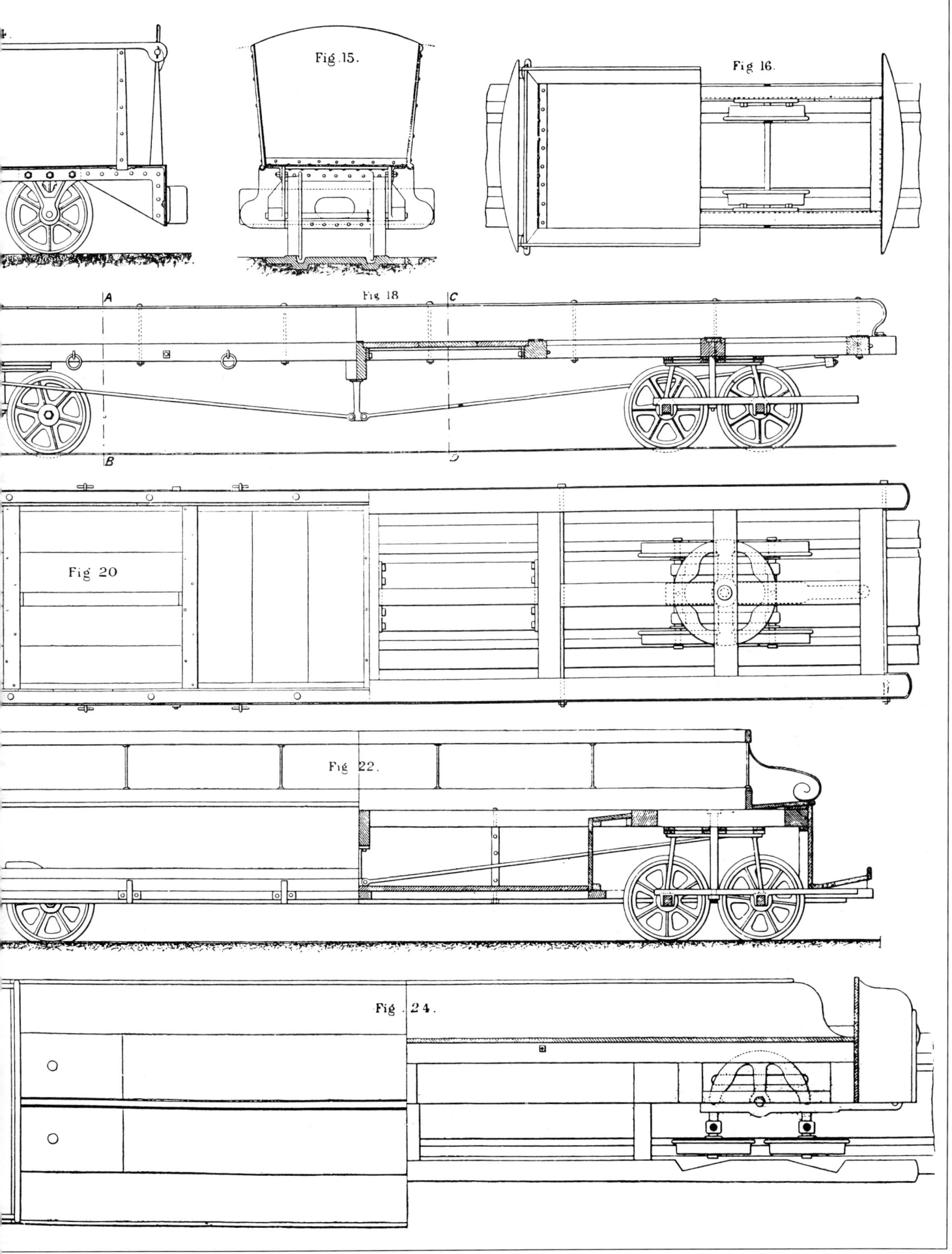

Fig. 15.

Fig 16.

Fig 18.

Fig 20

Fig. 22.

Fig. 24.

The lower platform of these wagons was made of spruce boarding ³/₄in thick and the whole lower assembly could be utilised as a flat wagon in its own right, without using the turntable and upper platform. As is shown in the drawing, the upper platform was constructed with a similar arrangement of framing to the chassis. In this instance, however, the outermost pair of longitudinal frames were constructed of the same material as their counterparts on the chassis, whilst the same material was used for the innermost pair but rotated through 90 degrees so as to give a cross-section of 3in wide and a depth of 2in. The centre member was 4¹/₂in wide and 2in deep. The upper platform was made of spruce boarding, but this time with a thickness of 1in. The bearing surface for the turntable consisted of two circular rubbing plates, 2ft 6in diameter and ¹/₂in thick, one being secured by means of screws to the underside of the framing on the upper platform and the other being similarly fixed to the appropriate supported portions of the lower platform. A captive pivot in the centre frame member for the upper platform could be lowered into a hole passing through the lower rubbing plate and its associated platform and centre frame member when it was desired to fit the turntable platform. This pivot had a shank diameter of 1¹/₂in and a length of 9in. In order to prevent the turntable revolving when it was not required to do so, locking pins could be engaged at either end of the upper (turntable) platform. These passed down into suitable lugs on the chassis above the drag irons for the towbars. These latter components were secured to the chassis cross members by means of bolts of 0.625in shank diameter. The tare weight of this type of wagon, inclusive of turntable platform, was approximately 889 lbs.

One type of four-wheeled wagon shown in *Engineering* was designed for the carriage of coal and was made mainly of wrought iron. As with the other four-wheeled wagons, diagonally opposite wheels were loose on the axle and the wheels, 2ft 6¹/₂in wheelbase and axles were the same as for the turntable wagon previously described. The capacity of these wagons was approximately 1 ton and their overall length was 7ft 10in, width 3ft 8in and height 4ft 4in. These wagons were of the dropside variety and their main frames consisted of 0.375in thick, 3in angle iron with a downward 90 degree mitre at each end. These end portions were strengthened with triangular gussets, once again of 0.375in thick wrought iron and the buffer plates were of the same material. These last mentioned items were continued at each side beyond the basic chassis width to finish with ends in the form of circular arcs. Two 0.625in bolts at each end secured a single buffer to each buffer plate. This single buffer was made of English elm in the form of a segment, 3ft 8in wide and 4¹/₂in long in the middle. When required, the towbar was passed through the aperture in the buffer and buffer plate and its end engaged in a suitable hole in an angle iron section, projecting 4in towards the middle of the wagon and 2¹/₂in deep. The four rivets securing this last mentioned angle iron can be identified as the lowest row in the end sectional view in the drawing. The towbars for inter-wagon coupling of this type of vehicle were merely 1¹/₂in diameter iron bars approximately 1ft 4¹/₂in long with their ends bent downwards at 90 degrees. These simply rested in place under their own weight. The axleboxes were of cast iron and were affixed to the main frames by means of three ³/₄in diameter bolts per bearing. The main frame rivets were ¹/₂in diameter and other rivets were 0.375in diameter.

Regarding the body of this type of wagon, the bottom plate was ¹/₄in thick and the sides and ends were 0.125in thick, with their uppermost outside edges bordered by arc section beading 1¹/₄in deep and ³/₄in maximum thickness. Further support was given to the ends of the body by means of two angle irons at each end secured to the end sheet and to the bottom plate. These angle irons were of the same material as the main frames, but with their longitudinal faces tapering down towards the top. Each body side plate was fitted with three hinges. These were also secured to underside of the bottom plate, which overhung the bottom of the body at both the sides and the ends. The hinges tapered towards the top (from 3in to 2in) and were ¹/₄in thick, each being secured by five rivets 0.375in diameter. The hinge bolts were 0.625in diameter and each was secured to the bottom plate by means of two ¹/₂in diameter rivets. The diameter of the main locking studs at the four uppermost corners was 1¹/₄in and the sides were normally held in place by pins passing through these studs. The tare weight of this design of coal wagon was 1,631 lbs. In addition, there was another design of iron coal wagon with similar chassis arrangements to the one which has just been described, but with a smaller body which was 6ft 3in long, 3ft wide and 1ft 8¹/₂in deep.

The Chatham Dockyard narrow gauge tramway was also noteworthy in that it featured a relatively early application of bogie vehicles, albeit of a rather primitive nature when compared with those which had been adopted shortly before on the Festiniog Railway. The first of these vehicles shown in the illustrations in *Engineering* was a trolley used to carry loads of up to 4 tons. Its length was 21ft whilst its overall width was 4ft and its height was 2ft 9in. The frame material for this vehicle was English oak and the longitudinal side pieces were 5in wide, with a rebate at the innermost upper corners for the floor, and 4in deep. The centre longitudinal member was made from the same section material but the floor rebate configuration was rather more complex. On the two end portions of the vehicle where the floor planking was longitudinal in configuration, there were two longitudinal rebates, one on each of the upper corners of the central member.

On the middle portion of the vehicle, where the floor planking was lateral in configuration, the height of the central member was reduced by the depth of the floor, namely 1¹/₄in

The transverse framing was of the same section material as the longitudinal framing (with suitable rebates for the floor), with the exception of the centre transverse member. This was 4¹/₂in wide and 8in deep and constituted the anchor beam for lateral and longitudinal iron trusses and tie rods. The vertical truss irons were 1¹/₂in diameter and the corresponding dimension for the tie rods was 0.875in

The longitudinal side members were surmounted by top side pieces, 8in deep and tapering in section from a width of 3¹/₂in at the bottom to a width of 3in at the top. These were affixed to the longitudinal side members by means of eight ³/₄in bolts on each side of the vehicle. Some components, namely the uppermost edges of the side pieces and the tops of the frame cross members, were protected by means of rubbing irons which were ¹/₄in thick and seven rings (held by 0.625in bolts) were provided on each side to enable the lashing down of bulky loads.

The bearing surfaces for the bogies consisted of two

A rare view (taken on 20th August 1893) showing one of the items of bogie rolling stock on the Chatham Dockyard Tramway. This vehicle appears to have been improvised in the manner described in *Engineering* in 1875 by means of fitting a dry-dock gangway with a central double seat and mounting the resultant assembly on two cast iron four-wheeled wagons of the type illustrated in the drawing reproduced from the 1875 feature. The later pattern of knuckle-ended towbar is of interest and permanent way of both the cast iron and conventional type is shown to advantage in this view.

(Public Record Office Ref. ADM 195/7)

circular iron plates, 2ft in diameter and $^3/_4$in thick. The uppermost of these was attached, presumably by means of countersunk screws, to the underside of the trolley's main frame timbers, whilst the other circular plate formed the upper structural portion of the bogie. From this last-mentioned plate, four iron pillars of 1.375in diameter, arranged in an isosceles pyramid configuration descended to meet the axle shanks (2in square section iron) to which they were riveted at their lower ends. Longitudinal bars connected the axles which were turned down at their extreme ends to a diameter of 1.875in.

The wheels, of 1ft 5$^1/_2$in nominal diameter and of the same basic pattern as the larger type used on the four wheeled wagons previously described, ran loose on these axles, each being allowed $^1/_4$in lateral play. The bogie pivot was 2in diameter and its upper end was captive in a recess in the second cross member from the end of the vehicle. The drawgear consisted of longitudinal bars of 1$^1/_2$in thick iron bolted to the middle of both axles on the bogie which also carried the lower end of the pivot. The outermost ends of the two bars carried the eyes for the towbars and it is suggested that these vehicles were drawn by means of the knuckle-ended towbars shown in accompanying illustrations.

A passenger vehicle was also depicted in *Engineering* in 1875 and this used the same bogie and wheel arrangements as the trolley. It had a central longitudinal seat and two sets of main frames. The upper longitudinal members were 17ft 6in long, 3$^1/_2$in deep and 4$^1/_2$in wide. Their end cross members flanking the bogie pins were of section measuring 5$^1/_2$in by 3$^1/_2$in and their middle cross member was of 8in by 4$^1/_2$in section timber. The lower longitudinal frames were 20ft long, 2$^1/_4$in deep and 5in wide. Their two end cross members were of 2$^1/_4$in by 4$^1/_2$in section timber and their middle cross member was of 2$^1/_4$in by 5in timber. The uppermost back rails for the seats were of teak, 3$^1/_2$in deep and 1$^1/_2$in wide, whilst the lower rails were of the same material, 5in deep and 2in wide. The stanchions separating the rails were of iron bar $^3/_4$in diameter. The vehicle was designed so that the seats could hinge upwards towards the centre revealing a compartment in which the workmens' luggage could be stowed.

The seats, toe guards and side panelling were all made from one inch thick teak, whilst the internal floor and ends of the luggage compartment were of one inch thick spruce. The stay-irons connecting the top and bottom frames at their ends were of 2in by 1in section, those supporting the footboards were of 1in by $^1/_2$in section, while those positioned on the underside of the lower main frame assembly were 19ft long, 2in wide and 0.875in thick. The irons on the inside of the upper longitudinal main frames were 3$^1/_2$in deep and 0.3125in thick and the flat stay irons inside the panelling were 1$^1/_2$in by $^1/_2$in. The normal capacity of this vehicle was 30 workmen but there was a larger and simpler design

which could carry no less than 50 workmen. The recorded dimensions of this vehicle were: length 36ft, width 4ft 7in, height to top of platform 2ft 1$^1/_2$in and to top of seat 3ft 6$^1/_2$in

Unfortunately, no details of the construction of these vehicles appear to have survived but it is known that another type of passenger vehicle was improvised by mounting a ships "brow" or trussed gangway on cradle assemblies carried by two cast iron four wheeled wagons (these assemblies were normally used for the carriage of long items such as ships' masts in a fashion similar to but safer than the means by which locomotive boilers could be transported at Crewe or Horwich). A longitudinal double seat was mounted on the upper side of the gangway and it is fortunate that an illustration of one of these improvised vehicles has survived to be reproduced here. Although these vehicles are likely to have been extremely uncomfortable to travel in as they were unsprung, it is probable that they stood up to the hard usage that they would have endured in a manner rather better than the early purpose built passenger vehicles with their primitive and delicate bogie design.

By the turn of the century, the intensity of usage of the narrow gauge tramway was at its peak as a result of the ship construction programme which preceded the Great War. Ten steam locomotives are known to have seen service on the little line although it cannot be ascertained today whether all were in use during any single period. It is known (from a report in the *Chatham and Rochester News* for 6th June 1908) that *Khartum* was involved in a collision with a standard gauge locomotive in May 1908 and sustained serious front end damage as a result. Surviving records do not indicate whether the engine was scrapped or rebuilt following the accident.

Unlike the situation which was to prevail at Woolwich Arsenal, however, there does not appear to have been a great degree of development in the design of rolling stock at Chatham. The most significant in relation to bogie vehicles appears to have been the predictable use of conventional sprung, outside framed bogies on some later wagons, but passenger accommodation remained rudimentary in contrast to the fine enclosed carriages which were to see service at Woolwich Arsenal. One enclosed carriage, fitted with windows, (for the conveyance of officers) is known to have been in use on the 18 inch gauge Dockyard system by 1908 as this was referred to in the local newspaper report on the accident involving *Khartum*.

After the cessation of locomotive haulage, some parts of the Chatham Dockyard tramway remained in use for hand-pushed four-wheeled wagons, as had been the case at Crewe. One of the hand-pushed wagons has now been placed on display in the Historic Dockyard Visitors' Centre as a small relic of an important landmark in British narrow gauge railway history.

Permanent Way at Chatham Dockyard

As has been the case with the Royal Arsenal Railways system it is possible to gain an appreciation of the extent of the 18 inch gauge railway system at Chatham Dockyard from the study of Ordnance Survey maps.

One particularly useful early example is a map of 1879 now in the Public Record Office at Kew.

The narrow gauge tramway tended to be concentrated in the western side of the Dockyard complex with the earliest functional sections dating from the early 1870s and initially relying upon hand or horse working. The narrow gauge system served such areas as the Ropery, the Rigging Store and the Covered Slips, and also extended into the part of the Dockyard which dated from the mid to late nineteenth century extension programme, with one solitary section reaching out eventually to the Coal Depot at the north eastern corner of the Dockyard complex, although this appears to have been constructed after 1879.

The rationale behind the use of so narrow a gauge which had prevailed at Crewe Works, namely the low radius of curvature and the restricted spaces inside shop buildings, was equally in evidence at Chatham and the same minimum radius curve of 25 feet for locomotive worked narrow gauge lines prevailed.

As was stated in *Engineering* in 1875, in considering the use of a narrow gauge tramway (the term for such a line which appeared to find favour with the Royal Engineers), Colonel Pasley, under whose direction the Dockyard was being extended at its northernmost end, divided the normal internal traffic within the Dockyard into three classes. The first of these was the carriage of light stores, such as the distribution of coal from the stores to boiler houses and other destinations. For this work he considered the existing roads and horse-drawn carts to be adequate. The second category comprised intermediate loads such as castings and forgings of up to 15 tons in weight. This traffic was of a frequently recurring nature and was highly destructive to the cart roads and pig-iron tramways then in use in the Dockyard. The third category comprised the exceptionally heavy loads such as marine boilers and stern-posts of ships. This type of traffic was so infrequent that on its own account it did comparatively little damage to the existing roads and pig-iron tramways in the Dockyard.

Colonel Pasley went on to criticise the standard gauge internal railway used at Portsmouth Dockyard on the grounds that the wagons used were too heavy for handling small quantities of stores which could otherwise be hand-pushed in a smaller wagon. He also believed that too few locomotive hauled trains were necessary for the system to be economic, and that there would be too many turntables if a purely standard gauge system were adopted at Chatham. Another argument which had been advanced in favour of the adoption of a permanent railway system at the Dockyard was that the ballast for the primitive wood or granite tramways then in use consisted of a type of pig-iron known as 'Seeley's Pigs'. This material was considered by some Members of Parliament and other influential persons as far too valuable a resource for such a use and they wished it to be replaced. It was therefore decided in 1868 to lay a trial length of cast iron tramplates on one of the main roads which had hitherto seen some of the heaviest traffic within the Dockyard. Rather surprisingly, in the light of what has been stated regarding 'Seeley's Pigs', the plates for the experimental railway were cast from the hard but brittle white iron furnished by this material and a few of the plates actually cracked in service. However this was of little consequence as the running surface offered was virtually unimpaired.

As the early experiment had been successful, it was decided in 1870 to lay a section of tram-plate railway one third of a mile in length linking the workshops in the older (southern) part of the Dockyard with two of the new docks then being opened. Soon afterwards, the narrow gauge network was extended in both the older and newer sections of the complex.

The method of construction of the tram-plate railway can be observed in accompanying illustrations. As can be seen, the main feature of this type of railway was that it could be combined in a double-track configuration with a road for ordinary vehicles. This was accomplished by having the composite road laid on a bed of Portland cement concrete mixed in a ratio of one part concrete to twelve parts of gravel. The outermost visible boundary consisted of granite pitching 9in deep and 4in wide. Two tram-plates would then be laid side by side, so as to leave a gap between them of 2ft 5½in width. This would be filled with 'half-sovereign' granite pitching to form a horse track between the tram-plates. During the early stages of the railway's existence the concrete bed was allowed to set with a template resting upon its upper surface, so as to provide a seating for the ribs on the underside of the tramplate. Blocks of creosoted fir or hardwood measuring 11in by 5in by 4½in were embedded in the concrete during the setting process and the tram-plates were spiked to these by means of ½in diameter spikes at their corners so as to key adjoining plates together. This measure was found to be unnecessary and the later practice was simply to hammer the tram-plates down, with the aid of wooden mauls, into the wet concrete and allow the latter to set around the ribs on the underside of the plates. By 1873 there was a distance of 1,480 yards of double track and horse roadway combined, in use together with 1,865 yards of single track railway.

In order to simplify the laying of narrow gauge railways constructed on this principle, the range of components utilised was reduced to a few standard types. The iron utilised for the tram-plates used after the experimental period was obtained at Woolwich Arsenal, where some at least of the plates were cast, from obsolete shot and shell. The standard type of straight tramplate was 6ft long and 2ft 8in wide and was designated by the letter 'A'. The longitudinal ribs which supported the grooves were 4½in wide and projected 1½in below the underside of the main body of the plate. Additional transverse strengthening ribs were located 5in from each end. Each 6ft plate weighed 1,060 lb, or 530 lb/yd for a single track section.

The curved sections were of four standard radii which were in reality two pairs of radii complimentary for double-track running. The two smaller radii were 25ft 7in and 30ft 8¾in and sections for these radii were denoted respectively by the letters 'B' and 'G'. Similarly, the two larger radii were 78ft 8in and 83ft 9¾in and these were allocated the letters 'E' and 'F' respectively. In single-track formations it was possible to use any of these curved components individually. The weight of these sections was 545 lb/yd. Points and crossings were catered for by means of four standard components denoted by the letters 'CL' and 'DL' (for left handed components) and 'CR' and 'DR' (for right handed ones). The 'CL' and 'DL' components arranged for a left handed turnout are shown in the accompanying illustration with crossings being constructed with the aid of two 'D' components. Each two-plate unit for a point or crossover weighed 3,256 lb. The tongues for the 'C' components were of wrought iron and weighed 59.3 lb per pair. These were located by pins cast integrally with the 'C' components and could be lifted away and re-located if an obstruction found its way into the widened groove where the

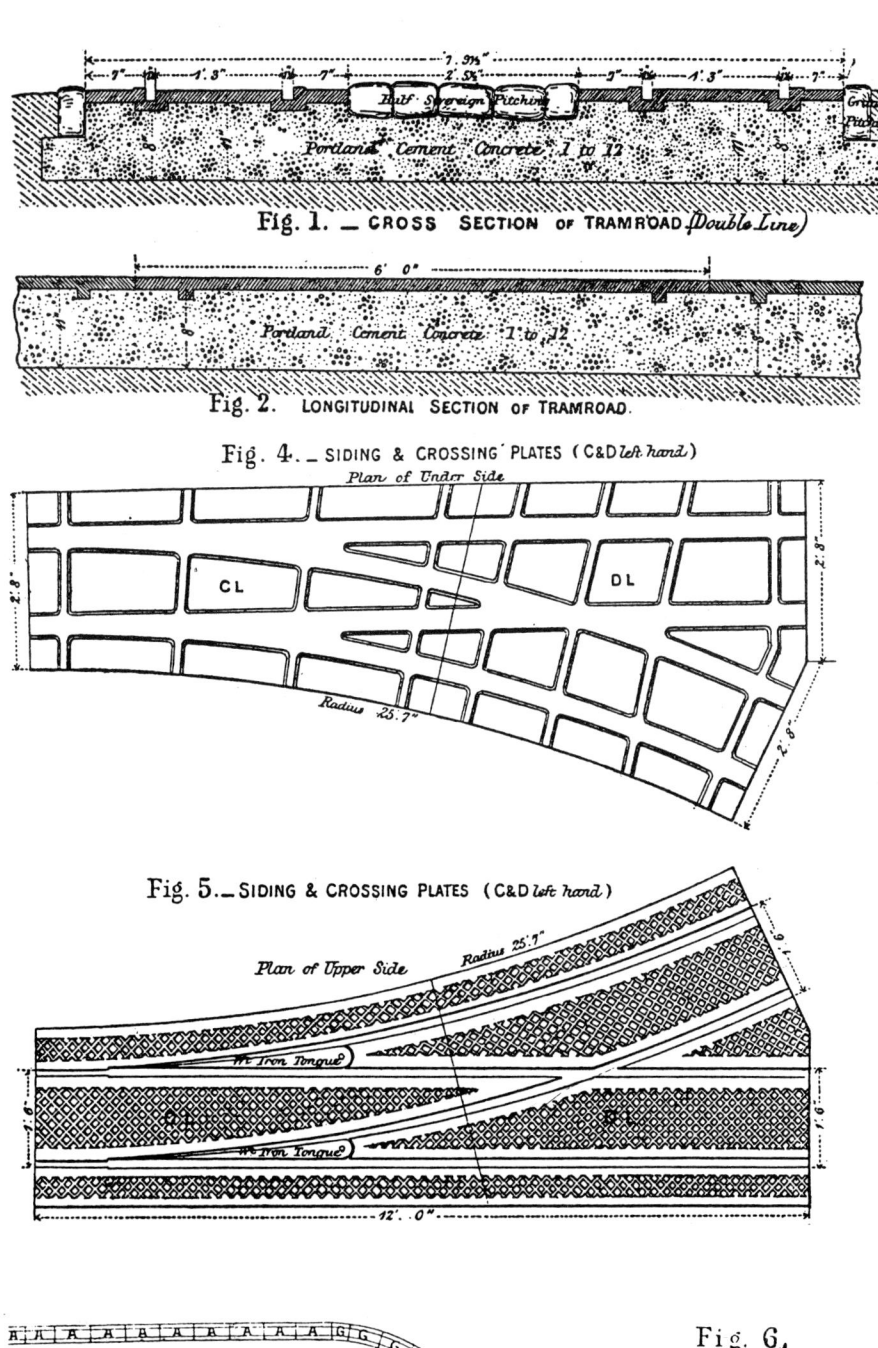

Fig. 1. _ CROSS SECTION OF TRAMROAD (Double Line)

Fig. 2. LONGITUDINAL SECTION OF TRAMROAD.

Fig. 4. _ SIDING & CROSSING PLATES (C&D left hand)

Plan of Under Side

CL   DL

Radius 25.7"

Fig. 5._ SIDING & CROSSING PLATES (C&D left hand)

Plan of Upper Side   Radius 25.7"

Wt Iron Tongue

Wt Iron Tongue

12'. 0"

Fig. 3._ STRAIGHT PLATE (A)

Plan of Upper Side   Plan of Under Side

6. 0"

A

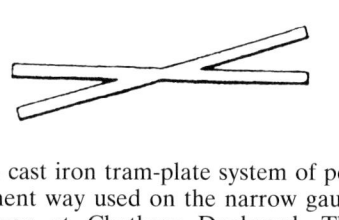

The cast iron tram-plate system of permanent way used on the narrow gauge railway at Chatham Dockyard. This illustration shows the main track components, including wrought iron tongues and cruciform filling pieces for pointwork, along with a schematic arrangement for tram-plates. Permanent way of this type also saw much use during the earlier period of operation at Woolwich Arsenal.

(Engineering)

Fig. 6.

Scale of Feet

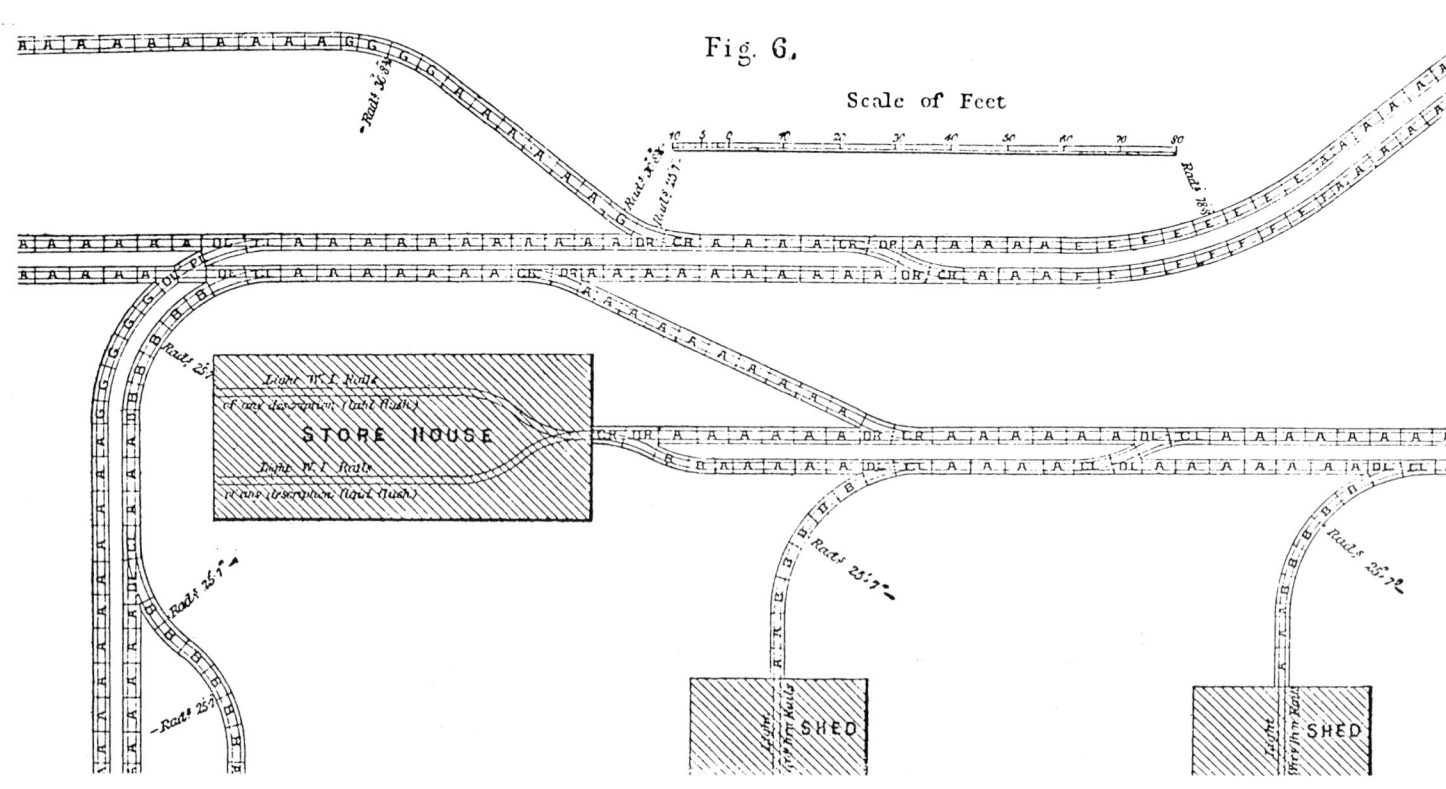

STORE HOUSE

SHED

SHED

An 1879 Ordnance Survey map showing the extent of the 18 inch gauge lines within Chatham Dockyard at that time. Apart from the standard gauge lines marked 'Railway', which were connected to the LCDR Dockyard branch opened in 1877, and the Sawmill Railway, all internal lines were 18 inch gauge and this network extended from the Factory and Repairing Basins in the north to the Gun Wharf at the southern end of the Yard.

(Public Record Office Ref. WO78/2342)

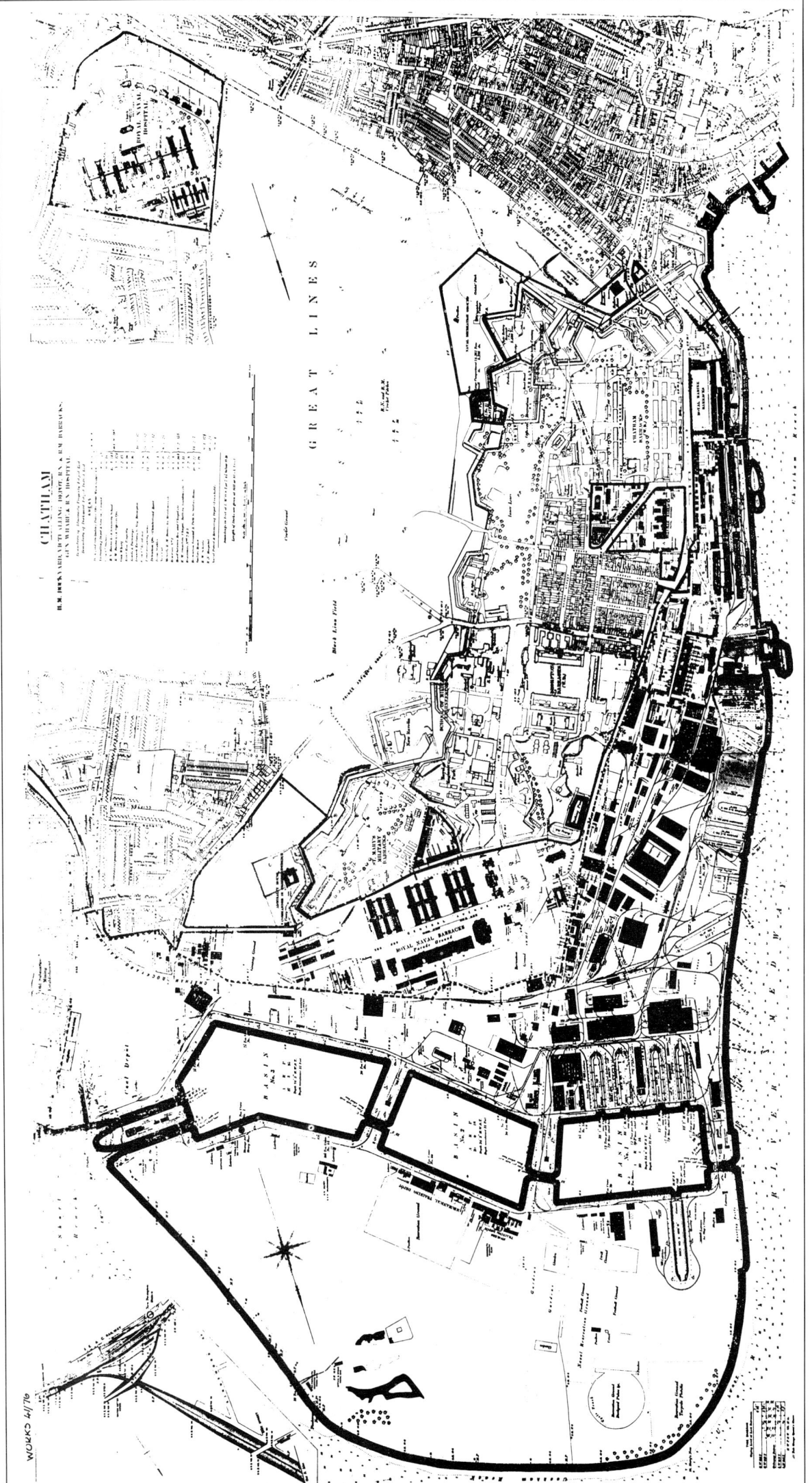

This 1911 Ordnance Survey map of Chatham Dockyard shows the internal railway system at a time when the 18 inch gauge contribution was at its zenith. By this time much of the narrow gauge network consisted of conventional rail, in some instances incorporated into a mixed gauge formation, and it was possible for an 18 inch gauge vehicle to travel from the Coal Depot (east of No.3 Basin) to the southern Gun Wharf.

(Public Record Office Ref. WORK 41/76)

The interior of one of the Royal Carriage Department buildings at the Royal Arsenal showing the cast iron tram-plates used during the early years of the narrow gauge railway there. Many were replaced by 41 lb per yd flat-bottomed rail during the first three decades of narrow gauge operation, although some survived to the end.

(Courtesy A. Turner)

A mixed gauge weighbridge in No.7 Building Slip at Chatham Dockyard, December 1989. The section of narrow gauge track to the west of this weighbridge was all hand-worked and the track to the east appears to have been purely standard gauge, at least in later years.

(Author)

Right: This view shows the inscription on the platform of the weighbridge which reads 'H. Pooley & Son Ltd. Birmingham & London No. 11915'.

(Author)

tongue was normally situated. Initially, the tongues were coupled beneath the turnout body by means of a rod (as was later to be the norm at Horwich) and sometimes equipped with point levers. However, this was found to be unnecessarily complex in use and it became standard practice simply to use uncoupled tongues which could be set to the required position by the train driver or an assistant with the aid of a stick or wooden pole.

The method of assembly of a track layout from constituent cast iron components is illustrated. The larger radius 'E' and 'F' curved sections tended to find favour on parts of the system used for passenger haulage, where speeds could reach 12 miles per hour. In order to reduce wear on the point and crossing components, triangular section wrought iron cross pieces were pro-

Two curved sections of tram-plate track in No.7 Building Slip (South side) at Chatham Dockyard.

(Author)

A section of mixed gauge track in No.7 Building Slip (North side) surviving in December 1989. The end-grain wood packing between the running rails is evident.

(Author)

The site of a narrow gauge wagon turntable where 18 inch gauge track entered the north-east corner of No.7 Building Slip.

(Author)

A 6ft straight tram-plate outside the Indoor Bowling Alley in Chatham, December 1989. The chequer-plate upper surface (initially to provide sufficient grip for horses) is evident, as are the two longitudinal ribs underneath the grooves. This view makes an interesting comparison with the 1875 illustrations in *Engineering*.

(Author)

duced which could be simply dropped into the groove crossing points. Even after 1875, however, their use does not appear to have been universal as the few relevant surviving photographs at Woolwich and Chatham do not show them.

As at Woolwich Arsenal, there was some conventional narrow gauge track. The mixed gauge track was mainly of pure conventional section as the standard gauge steam worked railway in the Dockyard did not use tram-plates for pointwork. The cast iron permanent way proved to be more to the Admiralty's liking than to that of the War Office and sections survived in use at Chatham even after the cessation of steam locomotive usage. Even today, some years after the end of the Dockyard's use as a base for Royal Naval shipping, traces of the narrow gauge railway system still survive, particularly in the older part of the Yard. At the time of writing this includes a rare section in No.6 Covered Slip incorporated into a mixed gauge straight portion by means of the use of a conventional rail to accommodate standard gauge vehicles.

Direct Military Uses for 18 Inch Gauge Steam Railways

During the 1870s there was a steadily growing interest shown by the War Office and the Royal Engineers in the use of 18 inch gauge railways for military purposes. The earliest narrow gauge steam operated railway built specifically for military field purposes in the United Kingdom was the peculiar portable system designed by John Barraclough Fell in 1871. The genesis of this idea can be traced to the year 1868 in which Fell patented a monorail system, substantially similar to the later Lartigue principle adopted by the Listowel & Ballybunion Railway in Ireland. This Patent (No. 766/1868) also allowed for the use of two bearing rails 'tied together with plates or cross-braces' and the gauge being used "generally not exceeding two feet". The locomotives to be used on the monorail were to have two boilers, one mounted either side of the main bearing rail as on the later Listowel & Ballybunion locomotives, and provision was made for the use of four horizontal guide wheels which would run on steadying rails placed at low level on either side of the bearing rail. When he came to considering suitable locomotives for use on the version of the system with two bearing rails, Fell envisaged either a variant of the double-boilered type or a single-boilered variety with the boiler above rail level and wheels and cylinders below the boiler. The engine would be provided or not, as the case may be, with guide and gripping wheels.

The only known practical application of the monorail part of the 1868 Patent was the Parkhouse Mineral Railway, constructed in that year to link a haematite mine with the Furness Railway main line just to the north of Roose station near Barrow. This horse-worked line was found in practice to have insufficient carrying capacity and so it was decided to replace it, by January 1870, with another guide-wheel equipped elevated line, this time embodying two carrying rails placed 8in apart. This was worked, at least during the last two years of its existence, by means of a stationary steam engine and an endless cable in conjunction with a Fowler's clip drum. A sub-committee of the Royal Engineers inspected the Parkhouse line on 6th September 1870 and they were impressed by its relative stability and smooth running in spite of the fact that an accident occurred on the day of inspection, caused by the inability of the clip assembly attaching the leading wagon to the cable, to release the train at the end of one journey. The Royal Engineers made a number of recommendations to J.B. Fell concerning the construction of an experimental portable railway on the Parkhouse model for evaluation. This type of line was to be locomotive worked with two bearing rails at least 15 inches apart and supported on trestles of heights in convenient multiples of 10ft, not exceeding four times this value. The rolling stock was to be provided with springing, for the benefit of men being conveyed, and with at least two guide wheels per vehicle. The guide rails were to be of iron, and wagons were required to be at least 7ft long and 6ft wide.

By the end of 1870 Fell had been requested by the Secretary of State for War to supply a detailed drawing and specification for a locomotive of 18 inch gauge, capable of handling gradients of 1-in-50, together with an assessment of the cost of its construction by a suitable manufacturer.

Following the interest shown by the Royal Engineers J.B. Fell took out two further Patents concerning this general type of railway in 1871. The first of these (No.

1/1871) concerned the type of locomotive to be employed. This was to have a single boiler placed over the rails and three axles, the forward one being placed in front of the smokebox and the rearmost one being placed behind the firebox. The purpose of this wheel configuration was to obtain the lowest centre of gravity possible. The horn plates on the main frames projected upwards, contrary to the normal pattern of locomotive construction, and four guide wheels were employed. The drawing accompanying this Patent Specification showed a tank locomotive with inside cylinders, but provision was made in the Specification for the use of outside cylinders and a separate tender, instead of the built-in water tanks, if either or both of these measures were deemed necessary.

The second of the additional Patents was No.1246 of May 1871 and this covered the special portable track-work. The system was, as specified by the Royal Engineers, supported on trestles of heights which were variable according to the lie of the land. The track and trestles could be constructed of wood, iron or a combination of both. There was also provision for points in the form of a simple hinged section supporting track, wagon tipplers utilising a hinged section with the hinge body in a horizontal plane, and turntables.

The experimental Fell railway adopted by the Royal Engineers was constructed at Aldershot in the first six months of 1872. Sadly, no official plan of the course of the line appears to have survived, but it is known that it followed a mile long course commencing at the Stores Department, close to the town centre. The initial section upon leaving this point was laid on low trestles on a steadily rising gradient until a severe left hand turn into a 770ft long viaduct was reached which was 25ft high at its deepest point. The line then turned to the left again, through a small cutting (the only significant earthwork to have been undertaken for its construction), past the upper stores area and then via curves in a respective rightward and leftward direction to a terminus at a road near Flagstaff Hill. According to the published account in *The Engineer*, it was hoped to extend the line to the North Camp and canvas camping ground, and to provide connections with the Basingstoke Canal and the LSWR, but none of the projected extension work was ever destined to be carried out. The Aldershot line thus remained purely experimental in nature.

In July 1872, the only locomotive to run on the Aldershot experimental Fell line was delivered from the makers. With Manning, Wardle locomotives being successfully employed on narrow gauge lines both at Woolwich and at Chatham by this time, it was not surprising that the same firm was chosen to supply the Aldershot engine. In laying down the basic design for *Ariel*, however, Fell chose to depart from the drawing

Right: Maker's side elevation view of Manning, Wardle No. 412 of 1872, the locomotive supplied for the experimental elevated line at Aldershot. The style of turnout was typical of the makers at this time with the domeless boiler and raised firebox. Other features of interest are the cylinders set below the level of the axles and the drive offset from the centre of the crankpin. The guide wheels and low position of the cylinders can also be seen in these views, as can the protective handrail around the footplate. No surviving drawings exist for the tender, which also had a protective handrail.

(Leeds Industrial Museum via G. Horsman)

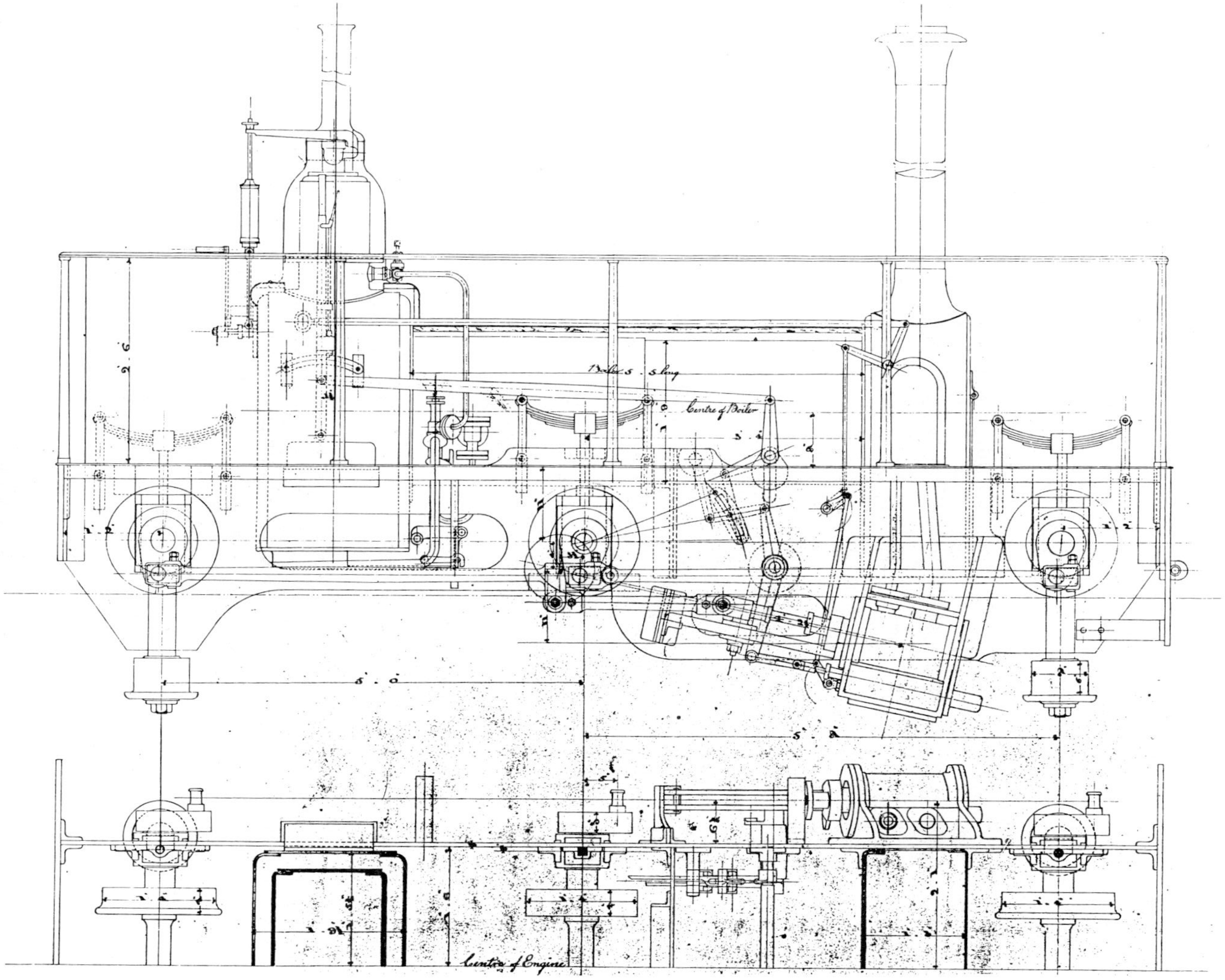

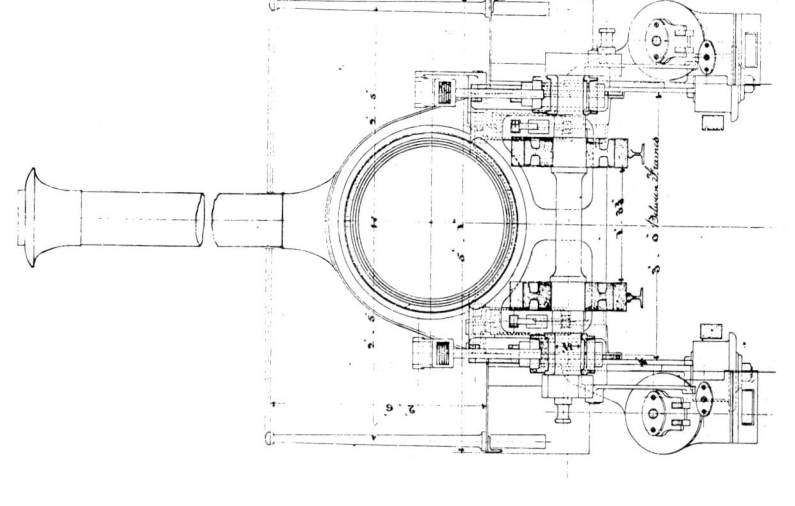

ORDER No 6720

Grate area = 2·9 sq. ft.
Heating surface = 76 sq. ft. viz. Box 14. Tubes 62
Total wheel base = 10-8.
Gauge of Railway = 1-6.

MANNING WARDLE & Co
BOYNE ENGINE WORKS
August 27th LEEDS 1872

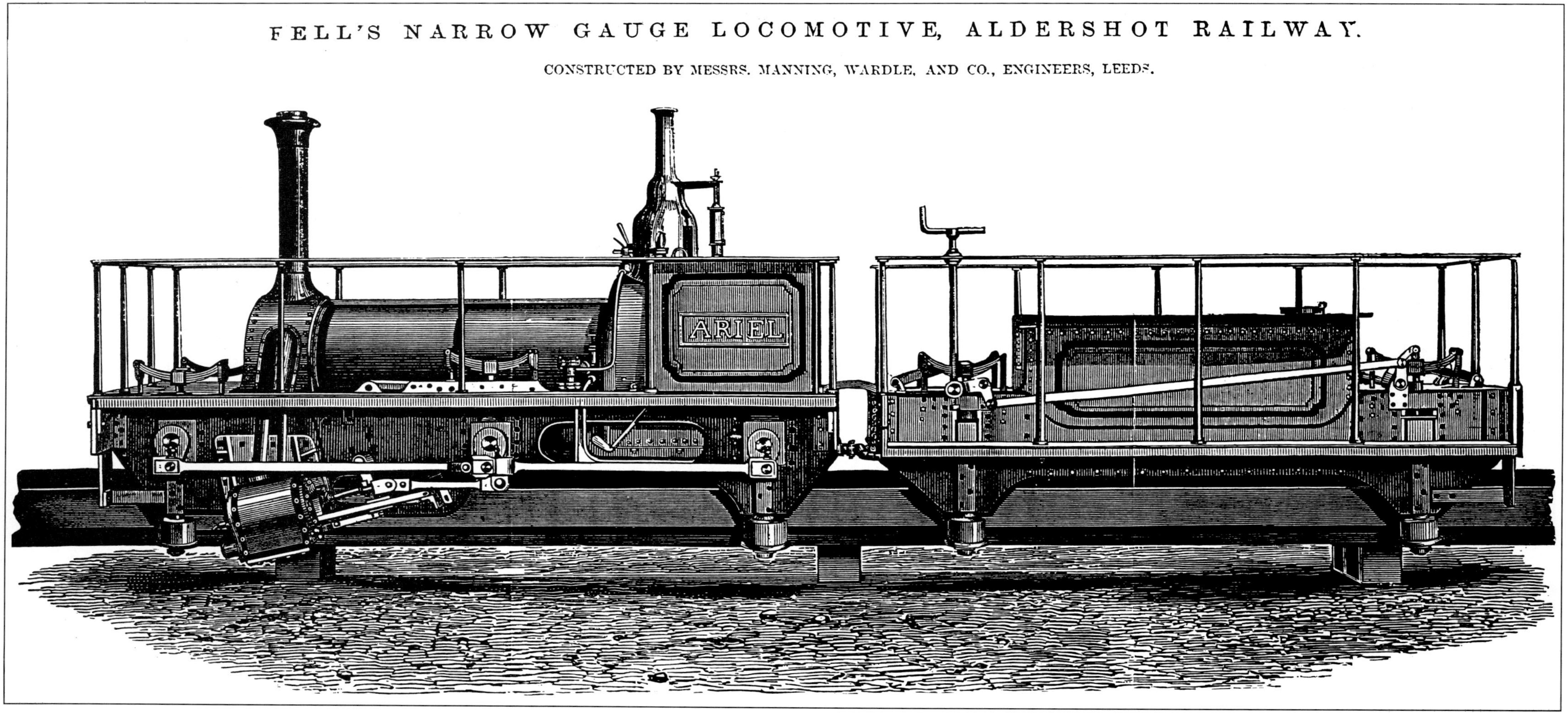

FELL'S NARROW GAUGE LOCOMOTIVE, ALDERSHOT RAILWAY.

CONSTRUCTED BY MESSRS. MANNING, WARDLE, AND CO., ENGINEERS, LEEDS.

An engraving of the Aldershot locomotive which appeared in *The Engineer* for 1st November 1872. The engine carried the name *Ariel*. Note the tender brake linkage.

(The Engineer)

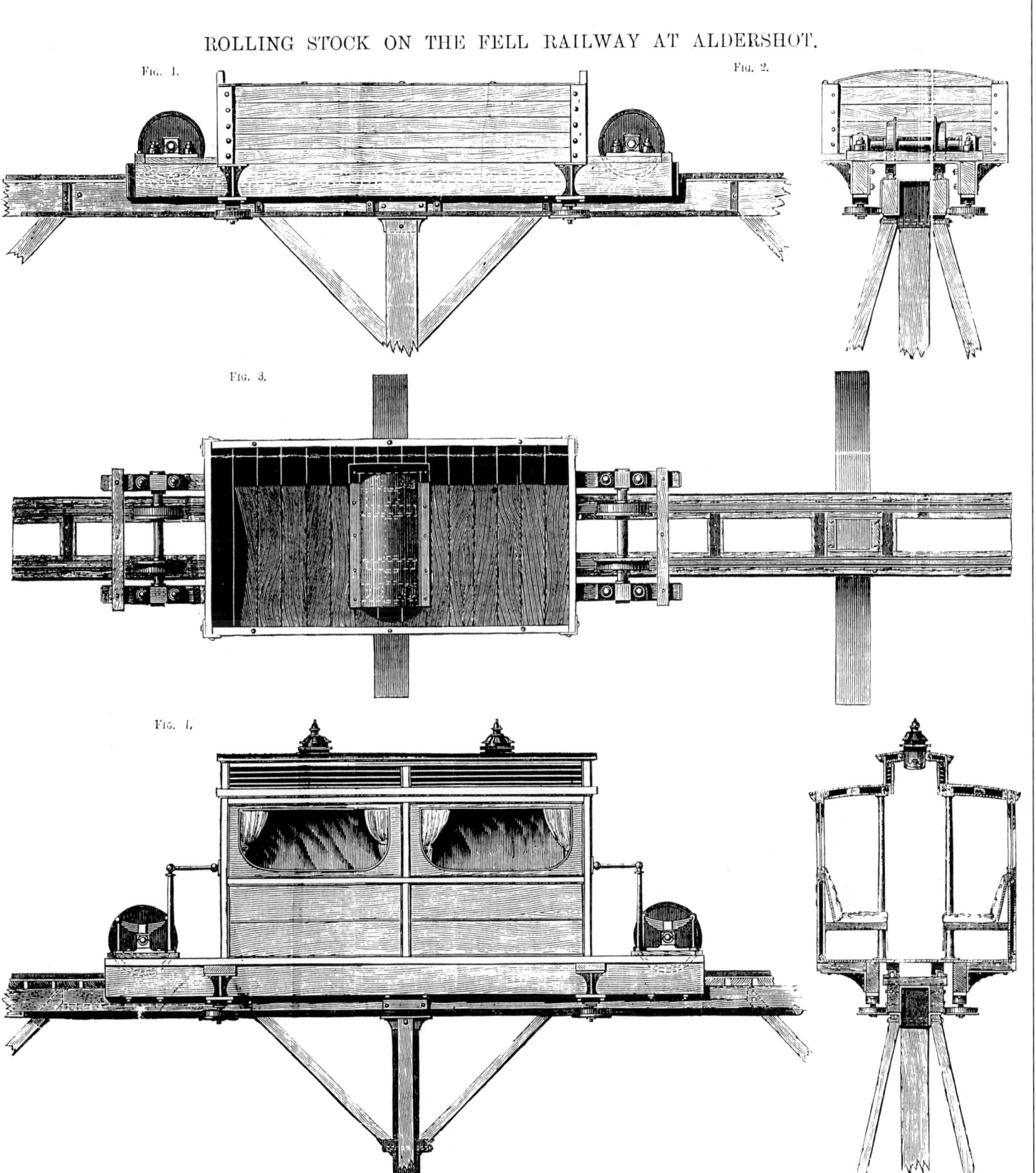

Fig. 1. Fig. 2.

Fig. 3.

Fig. 4.

The type of wagon used at Aldershot and a proposal for a carriage design (this latter was almost certainly never constructed). Both of these drawings are disproportionate when compared with the published dimensions.

(The Engineer)

which accompanied Patent Specification No. 1/1871 and opted for a configuration involving the use of outside cylinders and a separate tender which, incidentally, carried the brakes as the locomotive itself was unbraked. *Ariel* was Manning, Wardle No.412 and had cylinders measuring 6½in bore and 10in stroke and dri-

ving wheels of 1ft 4in diameter. The wheelbase of the locomotive was 10ft 8in and that of the tender was 8ft 2in. The firebox heating surface was 14 sq ft and 22 brass tubes of 1.875in outside diameter provided an additional heating surface of 62 sq ft giving a total of 76 sq ft. The locomotive and tender were each fitted with four flanged guide wheels which engaged upon timber side-rails, contrary to the original recommendations of the Royal Engineers Committee.

Two weeks after describing the locomotive, *The Engineer* featured engravings of the wagon design used at Aldershot and a proposed carriage which, in all

103

MR. FELL'S NARROW GAUGE RAILWAY AT ALDERSHOT.

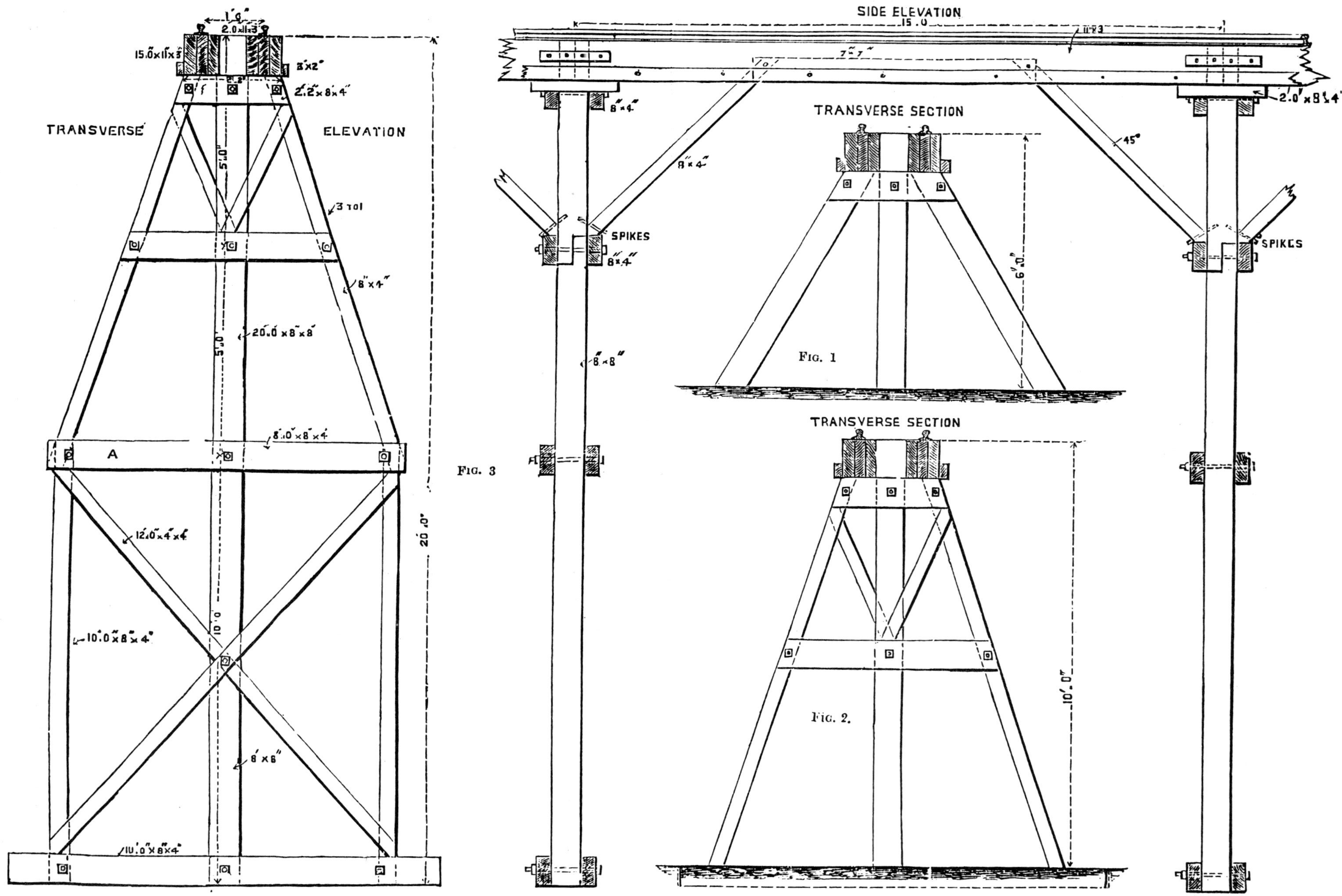

SIDE ELEVATION

TRANSVERSE SECTION

Fig. 1

TRANSVERSE SECTION

Fig. 2

Fig. 3

ELEVATION

TRANSVERSE

probability, never saw the light of day. The wagon was of the six-wheeled variety with the two end axles placed outside the body area and the centre axle contained within a covered recess occupying space which otherwise would have been part of the payload carrying area. In practice, some lateral play would have been required for the centre axle but no indication of such a measure was given in the feature. The wagons had oak main frames 13ft long, 10in deep and 5in wide. The bodies were made of 2½in thick planking and ¼in iron for the corner pieces. The body sides were comprised of five longitudinal planks whilst the ends had a sixth plank which had a curvilinear upper edge. The floor comprised a basic pattern of 15 planks with the necessary recess cut for the centre axle, which cut each of the three centre planks into two sections. The wagon bodies were 8ft long, 5ft 6in wide and 2ft high. Unfortunately the engravings which accompanied the description in *The Engineer* were disproportionate in comparison with the stated dimensions and were therefore unreliable.

Other details published at this time showed the design of the trestles used on the Aldershot line. The maximum height illustrated, 20ft, was somewhat less than the maximum height for the viaduct at Aldershot.

The main advantages claimed for the Fell system were that it reduced greatly the need for major earthworks and that such a line could be erected and dismantled with relative ease. In the latter part of 1872 a fair amount of evaluation was carried out. On 19th October of that year a number of test runs were carried out in the presence of, amongst others, General Sir F.E. Chapman, Inspector General of Fortifications, and Colonel Ogle of the Royal Engineers. The locomotive succeeded in hauling a load of 25 tons up an incline of 1 in 50 with an absence of undue vibration. Trains were run carrying passengers (officers and men), goods, such as on one occasion 590 cu ft of hay, or both. It appears from surviving records that a maximum of ten wagons were used in these tests but significantly there is no reference to purpose built passenger rolling stock, even for the carriage of officers. It was shown to be possible to run passenger trains at an average speed of 20 miles per hour, the maximum attained being 30 mph; mixed trains at 15 mph and goods trains at 10 mph. Some further runs were made eleven days later for the benefit of Mr J.B. Fell and his son, Mr Wardle, representing the engine's builders, and others, but these were curtailed by the inclement weather which prevailed on that day.

On 9th June the following year a further experiment was undertaken to test J.B. Fell's claims regarding the ease with which a railway of this type could be erected from its component parts. Fell had claimed that 500 man-days of labour were required to lay a mile of the type of railway used at Aldershot. Captain Luard of the Royal Engineers estimated the cost of a mile of this line, including the Patent Royalty, at £1,400. For the purposes of the experiment 29 men were utilised and it was found that they were able to erect 38 trestles at a spacing of 10ft with rails being laid as far as the 34th. Even if the last 40ft of structure completed without rails is disregarded, the length laid by 29 men in a day

was equivalent to approximately 450 man-days per mile.

During the period of almost one year in which the experiments were carried out it was recorded that the adopted method of construction of the trestles was altered, with iron strengthening brackets being used latterly, and that a point was constructed, with a radius of swing of 29ft 6in and serving lines 3ft 8½in apart. There appears to be no record as to whether a tippler section was ever constructed. The length of the bays, quoted as 15ft in the original diagrams, had been reduced to 10ft by the time of the final experiment, with the supporting timbers for the rails finally being one plank of 10in height and 5in width, as opposed to the original two side-by-side planks of 11in height and 3in width.

Although the results obtained at Aldershot supported the claims made by Fell in relation to his elevated railway, the Royal Engineers decided against ordering any more equipment of this type. By mid-1874, it had become clear that the Fell system was not likely to achieve a significant level of commercial application and there would never be a pool of suitable locomotives and rolling stock available which could be requisitioned at short notice for use on lines of this type. Moreover, Fell himself had forsaken the use of guide wheels on the 2ft 6in gauge Pentewan line in Cornwall which he had recently engineered. Although he was to further develop the construction of wooden rail-bearing structures at Pentewan Harbour and over the River Torridge on the 3ft gauge Torrington & Marland Railway in Devon, no more lines of Fell design were to be adopted by the British military authorities.

By 5th June 1874 the RE Committee had reported to the Inspector General of Fortifications advocating the use of the Aldershot line's materials so as to afford a means of instruction in the use of railways not equipped with guide wheels. Four years later a talk was given by a Mr John L. Haddan concerning monorail lines for military use. In that lecture, given on 20th May 1878, Haddan stated, in connection with his belief that the trestles used at Aldershot were too high, that failure of the Aldershot line was certain. In answering Haddan's criticism, Fell referred to the Report of the Royal Engineers Committee which indicated that the experimental targets set prior to the tests undertaken at Aldershot had been attained. Fell had since modified his view on the general principles of the construction of narrow gauge railways using locomotives relying solely on the bearing rails for adhesive purposes. He now favoured the use of gauges in the region of 3ft and the use of trestle viaducts in conjunction with, rather than instead of, conventional earthworks and ballast. This approach, as of necessity, dispensed with the scope, or need, for the use of guide wheels.

In conclusion, it can be said that there were a number of factors which ensured the failure of the Fell line at Aldershot. In addition to the non-standard nature of the equipment, already referred to in connection with the observations of the Royal Engineers Committee, such a line would have presented a relatively easy target for enemy artillery. There would also have been difficulties caused by severe winds and their effects upon the trestles and vehicles. Another difficulty from the point of view of safety was the possibility, and potential dire consequences, of an axle breakage causing derailment of an item of rolling stock. Finally, as was mentioned by Haddan, the potential for 'standardised' trestle heights and beam configurations would have

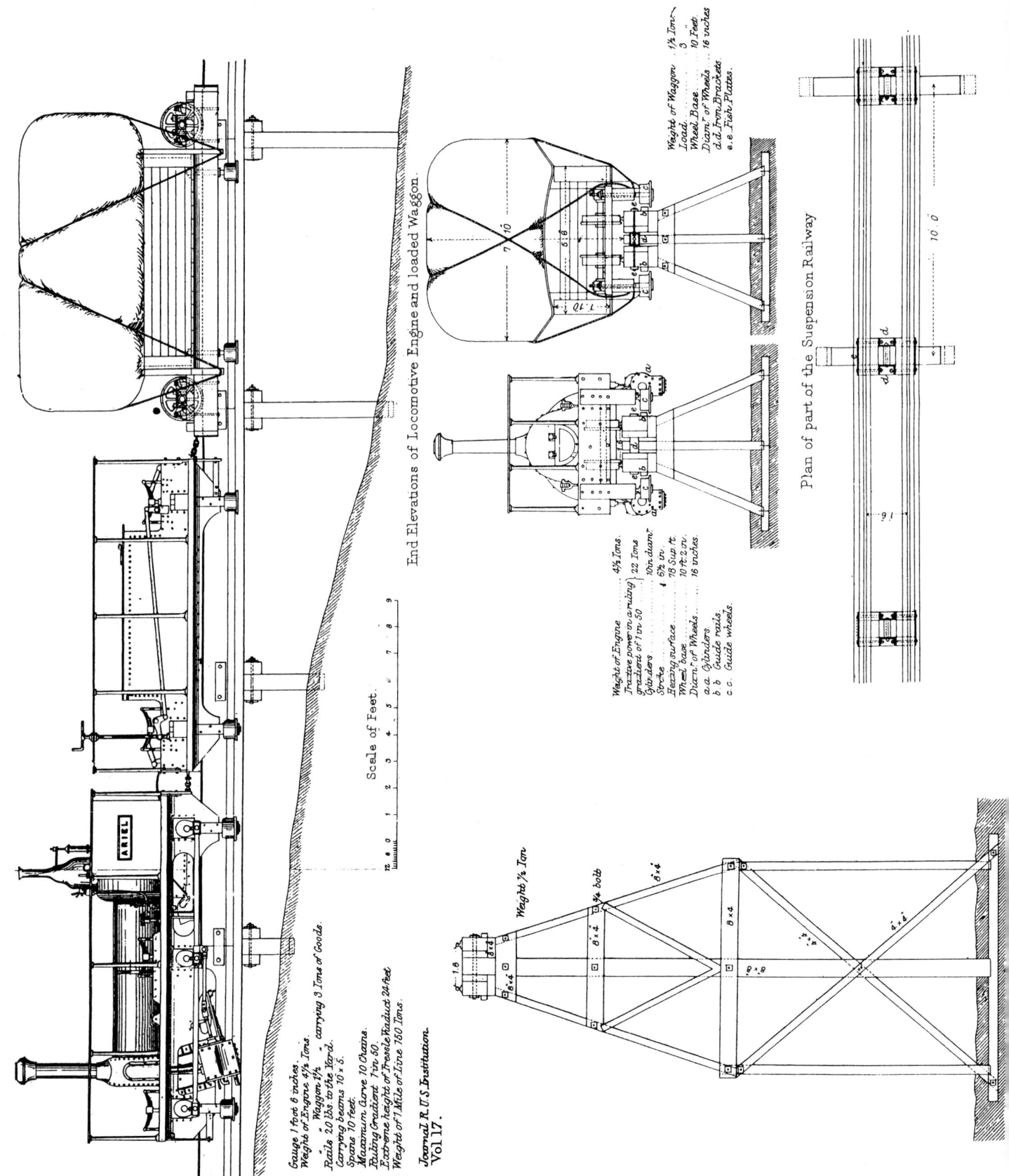

End Elevations of Locomotive Engine and loaded Waggon.

Scale of Feet.

Plan of part of the Suspension Railway

Gauge 1 foot 6 inches.
Weight of Engine 4½ Tons.
 "   " Waggon 1½ " carrying 3 Tons of Goods.
Rails 20 lbs to the Yard.
Carrying beams 10 × 5.
Spans 10 feet.
Maximum Curve 10 Chains.
Ruling Gradient 1 in 50.
Extreme height of Trestle Viaduct 24 Feet.
Weight of 1 Mile of Line 150 Tons.

Journal R. U. S. Institution.
Vol 17.

Weight of Engine .... 4½ Tons.
Tractive power in ascending
  gradient of 1 in 50 } .... 22 Tons
Cylinders .... 10 in. diam.
Stroke .... 6½ in.
Heating surface .... 78 Sup ft.
Wheel base .... 10 ft 2 in.
Diam.r of Wheels .... 16 inches
a.a. Cylinders
b b Guide rails
c.c. Guide wheels.

Weight of Waggon ... 1½ Ton.
Load 3
Wheel Base .... 10 Feet
Diam.r of Wheels ... 16 inches
d.d. Iron Brackets
e.e. Fish Plates.

Weight ½ Ton

been rather limited in the field, owing to the peculiarities of the lie of the land in any particular region.

Although the Fell line at Aldershot could only be described as unsuccessful, its place in British railway history was characterised by the fact that it pioneered the use for military field purposes of lines with bearing rails placed 18 inches apart. It may be argued that the use of guide wheels increased the effective gauge at Aldershot, but these only actually touched the guide rails when the vehicles concerned were on a curve.

As early as January 1872 an 18 inch gauge line was being projected in conjunction with fortifications works on the outskirts of Chatham. If completed in its original form this line would have linked the Convict Prison near Brompton Barracks with seven different works and would have crossed the LCDR main line in two different places (plus an interchange). In the event the line was completed circa 1880 linking only four works and not making any connection with the prison or crossing the main line. It will be discussed in subsequent paragraphs.

The next major development in the saga of 18 inch gauge steam locomotives intended solely for front line military use was brought into being by a series of related Patents taken out from 1873 to 1875. These Patents concerned the 'Steep Gradient Apparatus' invented by Mr Henry Handyside, the former Assistant Provincial Engineer to the Government of Nelson Province in New Zealand. As with Fell's system, the intention was to minimise the amount of earthworks necessary in the construction of railways. Unlike the approach to the problem adopted by Fell, Handyside's approach depended not upon the provision of a special form of permanent way but instead solely upon the use of specially adapted locomotives and rolling stock. Where the nature of the terrain to be crossed involved inclines of sufficient severity as to effectively prevent the haulage of trains of the desired weight, the Steep Gradient Apparatus would come into play.

In essence, the system enabled the locomotive to be used as a stationary engine to haul trains on heavily graded tracks. The main mechanical features were a winch fitted to the main frames of the locomotive and gripping struts capable of holding the engine on the incline when operating in a stationary mode. The design of these struts was arranged so that forward movement of the locomotive up the incline would release the grip and backward movement would tighten it. The normal mode of operation was that on lightly graded track, the winch would have wound the chain or iron rope used for haulage in, so that the buffers of the engine and those of the leading item of rolling stock were kept in close contact. Upon reaching the steeply graded section of track, a clutch lever locking the winch was released and the locomotive ran light up the incline to a suitable stopping point, paying out the chain or wire as it went. As soon as the locomotive had reached its point of rest, the gripping struts would be brought into use. The winch would then be operated by means of a pair of additional steam cylinders carried on the locomotive for this purpose. As soon as the leading item of rolling stock made contact with the rear buffers of the locomotive, the regulator to the winch cylinders would be shut off, either manually, via the driver's control, or automatically by means of a plunger fitted in one of the rear buffers of the engine. The gripping struts on the rolling stock would then be brought into play and these would hold these items in position whilst the engine surmounted the next section of the incline. The process would be repeated until the whole of the train had negotiated the entire incline.

The earliest proposal put forward in relation to the use of the Handyside system on a locomotive of 18 inch gauge was that put forward in *Iron* magazine for 17th October 1874. The feature in that edition was accompanied by a drawing of a proposed conversion of a Manning, Wardle locomotive. It will be seen that the main frames would have been extended rearwards by approximately 1ft to accommodate the winch assembly, with the centre axis of the drum being coincident with the rear of the original main frames. The cylinders for the winch would have been located between the two pairs of wheels on the engine and the gripping struts would have been located at the front of the locomotive actuated by a lever mounted on the right hand side of the locomotive. The fact that these Manning, Wardle locomotives were not designed for the additional rearward mounted weight imposed by the fitting of such a winch was illustrated by the need to provide rear supports which would be lowered into position at the same time as the gripping struts. The clutch lever for the winch would have been mounted at the rear of the right hand side of the footplate.

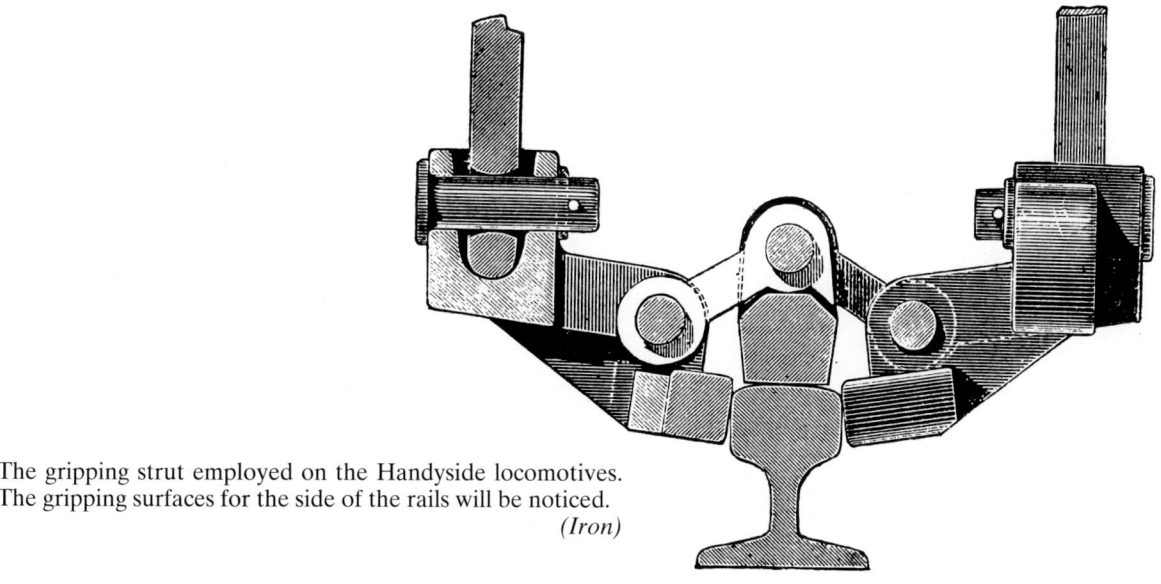

The gripping strut employed on the Handyside locomotives. The gripping surfaces for the side of the rails will be noticed.
(Iron)

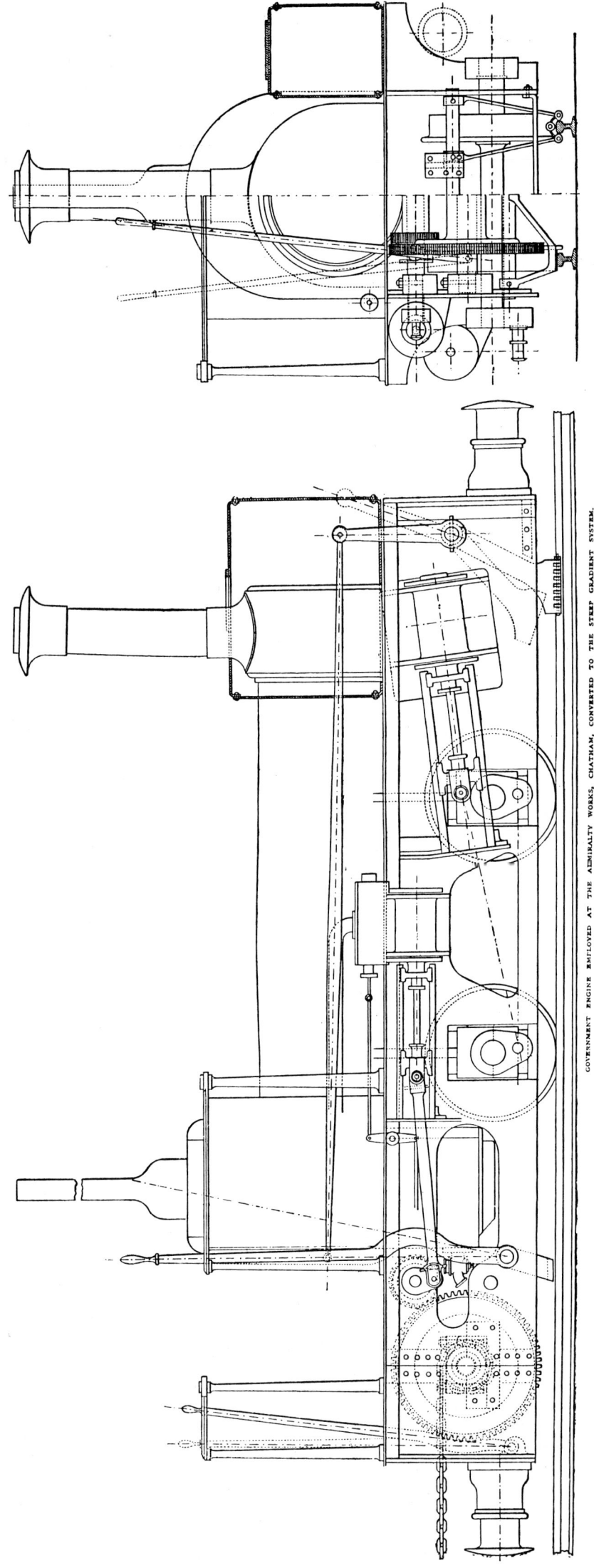

GOVERNMENT ENGINE EMPLOYED AT THE ADMIRALTY WORKS, CHATHAM, CONVERTED TO THE STEEP GRADIENT SYSTEM.

The proposed conversion of Manning, Ward e No. 448 *Burgoyne* to the Handyside steep gradient system. The saddle tank would have been replaced by two wing tanks (of differing dimensions) in order to transfer more weight to the front end. This conversion was never actually carried out and *Burgoyne* was still in use, according to Maker's records, in 1892.

(Iron)

It can be seen, from information contained within the Maker's records, that the engine selected for the proposed conversion was Manning, Wardle No.448 *Burgoyne*, a locomotive which had been supplied to the School of Military Engineering at Chatham on 21st April 1873. Although supplied to the Royal Engineers rather than the Admiralty, *Burgoyne's* design closely followed that of the Dockyard locomotive *Busy Bee*. It was to take rather longer, however, for the Royal Engineers Committee to formally consider Handyside's ideas in relation to 18 inch gauge military railway use.

In the period between the proposal of the Manning, Wardle conversion and the actual construction of an 18 inch gauge design of locomotive using the Handyside principle, some interesting developments took place. The most important of these was that the Handyside system found a commercial backer in the form of the Bristol locomotive manufacturing concern, Fox, Walker & Co. In 1875 the 'Handyside Steep Gradient Company Ltd' was registered with the subscribers being H. Handyside, E. Fox, F.W. Fox, E. Walker, W.F. Bath, H.L. Jones and J.F. Havenfield. Fox, Walker & Co. funded much of the development and undertook all of the construction of the documented Handyside locomotives. Standard gauge examples were to be tested at Avonmouth Docks in 1875 and in the following year on the Hopton Incline of the Cromford & High Peak Railway.

The occurrence of these tests encouraged the Royal Engineers Committee to show further interest in the Handyside system. It was recorded in one of the RE Committee Minutes (No. 3599 of 28th July 1876) that Henry Handyside had notified the committee of the impending Hopton experiments and in Minute No. 3603 of 25th August 1876 the Inspector General of Fortifications called for a report on the Hopton Incline demonstration. On 12th September 1876 a sub-committee consisting of Major Percy Smith RE and Captain Sale RE (Secretary) visited the Hopton-Incline tests and certain experiments were carried out for their benefit. The locomotive used was a 23 ton 0-6-0ST with cylinders 13in bore and 20in stroke, driving wheels 3ft 6in diameter and a wheelbase of 9ft 8½in. The winch cylinders were 9in bore by 12in stroke and the drum was equipped with 300 yards of steel wire rope. As an aid to engaging or disengaging the winch drum from its drive, as required by the operations of paying out the rope and subsequently hauling the wagons up the incline, epicyclic gearing was incorporated into the winch. When required, the wagons could be checked on the incline by a 'simple catch arrangement' details of which have not survived. The Handyside gripping strut was brought into play on the 1-in-14 Hopton Incline locomotive by means of a steam cylinder.

On the day of the sub-committee's visit, it was shown that the locomotive could haul a gross wagon load of 45 tons up the incline in seven minutes, with the equivalent net payload being 34½ tons. Haulage was undertaken in two stages from an approximate mid-point of the incline and from the summit. The locomotive descending light could be brought to rest from a speed of 6-8 miles per hour by application of the steam powered gripping strut in a distance approximating to its own length. When loaded with a gross weight of 50 tons and descending at 3½-4.0 miles per hour, the engine was brought to rest in a distance approximating to 1½ times its own length without damage to gripping

struts or rails. It was also observed, as a negative point, however, that defective manufacturing of the winch cylinders had restricted the maximum load which the winch could handle, the desired maximum loading being 56 tons for the Hopton Incline. The maximum resistance of the gripping strut to haulage was given as equivalent to 6-7 tons.

The opinion of the sub-committee was that for civilian use the Handyside locomotive could not compete with properly constructed fixed winding engines for haulage on inclines, yet the peculiar property of dual usage as a locomotive or fixed winding engine might make it particularly valuable in wartime. Their report went on to say: "It would enormously facilitate the construction of a field railway if inclines up to 1 in 10 could be allowed, and as fixed winding engines are out of the question under such circumstances, the use of this locomotive winding engine, or of some similar contrivance, seems the only way by which such steep gradients can be rendered practicable. Hence it seems that the system now under construction might be worked out so as to be of much use for military purposes."

One important reservation was expressed, however: "The application of steam power to the grip or brake seems undesirable, at least, for military purposes; it complicates the machinery and is unnecessary, as apparently the grip can be worked well enough by hand or the use of simple screw gearing."

The next reference to Handyside's work in the RE Committee proceedings was dated 24th November 1876 and this was mentioned in Minute No. 3727. By this stage an 18 inch gauge line had been proposed in association with the new Fort Borstall, then in the process of construction at Chatham. It appears that Handyside initially submitted his drawing for the proposed conversion of *Burgoyne* as a basis for a locomotive for this line, but the committee emphasised their opposition to the Manning, Wardle design for field railway use on the ground that it had insufficient power. It was decided instead to lay down requirements for a purpose-built trench locomotive. The desired locomotive was to be of 18 inch gauge and was to be carried on eight wheels in such a manner as to be capable of negotiating curves of 15ft radius. It was to be fitted with a winch with 200ft of steel wire rope of 0.625in or ¾in diameter and both Handyside and ordinary brakes. The axle loading was to be limited to 3 tons and the total locomotive weight was to be limited to 9 tons. The locomotive was to be capable of being dismantled so as to form two parts, each weighing less than 5 tons and to be able to stand on a 1 in 10 incline without sustaining firebox damage. A copper firebox and brass boiler tubes were to be fitted and the working pressure was to be 130 psi. The engine was required to ascend a 1 in 10 gradient at three miles per hour light and at two miles per hour with a load of 18 tons. It was also required to run on the level around curves of 40ft radius at a steady speed of eight miles per hour.

In answer to the requirements laid down by the Royal Engineers Committee, Henry Handyside proposed a rather peculiar eight-wheeled double-bogie locomotive driven by what appeared to be two three-cylinder Brotherhood motors arranged so that power was transmitted to the bogie wheels. Exclusive of the winch, the main influences behind the design of this locomotive appear to have been the double Fairlie principle and the Crewe Works locomotive *Billy* as

Handyside's Railway System.
Proposed Narrow Gauge Engine.

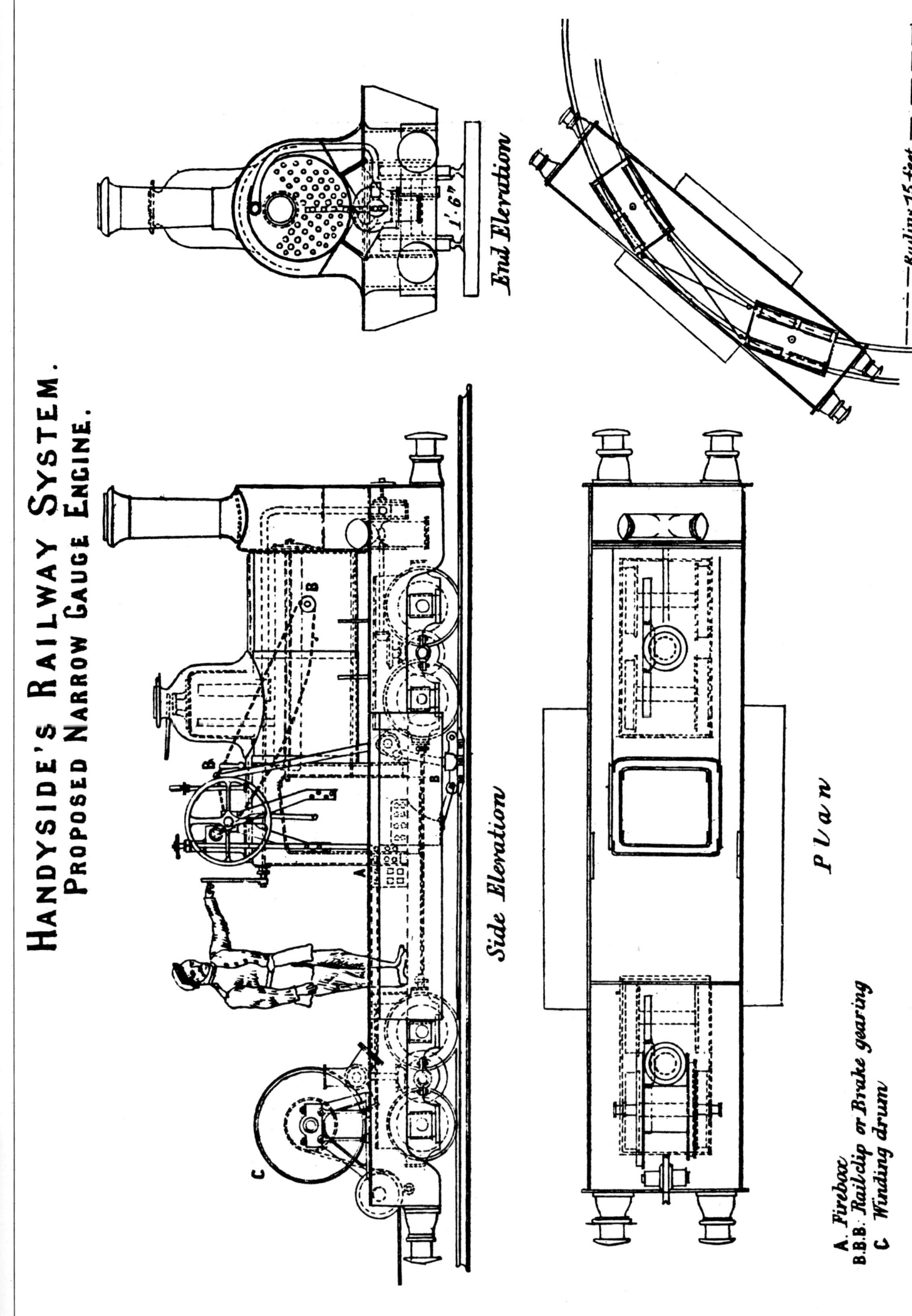

End Elevation

1' 6"

Side Elevation

Plan

Radius 15 feet

A. Firebox
B.B.B. Railclip or Brake gearing
C. Winding drum

originally constructed. The original drawings as reproduced in the committee's proceedings do not show how the locomotive would have been reversed and it may be that the front motor required reversing by dismounting from the footplate and manually rotating a wheel at the front end so as to rotate the slide valve spindle in relation to the crankshaft This would have been the case if the design of the motors had directly followed Patent Specification 2003 of 1873, although the rear motor could still have been reversed from the footplate. No details of the clutch mechanism for engaging or disengaging the winch or rear bogie were shown but the common power source for these components would have created constructional difficulties. A handwheel and chain mechanism was proposed for the gripping struts.

In view of the peculiarities inherent in this locomotive's design, it was of little surprise that the Inspector General of Fortifications decided, according to a minute dated 2nd January 1877, against ordering the construction of a prototype. The proposal of a fully adhesive wheel configuration at this initial stage was in itself a point of interest, however, and Arthur Percival Heywood was to follow a similar course, albeit allied with a different method for providing flexibility for the wheelbase, in his attempts to arrive at a suitable design

for a 15 inch gauge trench locomotive during the ensuing years.

The Handyside locomotives actually produced for use on 18 inch gauge trench railways were eventually turned out by Fox, Walker in the spring of 1878 as their Nos 399-404. The locomotives were given the classification HPTE (probably an abbreviation for 'Handyside Patent Trench Engine') by the Makers. *Iron* magazine for 11th May 1878 referred to experiments which were: "to be carried out at the Royal Arsenal, Woolwich to test the efficiency of a special kind of locomotive which has been constructed for the new trench railway. This railway is designed to be laid upon the surface of the ground wherever it may be found necessary to construct earthworks or to transport material, the ordinary methods of reducing irregularities by cuttings and embankments being out of the question in field operations. The engine is therefore designed to ascend and descend steep gradients, and is also fitted with an apparatus for hauling up and lowering down trucks. A hill too steep to be ascended with a load may be surmounted by the engine alone, and it may then wind up the load after it. An experimental railway running up and down hill in irregular fashion is being formed near the butts in the Government Marshes adjoining the Royal Arsenal, Woolwich for the purpose of the trial."

Further information about the six HPTE locomotives was furnished by the Secretary of the RE Committee in a minute dated 2nd May 1879. Here it was revealed that one of the locomotives had been sent to undergo trials at Chatham during that year. The locomotive cylinders were 8in bore and 10in stroke, with the dimensions of those of the winch apparently being unrecorded. The firebox heating surface was 24.15 sq ft whilst that of the tubes was 68.47 sq ft and the engine, complete with winch, weighed 8 tons in working order. The pony trucks supported bearing plates and were equipped with neither vertical nor side control springs. The trial railway consisted of a main continuous portion, incorporating three bridges, four points, several curves and some gentle inclines, of approximately a mile in length and a branch portion incorporating gradients of between 1 in 10 and 1 in 11. The line was described as using the same rails, fastenings and sleepers as standard for trench railways,

One of the six locomotives constructed by Fox, Walker & Co. of the Atlas Works, Bristol in 1878 using the Handyside Steep Gradient Apparatus. The Handyside system was intended for use on gradients of such a severity as to prevent the passage of a train but of such a magnitude as to allow the locomotive to ascend in the 'light engine' mode. In practice, defects in the design and construction of engine and winch ensured the eventual rejection of the system by the Royal Engineers.

(Courtesy F. Jones)

although it seems likely that some material was salvaged from the Fell line at Aldershot.

During the trials it was found that the maximum speed attained on the circular portion was twelve miles per hour, but this was considered excessive and half of this figure was recommended as a fair working speed, inclusive of stops for water, coaling and oiling. As regards haulage, it was found that the engine could surmount the 1 in 10 stretch without load, draw 10 tons up 1 in 18 and 50 tons on the level. It could also traverse 15ft radius curves satisfactorily and haul 10 tons up the 1 in 10 incline using the winch. The water consumption of the locomotive was estimated as 18 gallons per hour of normal working. During the same period and under the same conditions, 70 lb of coal would have been consumed, requiring the removal of clinker every two hours. The engine's coal capacity was 3 cwt and lubrication required 1½ pints of oil on starting, with a further pint required after each five hours of running.

Unfortunately, several faults were found with the design of the engine. The boiler pitch was excessively high, in order to clear the driving axle, and the steel haulage cable had of necessity had to pass rearward from the winch under most of the length of the locomotive's superstructure. The high boiler pitch, together with lack of side control springs on the pony trucks, made for potentially rough riding characteristics on poorly laid track or soft ground. The location of the winch at the front end meant that its controls were inaccessible from the footplate and there was also poor access to the oil cups for lubrication. The water capacity of 83½ gallons was felt to be inadequate as this provided sufficient water for less than five hours' normal working. The lack of a firebox damper resulted in a wasteful level of fuel consumption and the profile of the wheel treads was too narrow, resulting in a propensity to de-rail. There were also sundry additional defects, such as the steampipe

for the blower being supplied from too low a point in the boiler, and the lack of sufficient notches on the reversing sector.

By 1881 two of the Handyside locomotives had been assigned to the 18 inch gauge railway associated with construction work at Forts Borstall, Bridgewoods, Horsted and Luton during the 1880's decade.

The Inspector-General of Fortifications forwarded a report by Major Hogg RE (dated 30th April 1881) to the RE Committee and asked for their recommendations upon the subject of a more efficient locomotive for siege train purposes. In his report, Major Hogg highlighted defects in the construction of the main frames of the Handyside locomotives which were caused in part by the wish on the part of the Makers to keep the engine's weight down to 8 tons. The second of the Handyside locomotives to be set to work on the Fortifications had been repaired early in 1881, having suffered hard usage during the Woolwich experiments. During this overhaul, the winch assembly was removed and replaced by a cast iron weight of just under 18 cwt, a modification which was found to save the engine from rough riding on the level and gentle gradients, but which rendered it useless for haulage on gradients steeper than 1 in 30. The design of the winch engine was found to be defective on the first of the Handyside locomotives sent for use on the Fortifications line and the winch could not be made operational without much work being undertaken at Chatham by factory hands. A diagram appended to Paper VII of the Professional Papers of the Royal Engineers (1883) indicates that at least one Handyside had its water capacity increased to 106 gallons.

The Royal Engineers thus gained some usage from one of the Handysides in the 1879 trials at the School of Military Engineering and from two others on the Fortifications works, at least one of which had previously been used in trials at Woolwich Arsenal. The other three were regarded as unsuitable for field usage. Major Hogg then turned to the question of a more suitable locomotive for trench railways. He felt that the main priority at that stage was a design of locomotive to replace the Handysides on the Fortifications works and his recommendations involved the use of a locomotive with a water capacity of 200 gallons and no inbuilt winch. The cylinder dimensions were to be enlarged from those used on the Fox, Walker locomo-

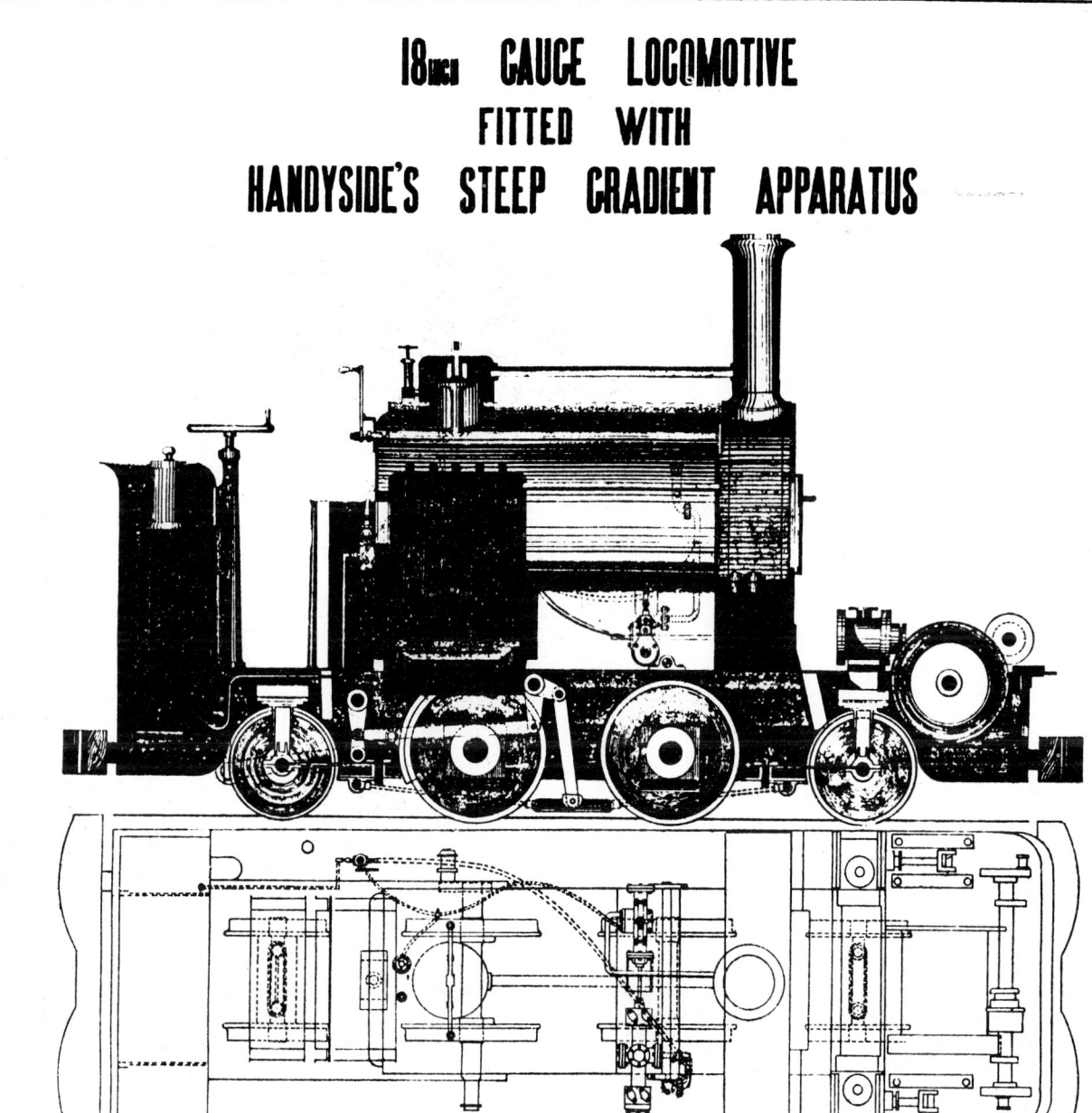

**18inch GAUGE LOCOMOTIVE
FITTED WITH
HANDYSIDE'S STEEP GRADIENT APPARATUS**

The basic general design of the Fox, Walker 'Handyside' locomotives (Nos 399 to 404 of 1878) was illustrated in this pair of drawings which accompanied RE Committee Minute No. 4847 of 2nd May 1879.

(RE Library, Chatham)

tives and the working pressure reduced to 100 psi. The boiler pitch was to be reduced by about 4 inches and the gross weight was to be about 10 tons or 12 tons if the locomotive were not to be used for siege train purposes.

Assuming the possibility of siege train usage, it was proposed to construct a tender truck carrying an improved design of crab winch, with a coiling mechanism, Handyside gripping struts, 300 yards of steel wire rope, a reserve tank for 200 gallons of water and a bunker for 6 cwt of coal. In addition a special tight coupling between locomotive and tender would have been necessary to take the strain off the steampipe joint between these vehicles.

Alternatively, Major Hogg felt that the design of a new locomotive for the fortifications works could be left to a reputable specialist maker, such as Beyer,

Peacock and that construction of the tender could be postponed indefinitely. Major Hogg himself was sceptical of 18 inch gauge locomotive-worked lines as being suitable for siege train purposes on grounds of safety and unit operational cost, a view which he was to repeat in *The Royal Engineers Journal* for September 1885

The Committee in answer to Major Hogg's report decided not to proceed with the construction of 18 inch gauge locomotives specifically designed for siege train purposes as they felt that metre gauge stock would be more appropriate for specially constructed locomotive-worked field supply lines. They felt, rather naively, that such stock could be readily procured in Britain in an emergency. The 18 inch gauge lines linking the Artillery and Engineer Parks to the front, it was felt, did not require the use of locomotives.

Some of the design faults on the Handyside locomotives were attributable to the fact that the threat of a conflict between Britain and Russia was a significant one at the time of ordering the engines. The design and construction of the locomotives was therefore somewhat hurried. The Russian threat had receded to a

This drawing of the 'Handyside' locomotives appeared in Paper VII of the RE Institution's Professional Papers of 1883. It suggests that the water capacity of the 'Handysides' working on the fortifications was later increased to 106 gallons.

Plate I

(RE Library, Chatham)

NARROW GAUGE ROLLING STOCK.

SECTIONAL SKETCH OF 18-INCH GAUGE LOCOMOTIVE

CARRYING STEAM WINDING CRAB
AND FITTED WITH HANDYSIDE RAIL-CLUTCHES.

Gross weight in driving order . . . . 8 Ton

Per centage carried by driving wheels . . .62.

Rail traction with 140 lbs. boiler pressure . 1 Ton

Cylinder diameter . . 8 Inches

Driving wheel ditto . . . 2 Feet

Stroke . . . . 9 Inches

Total heating surface . 113 Sq.ft

Grate area . . . . 4.42 Sq.

Curve radius traversable at low speed. 16 Ft

85 TUBES 1 5/16 INT: DIAM:

P

COAL 3 CWT.

TANK 106 GALL.ᴮ

FEET.

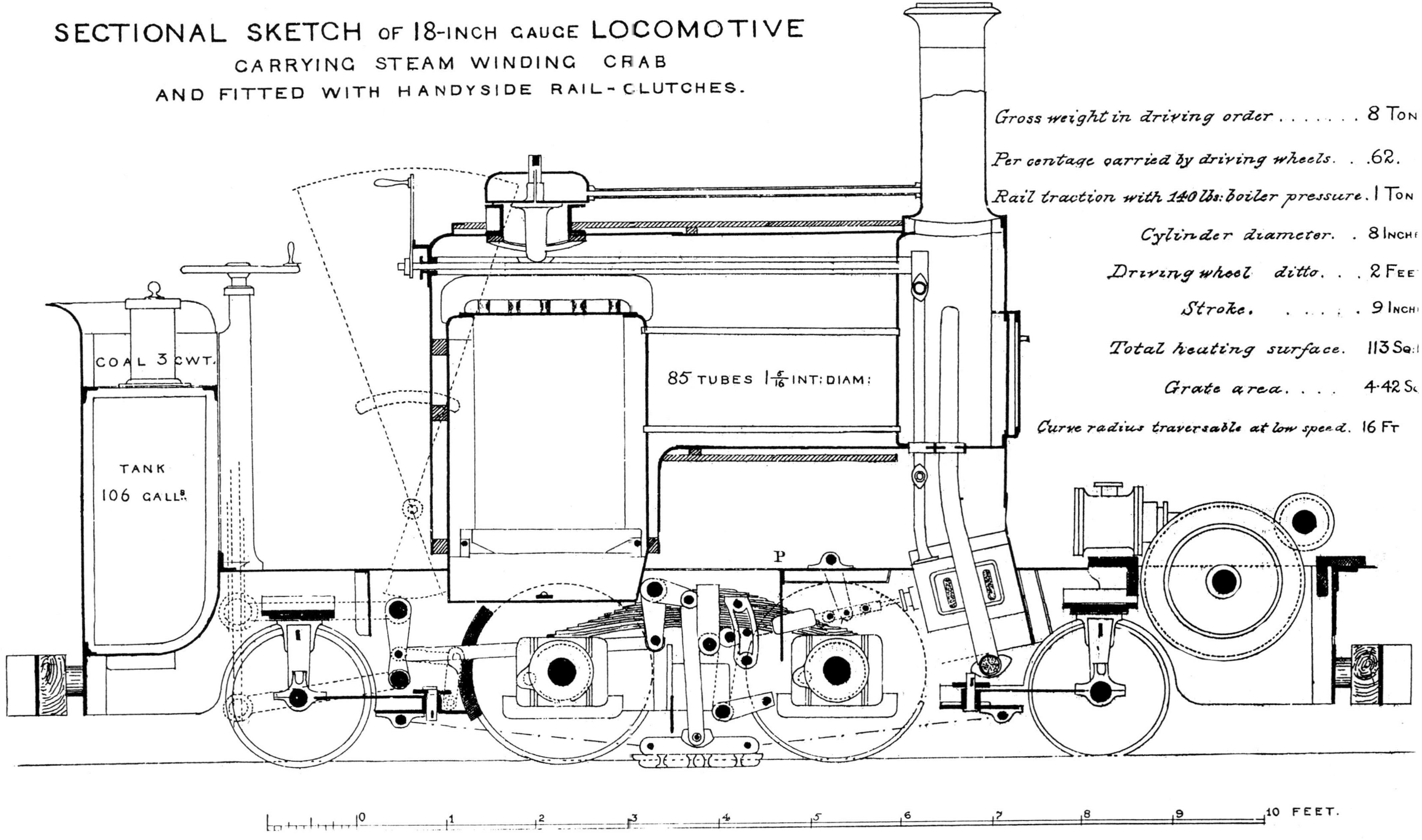

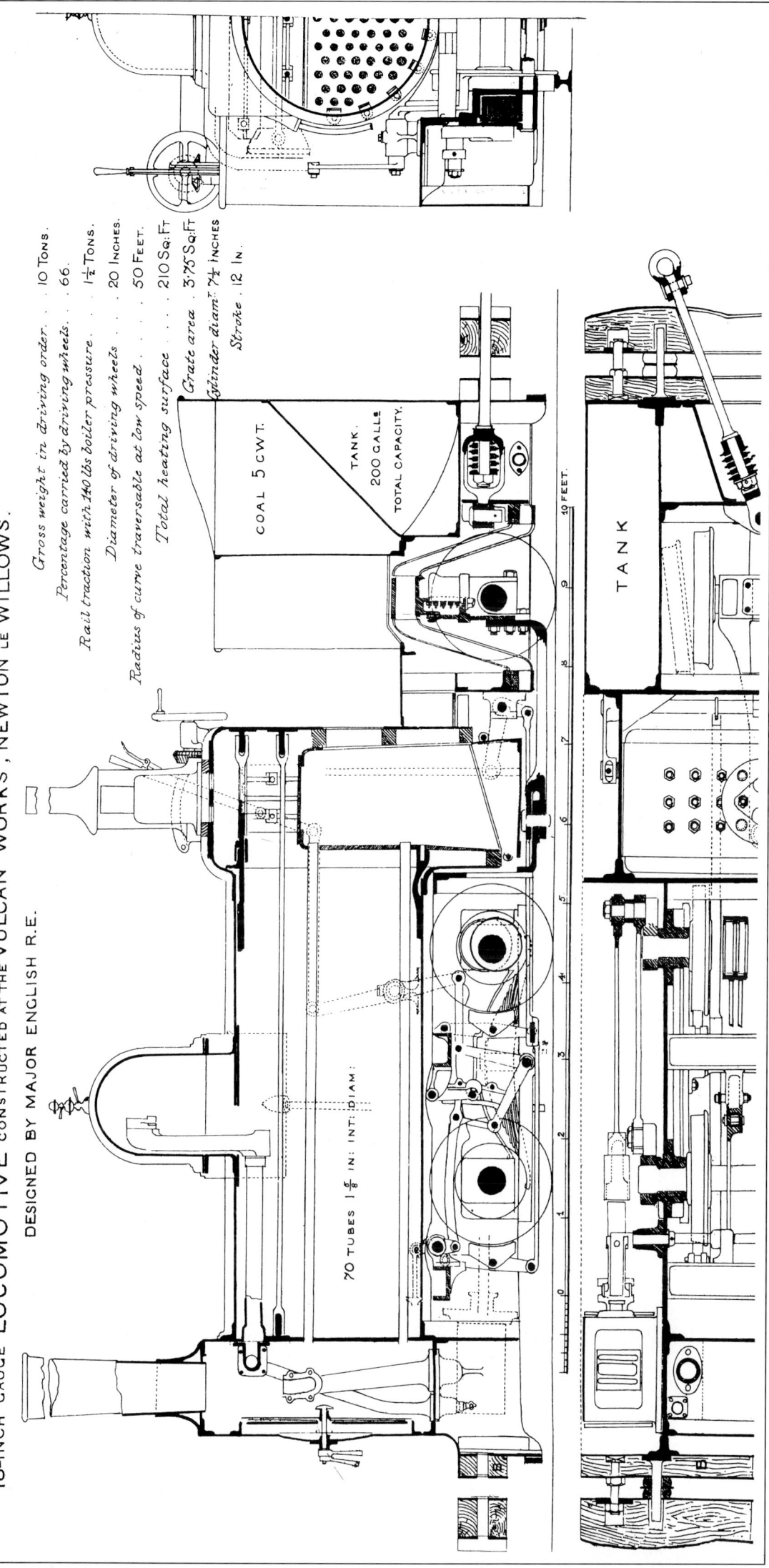

Plate II.

NARROW GAUGE ROLLING STOCK.

18-INCH GAUGE LOCOMOTIVE CONSTRUCTED AT THE VULCAN WORKS, NEWTON LE WILLOWS.

DESIGNED BY MAJOR ENGLISH R.E.

Gross weight in driving order	10 TONS.
Percentage carried by driving wheels	66.
Rail traction with 140 lbs boiler pressure	1½ TONS.
Diameter of driving wheels	20 INCHES.
Radius of curve traversable at low speed	50 FEET.
Total heating surface	210 SQ. FT.
Grate area	3.75 SQ. FT.
Cylinder diam. 7½ INCHES
Stroke 12 IN.

COAL 5 CWT.

TANK. 200 GALLS. TOTAL CAPACITY.

70 TUBES 1⅝ IN: INT: DIAM:

TANK

10 FEET.

This drawing appeared in Paper VII of the 1883 Professional Papers and shows simplified drawings of *Vulcan* (Vulcan Foundry 939 of 1883) for the Chatham Fortifications line. The English patent trailing truck (Patent No. 3869 of 1883) can be seen and this comprised a longitudinal crankshaft which compressed the suspension spring to apply side control when a curve was being negotiated. First used on *Vulcan*, this device was later adopted by John Fowler & Co. on several of their narrow gauge locomotive designs. Although not of good draughtsmanship quality, this drawing highlights several features important to prospective modellers, such as the Belpaire boiler, the lateral position of the reversing column and its associated reach rod and the position and size of the boiler-mounted sandboxes.

(RE Professional Papers)

A Maker's photograph of *Vulcan* (Vulcan Foundry No. 939 of 1883). The failure of the Fox, Walker Handyside locomotives ensured that no further 18 inch gauge locomotives would be designed so as to be able to work in the parallels during a siege. This Vulcan Foundry design was originally produced to work on the Chatham Fortifications line and therefore the minimum permitted curve radius was eased to 35 ft as against the 15 ft permitted for the Handysides. A satisfactory performance by locomotives of this design on the Chatham Fortifications line, and at Suakin, ensured that 18 inch gauge remained the War Office standard for trench railways until 1896, contrary to the view supported by Major Hogg of the Royal Engineers.

(Courtesy F. Jones)

significant degree during the period from 1878-81. It appears that some of the Handysides were sold circa 1890–6 after completion of the Fortifications works and were probably scrapped at this time. One example, however, is known to have worked at the Royal Arsenal and survived sans winding gear and front pony truck into the Edwardian period. In order to provide more suitable motive power for the Fortifications line, two specially designed locomotives were constructed by Vulcan Foundry Co. Ltd of Newton-le-Willows.

Right: The Maker's drawings of the Vulcan Foundry 0-4-2 back tank locomotives *Mars* and *Venus* (Nos 1160 and 1161 of 1885). These drawings are of better quality than the preceding ones but do not highlight the Belpaire firebox. The English patent link motion, a close relative of the Gooch variety, is shown to advantage however.

(The Engineer)

A Maker's photograph of *Mars* (Vulcan Foundry No. 1160 of 1885). This locomotive and its sister, *Venus* (Vulcan Foundry No. 1161 of 1885) were originally sent to the Chatham Fortifications line to replace *Vulcan* and *Mercury* after their departure to Suakin during the ill-fated Sudan Military Expedition of 1885. *Mars* and *Venus* remained at Chatham until about 1888 and appear to have been put into storage at Woolwich for the next sixteen years. From the number of 18 inch gauge steam locomotives in ordinary service on the RAR at the time of *Narrow Gauge Railways Two Feet and Under* it would appear that *Mars* and *Venus* never became part of *RAR* stock. The Chatham Fortifications line was still shown on an Ordnance Survey map of 1904, but it probably fell out of use during the 1890s.

(Courtesy F. Jones)

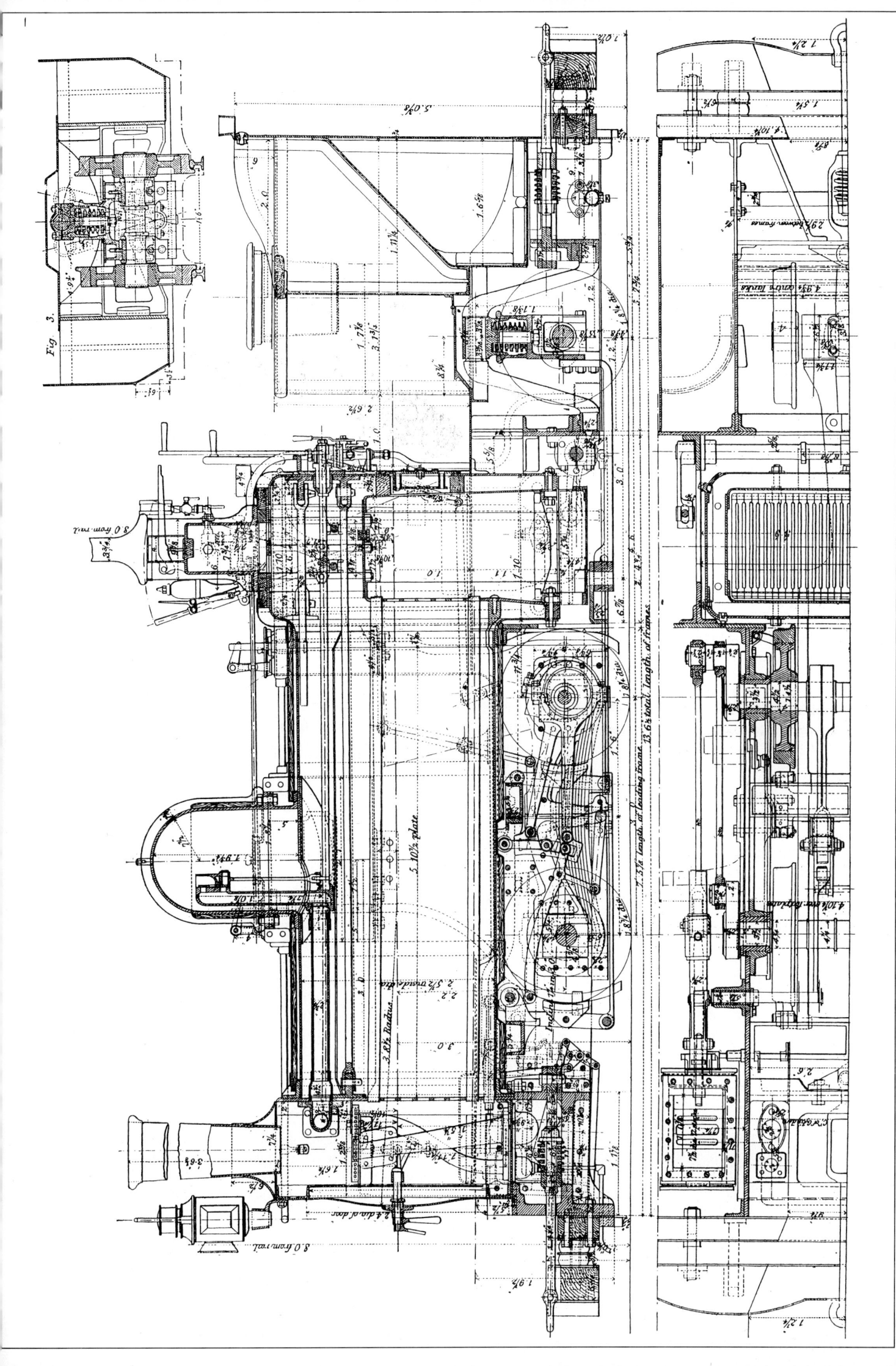

Fig. 3.

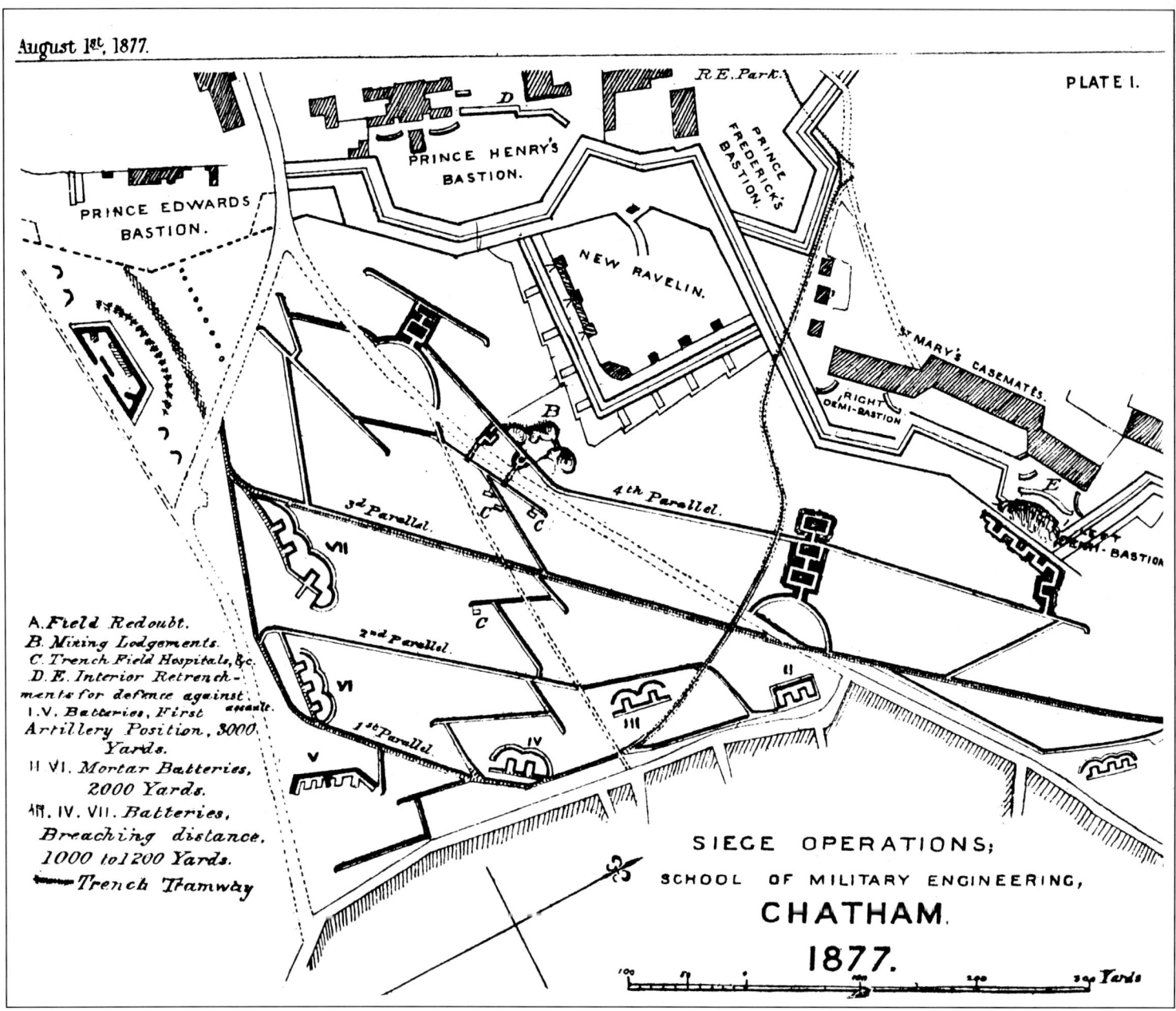

PLATE I.

PRINCE EDWARDS BASTION.

PRINCE HENRY'S BASTION.

R.E.Park.

PRINCE FREDERICK'S BASTION.

NEW RAVELIN.

ST MARY'S CASEMATES.

RIGHT DEMI-BASTION

3d Parallel.

4th Parallel.

2nd Parallel.

1st Parallel.

A. Field Redoubt.
B. Mining Lodgements.
C. Trench Field Hospitals, &c.
D.E. Interior Retrench-
ments for defence against
assault.
I.V. Batteries, First
Artillery Position., 3000
Yards.
II VI. Mortar Batteries,
2000 Yards.
AII. IV. VII. Batteries,
Breaching distance.
1000 to 1200 Yards.
Trench Tramway

SIEGE OPERATIONS;
SCHOOL OF MILITARY ENGINEERING,
CHATHAM.
1877.

This plan of siege operations at the School of Military Engineering was originally reproduced in *The Royal Engineers Journal* for August 1877. 18 inch gauge track was laid in the 1st and 3rd Parallels and rolling stock on these lines would have been manually propelled.

(RE Library, Chatham)

These engines were Maker's Nos 939 of 1883 and 1075 of 1884 (respectively *Vulcan* and *Mercury*).

The Vulcan Foundry locomotive design was described in *The Engineer* for 31st July 1885 and credit for the origination of the design was ascribed to Major English RE. The cylinders were 7½in diameter and 12in stroke. The driving, coupled and carrying wheels were all, rather unusually, of the same diameter of 1ft 8¼in and the wheelbase was 3ft coupled and 7ft 6in in total. The tanks held 200 gallons of water and the bunker had capacity for 6 cwt of coal. The heating surface was 222¾ sq ft made up of 204 sq ft for the tubes and 18¾ sq ft for the firebox. The weight of the locomotive in working order was 10 tons.

The Fortifications railway at Chatham was described in a letter which appeared in the August 1885 issue of *The Royal Engineers Journal*. Here it was claimed that *Vulcan* and *Mercury* could each manage a load of 60

tons, exclusive of the tare weight of the rolling stock, at a speed of 15 mph. It was also stated that one of these locomotives could take a net load of 13 tons of ballast on a line with a ruling gradient of 1 in 35 and haul the same load over a distance of 1.7 miles with a mean gradient of 1 in 85 at a speed of 12 mph. In a working day, each locomotive would make eight trips over the line, carrying 104 tons of ballast in nine hours. From this performance, the conclusion was drawn that a locomotive of this type could handle in excess of 22,000 gallons of water per day and, allowing ten gallons per head amongst the troops in camp, this would suffice for two battalions and the headquarters staff. The argument was advanced that water transportation should take place in wagons equipped with 500 gallon tanks, and the water could be distributed to each company by breaking down the train into its constituent wagons at the main rail-head and moving one wagon to each company by means of portable rails.

Further details in relation to the Chatham defences line were advanced and it was revealed that there were passenger trains on this system whose passengers consisted of convicts, who supplied labour for the Fortifications construction, and the warders who guarded them. It is recorded that the locomotives were each capable of handling eleven carriages, each with a capacity of twenty men comprising two warders and 18 convicts, at a speed of 10 miles per hour on a gradient of 1 in 43. The carriages each had a tare weight of 2½ tons. Drawings of the carriages and wagons used on the line are reproduced in accompanying illustrations. Records relating to the final disposal of these vehicles do not appear to have survived.

It was pointed out in *The Royal Engineers Journal* that, making allowance for the fact that the tare weight of troop carriages would be only 1½ tons, and that a full compliment of arms and kit for twenty men for each carriage would weigh half a ton, the locomotives used on the Chatham Fortifications railway could each draw a troop train of 13 carriages, holding 260 men, round 50 feet radius curves and over the same 1 in 43 gradient that was present on the section of line used by convict trains. This, it was argued, would prove to be most useful in the military context, particularly in hilly country where even a metre gauge line would require cuttings and embankments to ensure that curve radii were not prohibitively low. The letter describing the performance of *Vulcan* and *Mercury* prompted further comments by Lt Col. (formerly Major) Hogg who, as has been noted, did not share the War Office's enthusiasm for 18 inch gauge lines.

Contrary to the view expressed by the RE Committee in 1881, it was decided to send *Vulcan* and *Mercury* to the Sudan as part of the abortive Suakin Expedition of 1885 for use on the 18 inch gauge line there. Part of this line was shown in *The Royal Engineers Journal* for March 1886, although it had been removed by this time. Although (as has been discussed) both of these engines are believed to have returned to the United Kingdom for use in Thomas Russell Crampton's experiments at Woolwich in 1886, two further similar locomotives were constructed in 1885, these being Vulcan Foundry Nos 1160, *Mars* and 1161, *Venus*. These two locomotives were delivered to Chatham where they worked for at least three years. Their later careers will be dealt with shortly.

A feature written by Capt. H.G. Kunhardt in the July 1885 issue of *The Royal Engineers Journal* was of interest in that it reflected the writer's experiences with the locomotive-worked 18 inch gauge line at Suakin. He said that the engines were: "only capable of hauling 25 tons at a speed of eight miles an hour" and that such lines: "may be useful in arsenals or dockyards, or for connecting engineer parks with the trenches during the siege of a large fortress, but for such purposes as supplying an army in the field with men, ammunition and stores at a distance of more than five miles from the base, they are totally unsuitable. At Suakin a 1'8" (sic) engine and train, working day and night, was only just able to supply the headquarter camp and two regiments with water at a distance of 1½ mile from the base". The operational limitations of the 18 inch gauge locomotive-worked line for direct military use had therefore become more widely realised, although (as we shall see in the next paragraph), the War Department refused at this stage to turn its back on the prospect of utilising such systems.

The main point of interest at this stage of the discussion is that a *Manual of Military Railways* for the year 1889 survives in the Royal Engineers' Library at Chatham. In the section of the Manual devoted to trench tramways, a gauge of 18 inches is still advocated, together with a locomotive of the 0-4-2 tank configuration. The quoted dimensions for such a locomotive are identical to the Vulcan Foundry design as regards cylinder dimensions, water capacity, wheelbase and minimum radius of suitable track curvature of 50ft. This last requirement emphasises the fact that locomotives were seen by this stage as a means of moving men and supplies to, but not inside, the trenches themselves. The weight in working order is quoted in Paragraph 43 of the Manual as 9¾ tons on the basis of a 7¾ ton weight empty. The succeeding Paragraph 44, however, lists the stores necessary for a 30-gun siege train and gives the weight of three stored locomotives as being exactly 24 tons. Since these locomotives would be empty and weigh 8 tons apiece, adding the same figure used above for coal and water of 2 tons would bring the total back to the figure quoted in *The Engineer* for the Vulcan Foundry locomotive, *Mars*. The coal capacity quoted in the Military Manual for trench locomotives was 5 cwt, less than the original figure for *Mars*, but this may have been the result of over-optimism on the part of the Makers. The net load of 30 tons on a 1-in-50 gradient was the same as the Makers' quote for *Mars*.

The *Manual of Military Railways* of 1889 which has already been referred to sheds further light on the intentions of the Royal Engineers at this stage. Rather surprisingly, despite the existence of the Chattenden & Upnor Railway at this time, there was no mention of the use of 2ft 6in gauge as a military standard and discussion of trench tramways, as these systems were termed, centred around lines of 18 inch gauge.

The main uses for such a system, as detailed in Paragraph 38 of the Manual, were communications between artillery and engineer parks and the batteries and advanced trenches. Such a railway, laid in the parallels and approaches, would have been of use for the transportation of ammunition to the siege battery magazines and engineer material, and for the removal of sick and wounded to the rear, further away from immediate danger.

There was also a design shown for a gun trolley for use on such railways. In order to mount a gun on such a trolley, three gun detachments, each consisting of eight men and one NCO, would have been required and the gun and limber needed four ramps to raise it to the level of the trolley. Once raised to the level of the trolley, scotches would have been used to hold the gun and limber wheels in position whilst the trolley was run into place underneath the gun. Two skids were to be placed in a transverse position on the platform of the trolley, the smaller skid (2ft 9in x 9in x 6in) being located as to rest beneath the trail section of the gun and the larger skid (2ft 9in x 1ft 6in x 6in) being located as to support the trunnions, this latter skid being placed a small distance behind the longitudinal mid-point of the trolley. The limber shafts would then have been raised in two movements the first of which would lower the trail of the gun onto the forward skid and the second of which would unhook the limber from the gun carriage. At the end of these movements, the scotches securing the limber would have been knocked away and the limber would have been removed, along with its ramps. The last stage in the loading drill would have been to lower the gun carriage and this was accomplished by first pulling on the drag ropes for the gun, so as to enable the gun scotches to be knocked away, and then gradually lowering the gun onto the rear skid so that its wheels moved down the ramps, with the trolley moving forwards slightly during this process. The trolley stores consisting of two ramps, four scotches, two mauls and

Contemporary engravings of *Mars* (Vulcan Foundry No. 1160 of 1885). These views show the rocker shaft drive used in order to actuate the valves. The chimney and safety valve bonnet both extended to a height of 8ft above rail level.

(The Engineer and Engineering)

four handspikes could then be loaded, the two ramps being those which had supported the gun wheels.

The operation of unloading the gun trolley would have consisted firstly of bringing up the limber (and two associated ramps) and unloading the stores from the trolley. One pair of ramps would then have been placed to the rear of the gun wheels and the other pair to the rear of the limber wheels. The ramps would then have been hammered up tight by means of mauls. The distance between the butt of the limber ramp and the tip of the gun ramp was to be 2ft 6in.

The next stage in the procedure would have been to tie the drag ropes to the wheels of the gun, after which the gun would have been dragged a small distance up the ramp so as to clear the trolley. Scotches would then have been fixed to secure the gun wheels and the limber would be brought up its ramps until its hook could be engaged with the eye on the trail of the gun. The limber personnel would then bear down on the shafts until the extreme end of the trail was being supported by the limber. At this point, the 'keying up' process joining the gun and the limber would take place. The gun and limber would have been run up their ramps until well clear of the trolley at this stage and scotches applied to maintain this position. The trolley would then have been run away in a rearward direction. Finally, the gun and limber would have been raised a little further by means of the drag rope, so as to enable the scotches to be knocked away, and then both would have been lowered gradually to the ground.

The use of locomotives was not contemplated in the

A siege gun trolley of a design undergoing trials at the School of Military Engineering in 1877. This trolley, which was designed by the Secretary of the RE Committee, was of timber construction with cast-iron bogie frames and weighed approximately 1¼ tons. Although these trolleys were unsprung, the general design of the bogies was similar to those used at Woolwich Arsenal and it is almost certain that these vehicles were constructed in the Royal Carriage Department there.

(RE Library, Chatham)

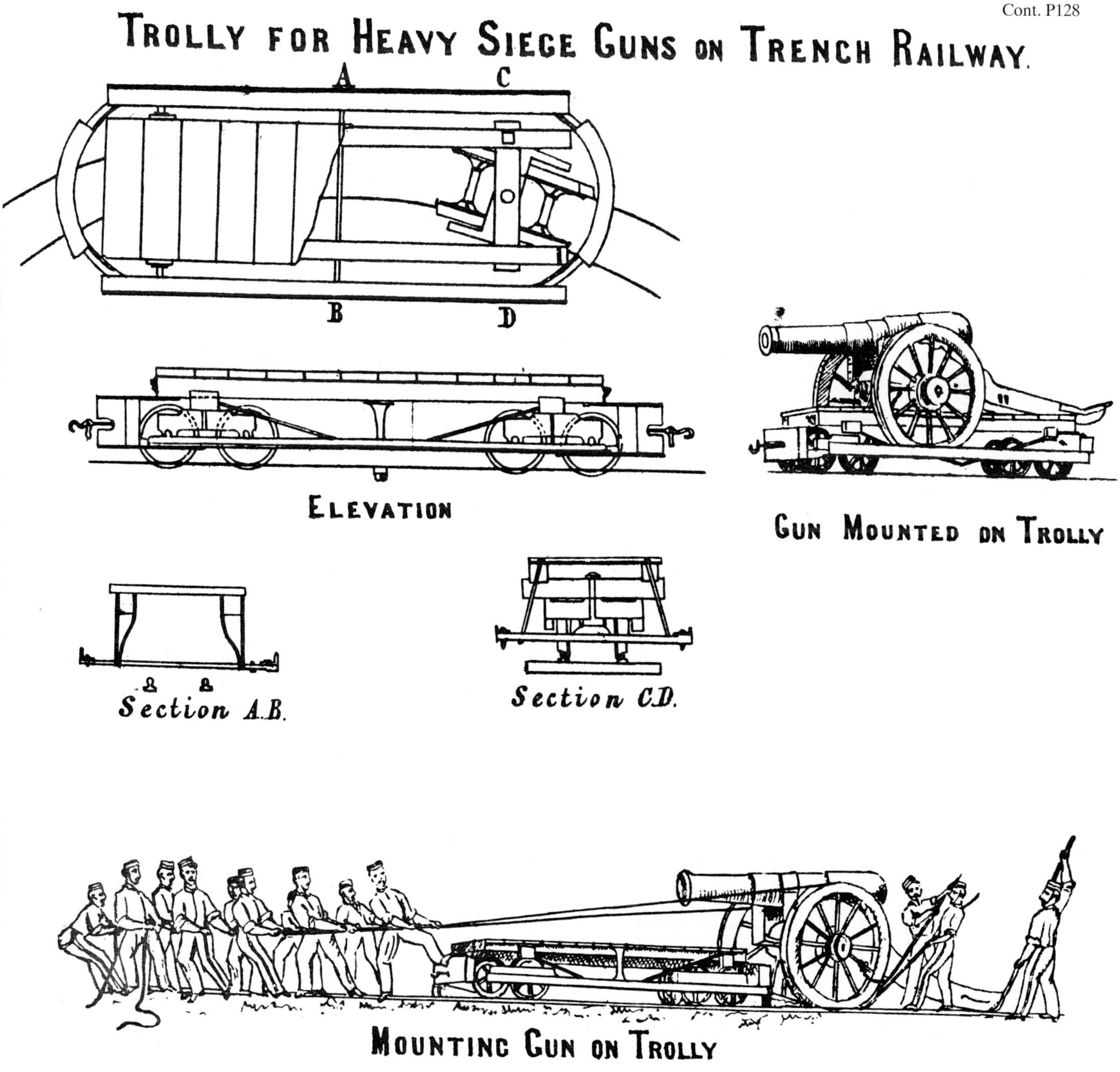

approaches and parallels (the drill described above specified manual rope haulage for the gun trolleys), but locomotives were envisaged for working the lines from the engineer parks up to a fortress within the zone of fire, from which wagons could be moved by means of manual effort into the parallels.

Some details were also given in the 1889 Manual regarding the permanent way to be used by 18 inch gauge military railways. A convenient rail size was, it was claimed, 24 lb/yd with rails being supplied in 18ft lengths. Steel sleepers were to be preferred, but if these were not available, then suitable sleepers could be cut to a length of 3ft 6in out of 7in by 3in deal battens. A sleeper spacing from centre to centre of 2ft was recommended for average soil, with closer spacing or longitudinal sleepering being the preferred course of action where the ground was swampy. Points and switches for such railways were kept in the siege equipment store. In some military situations there could have been a need to avoid noise and this was made possible by means of provision for the use of T-headed screws to secure the rails to wooden sleepers. The screws could be fixed to the sleepers (to the correct

Cont. P128

TROLLY FOR HEAVY SIEGE GUNS ON TRENCH RAILWAY.

ELEVATION

GUN MOUNTED ON TROLLY

Section A.B.

Section C.D.

MOUNTING GUN ON TROLLY

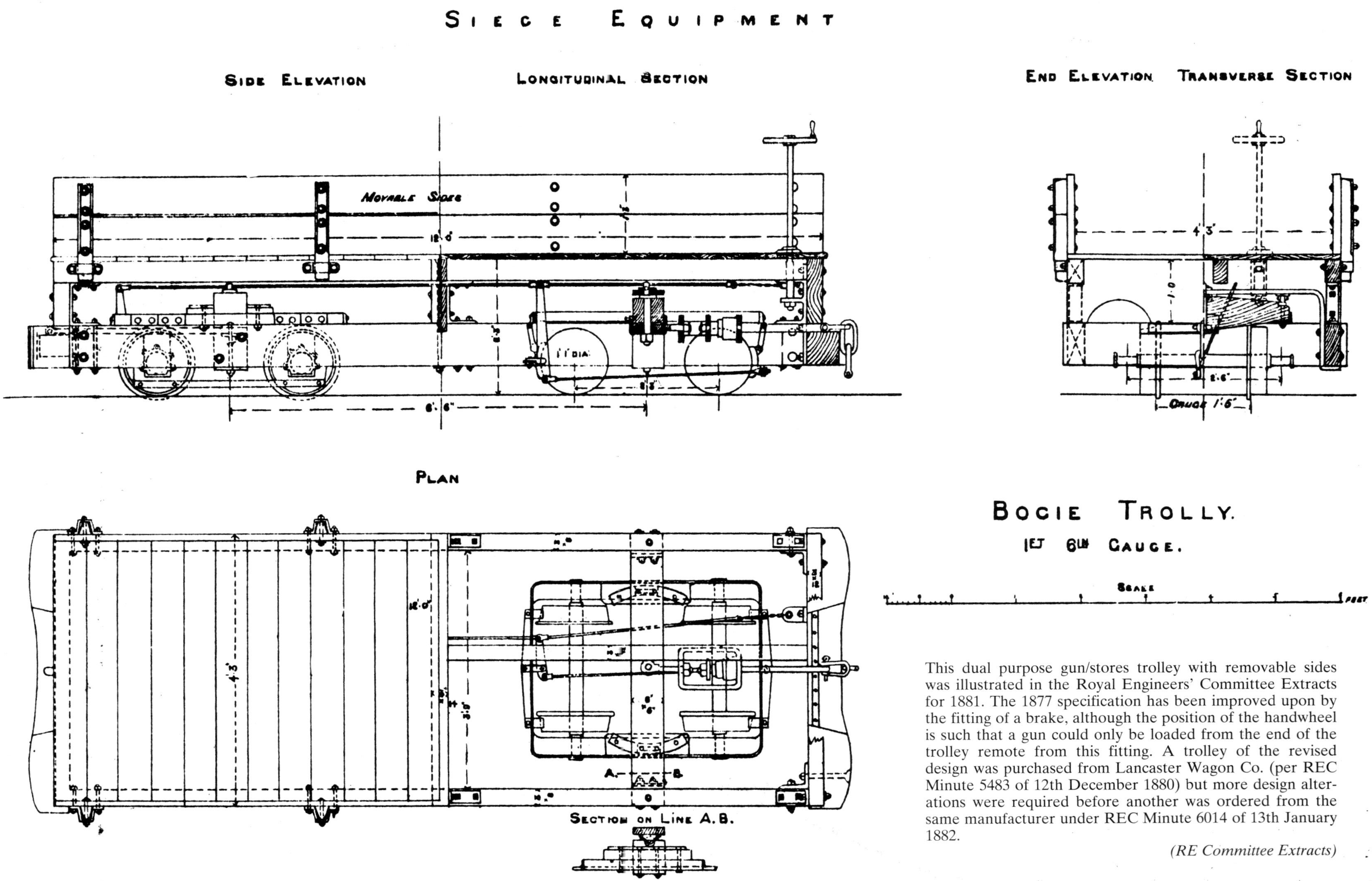

SIEGE EQUIPMENT
SIDE ELEVATION
LONGITUDINAL SECTION
END ELEVATION
TRANSVERSE SECTION
MOVABLE SIDES
12'0"
6'6"
1'1" DIA
4'3"
GAUGE 1'6"
PLAN
SECTION ON LINE A.B.
BOGIE TROLLY.
1FT 6IN GAUGE.
SCALE
FEET

This dual purpose gun/stores trolley with removable sides was illustrated in the Royal Engineers' Committee Extracts for 1881. The 1877 specification has been improved upon by the fitting of a brake, although the position of the handwheel is such that a gun could only be loaded from the end of the trolley remote from this fitting. A trolley of the revised design was purchased from Lancaster Wagon Co. (per REC Minute 5483 of 12th December 1880) but more design alterations were required before another was ordered from the same manufacturer under REC Minute 6014 of 13th January 1882.

(RE Committee Extracts)

CHATHAM DEFENCE WORKS TRUCK
TIPPING ON EITHER SIDE
CAPACITY 20 CU:FT: WEIGHT 9 CWT.

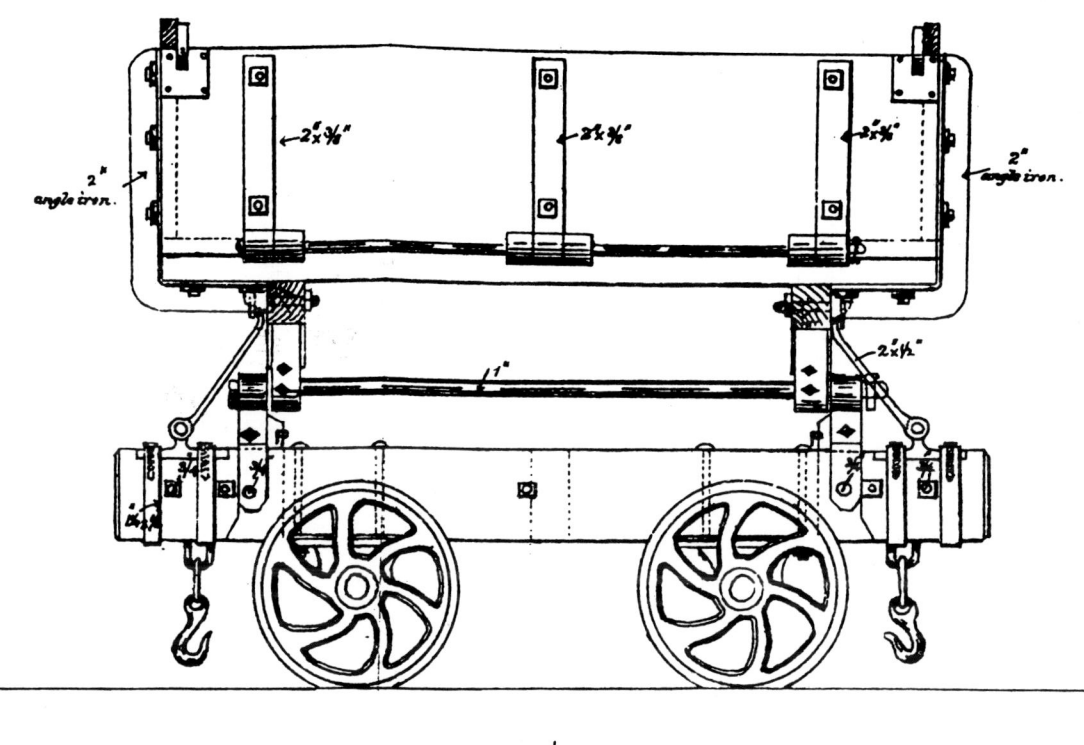

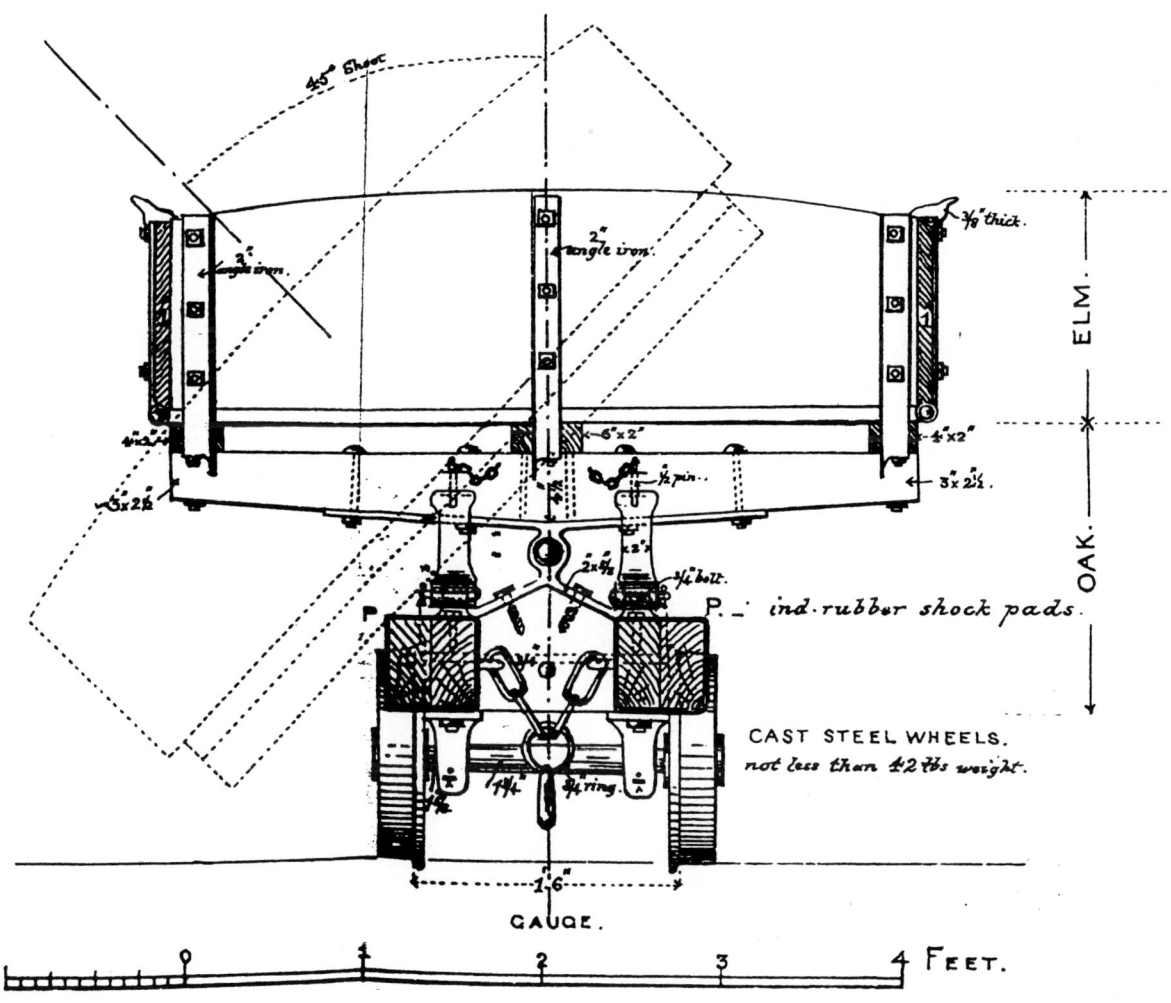

A four-wheeled tipping wagon used on the Chatham Fortifications works during the 1880s. No maker is named on the drawings and it may be that these wagons were built locally.

(RE Professional Papers, 1883)

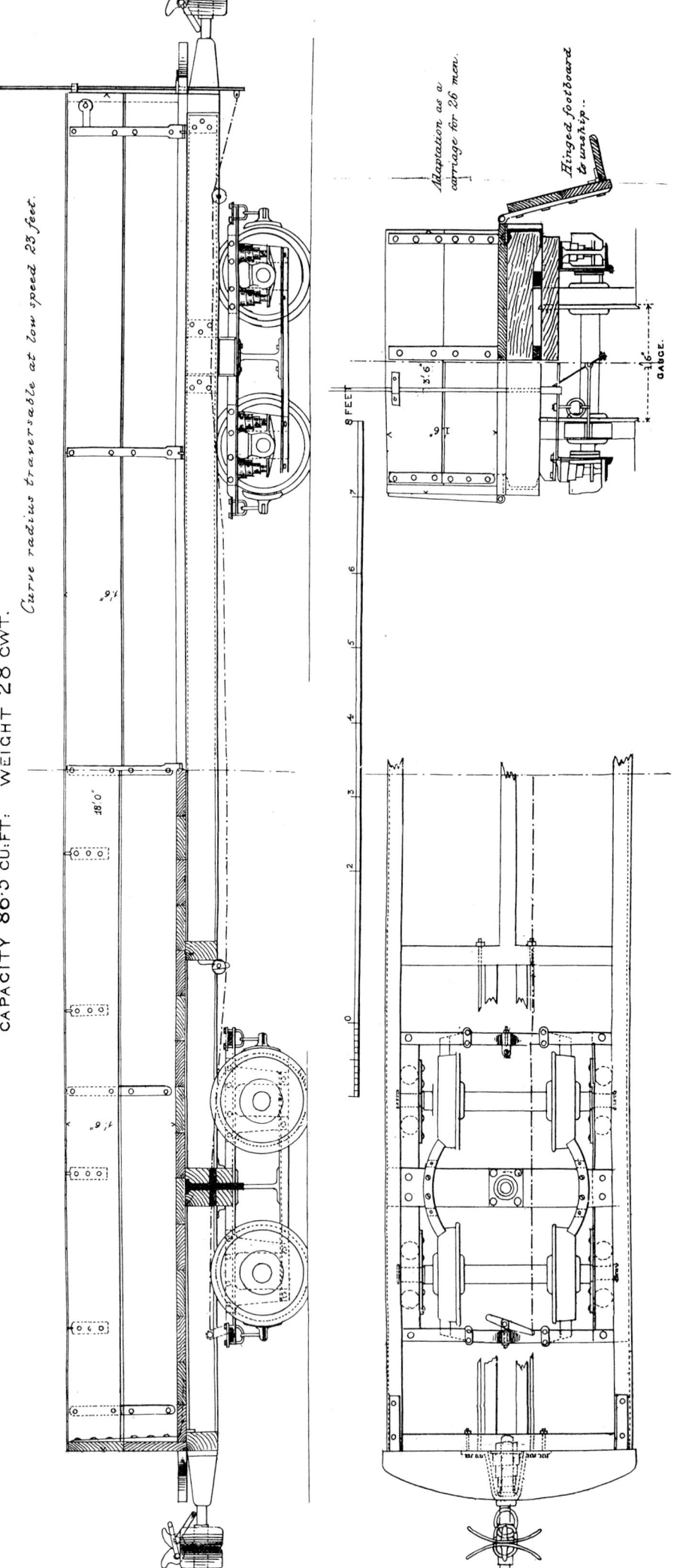

18-INCH GAUGE **BOGIE WAGON** FOR GENERAL USE.

Designed and constructed by the Lancaster Wagon Company.

CAPACITY 86·5 CU:FT: WEIGHT **28** CWT.

Curve radius traversable at low speed 23 feet.

Adaptation as a carriage for 26 men.

Hinged footboard to unship.

GAUGE.

This general purpose bogie wagon design for use on the Chatham Fortifications works was constructed by Lancaster Wagon Co. circa 1882. As can be seen on the drawings, these wagons could also be used for the carriage of workmen by lowering the dropsides.

(*RE Professional Papers*)

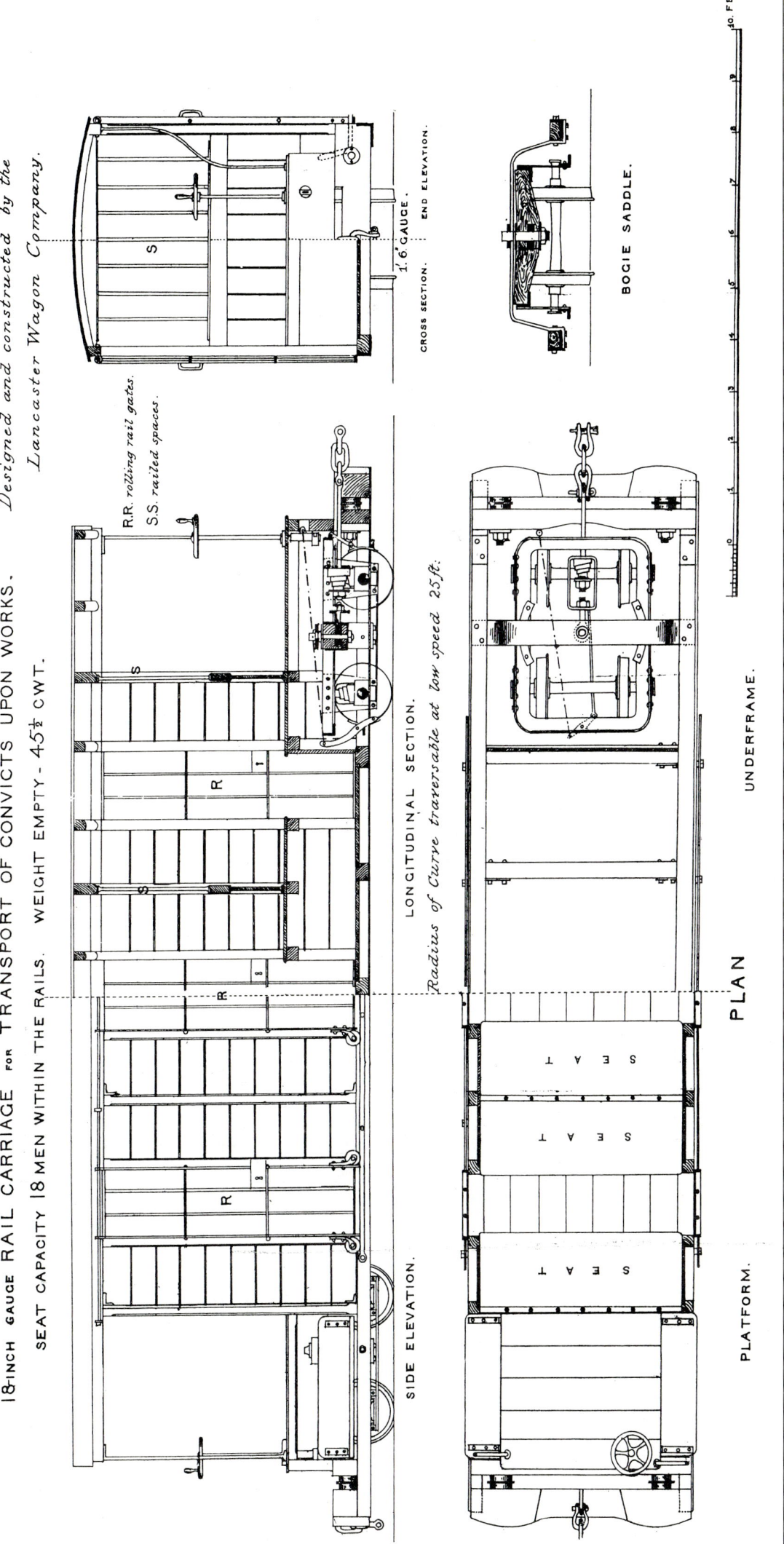

NARROW GAUGE ROLLING STOCK.

Plate V.

18-INCH GAUGE RAIL CARRIAGE FOR TRANSPORT OF CONVICTS UPON WORKS.
SEAT CAPACITY 18 MEN WITHIN THE RAILS.   WEIGHT EMPTY - 45½ CWT.

Designed and constructed by the
Lancaster Wagon Company.

R.R. rolling rail gates.
S.S. railed spaces.

SIDE ELEVATION.

LONGITUDINAL SECTION.

Radius of Curve traversable at low speed 25 ft.

CROSS SECTION.   END ELEVATION.

1' 6" GAUGE.

BOGIE SADDLE.

SEAT   SEAT   SEAT

PLAN

PLATFORM.   UNDERFRAME.

40. FEET

These bogie convict carriages were used on the Chatham Fortifications line and were constructed by Lancaster Wagon Co. circa 1883. The basic design owes much to the influence of Charles Easton Spooner, a fact emphasised by the 'well' configuration of the chassis.

(RE Professional Papers)

125

gauge) in the engineer park and screwed down by means of a key to take hold of the bottom of the rail section when the rails reached the trenches. By this means hammering could be dispensed with. Where average soil was present it would not have been necessary to ballast railways of this type, although it would have been necessary to cut a drainage trench along the reverse side of the parallel where the track ran.

As a result of previous awareness (per REC Minute 4403 and subsequent programme of trench railway experiments of April 1879), and of demonstrations carried out at the Duke of Sutherland's residence in July 1879 with some 500 mm gauge equipment previously used at the RASE Kilburn show, the Royal Engineers were impressed by the Decauville-inspired portable tramway system produced by John Fowler & Co. under Alfred Greig's patent No. 1189 of 1879. This consisted of steel rails, weighing 15 to 22 lb/yd held together by corrugated steel sleepers. The chairs holding the outside flanges of the rail were riveted to the corrugated sleeper, whilst those holding the inside flange of the rail were formed by means of a hooked bolt which passed through the corrugation in the sleeper and under the rails to be secured by a nut screwed from the extreme outside edges of the sleeper. At one end of each length of track was a double sleeper, upon which the ends of the rails of the neighbouring length of track would rest. Curves, siding pieces, portable turntables and level crossings could all be supplied ready for use, as could ramp transfer sidings. The first 18 inch gauge track of this type was acquired on approval by the RE Committee in 1879, with purchase being finally authorised in 1881 (ref. REC Minutes 5758 and 5799).

Paragraph 44 of the 1889 Manual considered the personnel and materials necessary for laying 18 inch gauge military tramways. For a unit of siege train (30 guns) and 5½ miles of single track, the following plant would have been required (with the tare weights in brackets): three locomotives (24 tons); 25 bogie gun trolleys (54.35 tons); 20,333 rails 18ft long and 24 lb/yd (200 tons); 30 switches and 15 crossings (1.63 tons); 11,000 deal sleepers 3ft 6in x 7in x 3in (95¼ tons); 100,000 T-headed coach-screws (16.18 tons) and 3,500 pairs of fish-plates each with four bolts (6.11 tons). In addition, the platelayers' tools would need to be drawn from the siege-trains' stores. From the point of view of personnel required for laying an 18 inch gauge military tramway, it was expected that the Royal Engineers would need to supply one NCO and two sappers, whilst the Infantry would be required to provide one NCO and twelve men. This compliment of personnel, it was argued, could lay between 100 and 150 yards of track per hour, provided that the track was in a parallel or in open country where a formation had been made.

The 1889 Manual provides an interesting insight into the configuration that British trench railways would have adopted had Britain been involved in a major European conflict at this time. From the railway historian's point of view, however, these railways were destined to become for the most part just another 'might-have-been' as the general lack of adoption of the 18 inch track gauge eventually sealed their fate. There was to be one last overseas example of the British 18 inch gauge military railway and this was, as with the Suakin line, in the Sudan. Some of the 18 inch gauge equipment from the Suakin line was apparently moved along the coast to the small port of Trinkitat, where it was used in the construction of a line to reach some water wells at El Teb. As has already been mentioned, the one steam locomotive definitely known to have worked on this line was *Rameses* (Bagnall No. 1452 of 1896), which was photographed circa 1921, having probably been out of use after about 1904.

During the early 1890s, official support for the employment of 18 inch gauge lines for siege purposes waned considerably. This process culminated in a letter (ref. 57/General No. 6434) of 31st January 1896 from the Deputy Inspector of Fortifications, H.F. Turner, to the President of the Royal Engineers Committee. In this letter, it was outlined that the break of track gauge on a siege railway between the local standard and the 18 inch gauge should normally take place at the artillery depot or field arsenal. Forward of this, 18 inch gauge track of a portable nature (ie Greig's patent) for manual or horse propulsion would be used. Thoughts of using 18 inch gauge locomotives on siege operations were therefore finally discontinued at this stage. On 2nd February 1900, the RE Committee sent a memo to the IGF pointing out that the latest heavy howitzers had proved too large for 18 inch gauge gun trolleys and that in future 2ft 6in lines, suitable for horse or locomotive haulage, should be used for expeditionary and front line siege transportation purposes.

The views of Major Hogg and his supporters had prevailed and during the early Edwardian period 2ft 6in gauge, as exemplified by the Chattenden & Upnor Railway, was the preferred siege standard. By the time of the 1914-18 War, however, the flexibility and popularity of the nominal 2ft gauge line had ensured that the WDLR's of the Western Front, as their German counterparts, were constructed mainly to this gauge.

In the domestic military context, the 18 inch gauge steam operated railway still had a few tasks to perform. The period shortly after the turn of the century saw the establishment of a standard gauge military railway at Longmoor Camp, near Bordon in Hampshire and the task of moving barrack huts from Longmoor to Bordon has been mentioned. The following year, 1905 it was decided to upgrade the 18 inch gauge line for use in the construction of the standard gauge system and three steam locomotives were requisitioned. These were the former Chatham Fortifications engines, *Mars* and *Venus* and the RAR Fowler engine, *Flamingo*. After the completion of the task of construction, the narrow gauge railway was re-routed and a 1910 Ordnance Survey map shows that it had been re-laid within the Camp. The 18 inch gauge track remained on this site until about 1919 and much use was made of it for training purposes during World War One.

By 1920, *Venus* and *Flamingo* had both been cut up for scrap although, as previously mentioned, *Mars* was retained to supply hot water to a camp bath house, being retired from this activity in 1924. After a period in the 1920s when thought was apparently given to the idea of preserving the locomotive intact, the chassis was scrapped but the boiler was retained as an instructional exhibit, primarily to demonstrate the constructional configuration of the Belpaire firebox. Today, this boiler survives in the Museum of Army Transport at Beverley as a lasting reminder of the type of locomotive which would have seen use on 18 inch gauge field railways in the event of Britain's involvement in a major European conflict in the 1880s. If it is assumed that the boiler barrel of *Mars* was not replaced during the engine's working career, then it follows that this is the earliest specimen of the Belpaire design now extant in the United Kingdom.

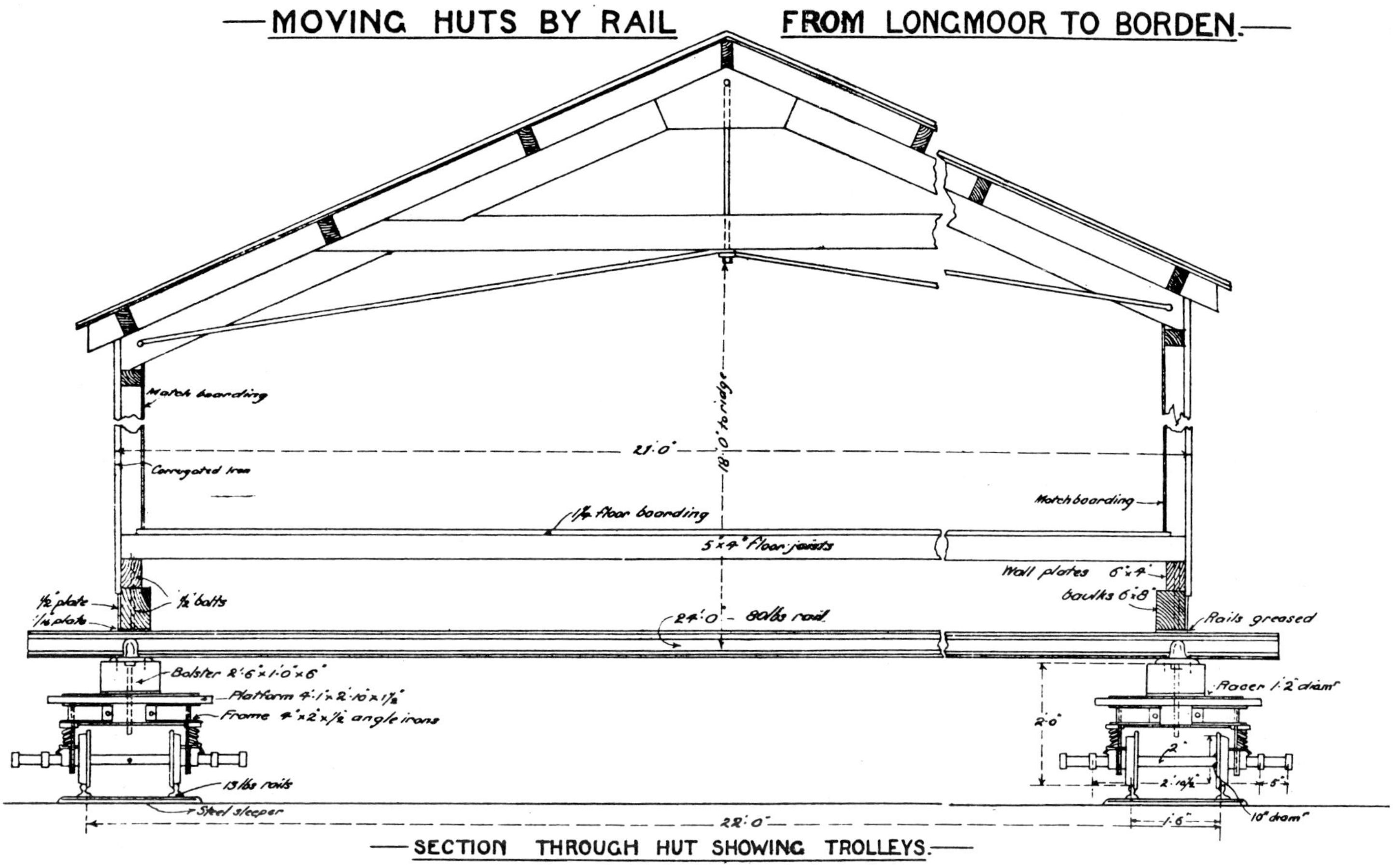

Match boarding

21'·0"

Corrugated iron

18'·0" to ridge

1¼ floor boarding

Match boarding

5"×4" floor joists

½ plate
¼ plate
½ bolts

Wall plates 6"×4"
baulks 6"×8"
Rails greased

24'·0" — 80lbs rail

Bolster 2'·6"×1'·0"×6"
Platform 4'·1"×2'·10"×1¾"
Frame 4"×2"×½ angle irons

Racer 1'·2" diam"

2'·0"

13lbs rails
Steel sleeper

2'·10½"
1'·6"
10" diam"

22'·0"

— SECTION THROUGH HUT SHOWING TROLLEYS.—

This cross-sectional diagram of the method of moving 68 barrack huts from Longmoor to Bordon appeared in *The Royal Engineers Journal* in 1904. Each hut, of over 30 tons in weight, was mounted on seven cross beams which were each supported by two bogies. It was found to be possible to move four huts in a day using a donkey engine pulling on anchor points 400 yds apart for most of the distance, and with additional help from a Fowler ploughing engine where necessary. One hut, which became dislodged during the operation, was utilised as a Police Station at Whitehill. After completion of the hut moving operation in 1905, one of the parallel 18 inch gauge lines was lifted, whilst the other was relaid to become a locomotive-worked construction line.

(RE Library, Chatham)

These two views, although of indifferent quality, are of such a historic value as to justify inclusion in this Volume. They show *Mars* (Vulcan Foundry No. 1160 of 1885) on arrival from the Royal Arsenal to commence work on the upgraded Bordon–Longmoor 18 inch gauge line used in the construction of the standard gauge Longmoor Military Railway. The virtually unaltered condition of the engine from its original state suggests that it may have done comparatively little work on the RAR.

(Courtesy R. Redman)

The Deptford System

The last of the 18 inch gauge steam-operated military service lines to be opened in the United Kingdom was the system which served the Royal Army Service Corps Depot at Deptford. This site had formerly been the City of London Corporation's Foreign Cattle Market and from 1900 it had been connected to the LBSCR's Deptford Wharf branch by means of a standard gauge tramway passing through Grove Street. Shortly after the outbreak of World War One the site was requisitioned for use as a ration depot.

Some accounts suggest that narrow gauge trackwork existed at the site as early as this time, but the first steam locomotives were only ordered in 1915. As some measure of compensation for their being passed over as a choice of supplier for steam locomotives for the Royal Arsenal Railways, the contract to supply motive power for the Deptford system was awarded to the Leeds concern, Hunslet Engine Co. Ltd. In all, a dozen locomotives were delivered in three batches over a two-year period. They bore running numbers from 1 to 12 on cabside plates and their identities were: Nos 1 to 3 - Hunslet Nos 1196 to 1198 of 1915; Nos 4 to 8 - Hunslet Nos 1207 to 1211 of 1916, and Nos 9 to 12 - Hunslet Nos 1288 to 1291 of 1917, all respectively.

The design of these locomotives was basically an enlargement of a much earlier Hunslet engine; *Jack* (No. 684 of 1898). In coming up with their basic specification for an 18 inch gauge steam locomotive, Hunslet declined to follow the precedent set by their Leeds neighbours, Manning, Wardle and adopted the forward-hung well tank configuration, in conjunction with outside Walschaerts valve gear. This was in preference to a saddle tank and inside Stephenson/Howe link motion. The general design was an attractive one which has proved popular over the years with narrow gauge enthusiasts and modellers alike.

The engines were constructed, as would have been

expected, to the 0-4-0 wheel arrangement with a wheelbase of 3ft 6in. The flycranks were counterbalanced, very much in the fashion of those on the Darjeeling–Himalaya Railway B class locomotives and the wheels were 1ft 6½in diameter. The capacity of the well tank was rather low, at 58 gallons. The boiler pitch was relatively high at 3ft 5¼in when compared with the Manning, Wardle engines at Woolwich Arsenal. The boiler was of the domed variety and two boiler-mounted sandboxes were fitted. On the Maker's photograph of No. 1198, the dome was shown as polished brass, whilst the livery of the locomotives as built was recorded as khaki. The locomotives were oil-fired, with a capacity for 25 gallons of oil and the maker's characteristic pattern of cab was fitted, this having a similar cutout profile to the ones fitted to such familiar Hunslet products as *Britomart* and *General Machado*.

As used in the early days of steam operation at Deptford, the locomotives carried wire spark arresters which could be seen above the top of the chimney, but these ultimately gave way to Austrian style spark arresters shown in an accompanying illustration.

The rolling stock at Deptford consisted of over 500 four-wheeled wagons apparently supplied by two companies, P.W. Maclellan Ltd of Glasgow and the Bristol Carriage & Wagon Company. These timber-framed vehicles had frames 3½in wide and 4½in deep extending to a length of 7ft over the dumb buffers. There were three cross-members, two of which took the drawhooks and were of 8¾in by 4½in section, and the third of which was the middle member of 3in by 3½in cross section. In order to provide additional strengthening, 0.375in thick mild steel plates 6ft in length were bolted to the outsides of the solebars, extending over their full depth. The outer faces of the beams carrying the drawhooks were similarly strengthened, but this time the depth of the plate was only 4in and its width was 1ft 2½in. Three link couplings were fitted and the drawhooks were sprung with the conventional design of coil springing used for this purpose. The main frame assembly was stayed by means of two longitudinal ³⁄₄in diameter bolts passing through the bufferbeam

An illustration from a Hunslet catalogue showing Deptford Special Reserve Depot 0-4-0WT No.3 (builders' No. 1198 of 1915) as built.

(Author's Collection)

members and a single lateral 0.625in bolt slightly displaced from the vehicle's mid-point. Tenons and fang bolts (0.625in diameter) secured the bufferbeams to the main frames and the dumb buffers were enlarged to a width of 9¾in inclusive of the sheet steel cladding which was ½in thick. The disc wheels were 1ft 6in in diameter and ran in plain bearings of a rather peculiar pattern. They were cast in pairs as a single unit and secured to the solebars by means of two pairs of two bolts arranged so as to flank each axlebox. The wheelbase of each wagon was 2ft.

In order to assist in the trans-shipment of goods from the Depot into steamers on the River Thames the Deptford wagons were designed so that their bodies could be removed by a dockside crane and loaded on board the delivery vessel. In order to achieve this, the body of the wagon rested on two cross-members mounted on the upper portion of the main frame. These were 4ft 2in wide and 4½in deep and their surfaces facing either end of the wagon were tapered so that the length of each of the cross-members was 4½in at the bottom and only 3½in at the top. The detachable body was of the three-plank variety, each of the constituent planks being 10in deep and 2in thick. The sides of the body could hinge about their lowermost edges and were secured in the vertical position by catches and when lowered, by chains. The body could be lifted by means of the insertion of chain hooks into eyes at the ends of two 4in wide bars of ¼in thick steel which passed underneath the floor and up at either end, some 2ft 6in apart from one another. The tare weight of a Deptford wagon was approximately 1 ton 4 cwt and it was reckoned that each could hold a load of 2½ tons. An interesting feature of the wagons' construction was that they were not fitted with brakes in spite of the fact that no brake vans appear to have been used on the 18 inch gauge internal system at Deptford.

There appears to have been no semaphore signalling on the narrow gauge line at Deptford and train routes (presumably destinations) were indicated by boards mounted on the locomotive in front of the chimney. These appear to have corresponded to the letters allocated to particular storage areas in the Deptford complex. Unlike the RAR system, however, there does not appear to have been any mixed gauge track and this would certainly have been an advantage from the point of view of operational simplicity. The basic principle advocated in *Narrow Gauge Railways Two Feet and Under* in relation to the ideal track layout for a military service system of this type was taken to its logical conclusion at Deptford where the track was arranged so that circular patterns of operation prevailed and train reversals were kept to a minimum.

As with the RAR, the cessation of hostilities in November 1918 resulted in a scaling down of operations, although the immediate effect with regard to the narrow gauge locomotives and rolling stock was rather less drastic than had been the case at Woolwich. By 1921, three of the locomotives, Nos 10-12, and 75 wagons, all apparently of P.W. Maclellan parentage, had been sold to the Sand Hutton Light Railway in Yorkshire, where they were joined in 1927 by another of the Deptford locomotives, No.4. The further history of these items will be considered in Chapter 3. The use of the Depot, meanwhile, had changed from the storage and distribution of rations to that of paper for newsprint. Control of most of the site passed, initially on a leasehold basis in 1926, to Convoys Ltd and this company continued for some years after this date to employ the remaining narrow gauge equipment for paper handling purposes. Eventually, however, the development of suitable road based handling equipment rendered the little railway obsolete and a visit to the site by the late Mr B. Derek Stoyel on 22nd January 1938 found locomotive Nos 1, 3, 5, 6, 7, 8 and 9 still extant in good external condition but out of use. The ultimate date of disposal of these locomotives is apparently unknown, but it is unlikely that they survived for much longer, as they would have presented a comparatively easy target for one of the drives for scrap metal during World War Two. The wagons likewise passed into history, but the system itself has taken rather longer to completely disappear from the landscape and traces remain extant at the time of writing.

The accompanying photographs were taken by kind permission of Convoys Ltd who now own the site and they show the extent of the surviving remains of the Deptford Special Reserve Depot system. For the most part these remains are concentrated on the jetties and, apart from the removal of the point levers and an accumulation of surface rust, the track in this area is largely in the same condition as when the last steam locomotives would have run over it during the 1930s.

With the completion of the discussion of the Deptford system ends the consideration in this Volume of military and military service lines. In final conclusion it can be said that the railways in this Chapter made an important contribution to British military and naval history, but they failed to establish the 18 inch track gauge as a universal standard. In the end, the passing of these lines was a product of several factors,

Two Hunslet 0-4-0 well tank locomotives shown on the Deptford system during World War One. The destination of a train was indicated by the target attached to the chimney (in a manner akin to the RAR duty boards). The wire mesh spark arrester used initially at Deptford can be seen.
(Imperial War Museum)

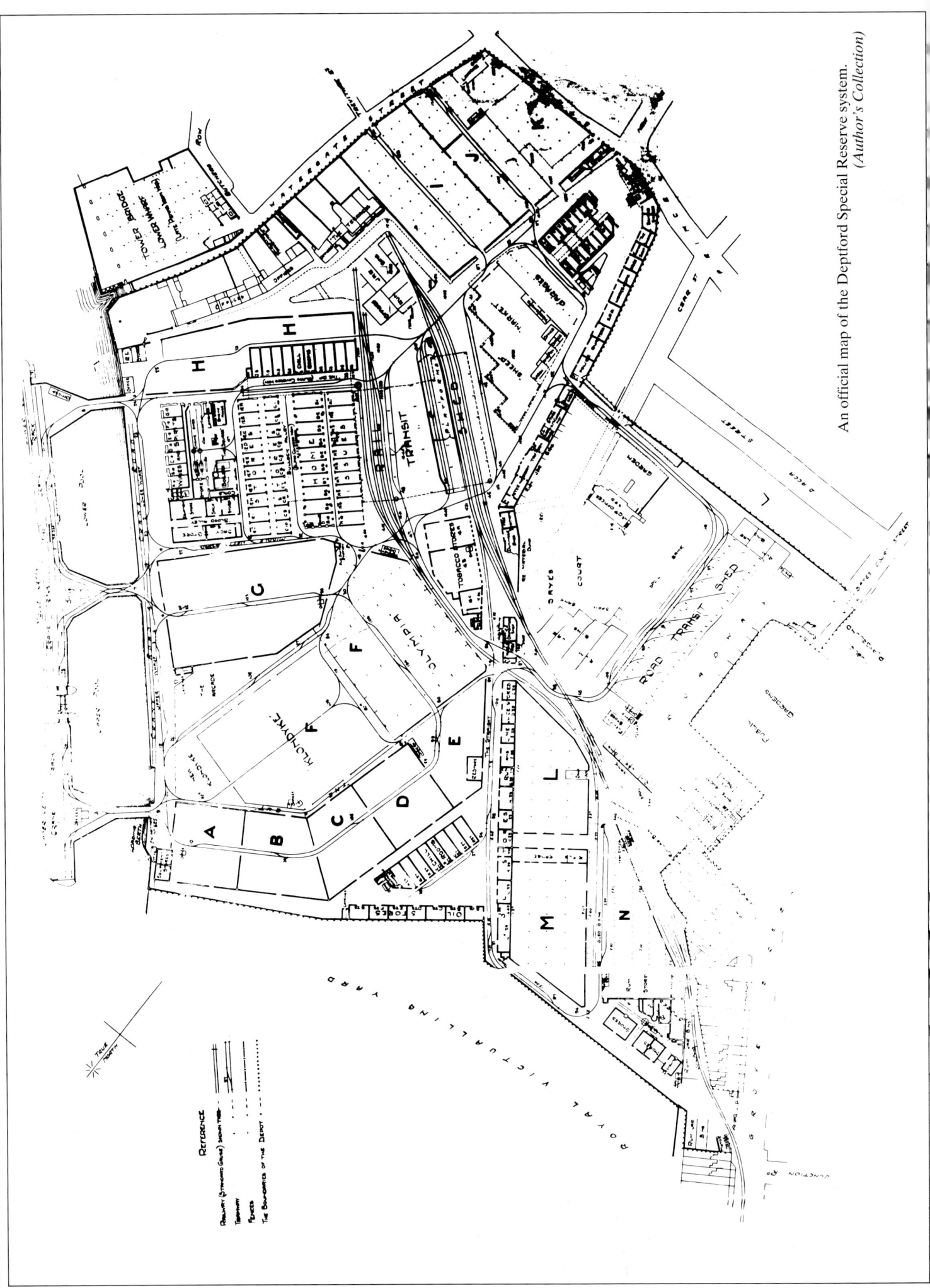

An official map of the Deptford Special Reserve system.
(Author's Collection)

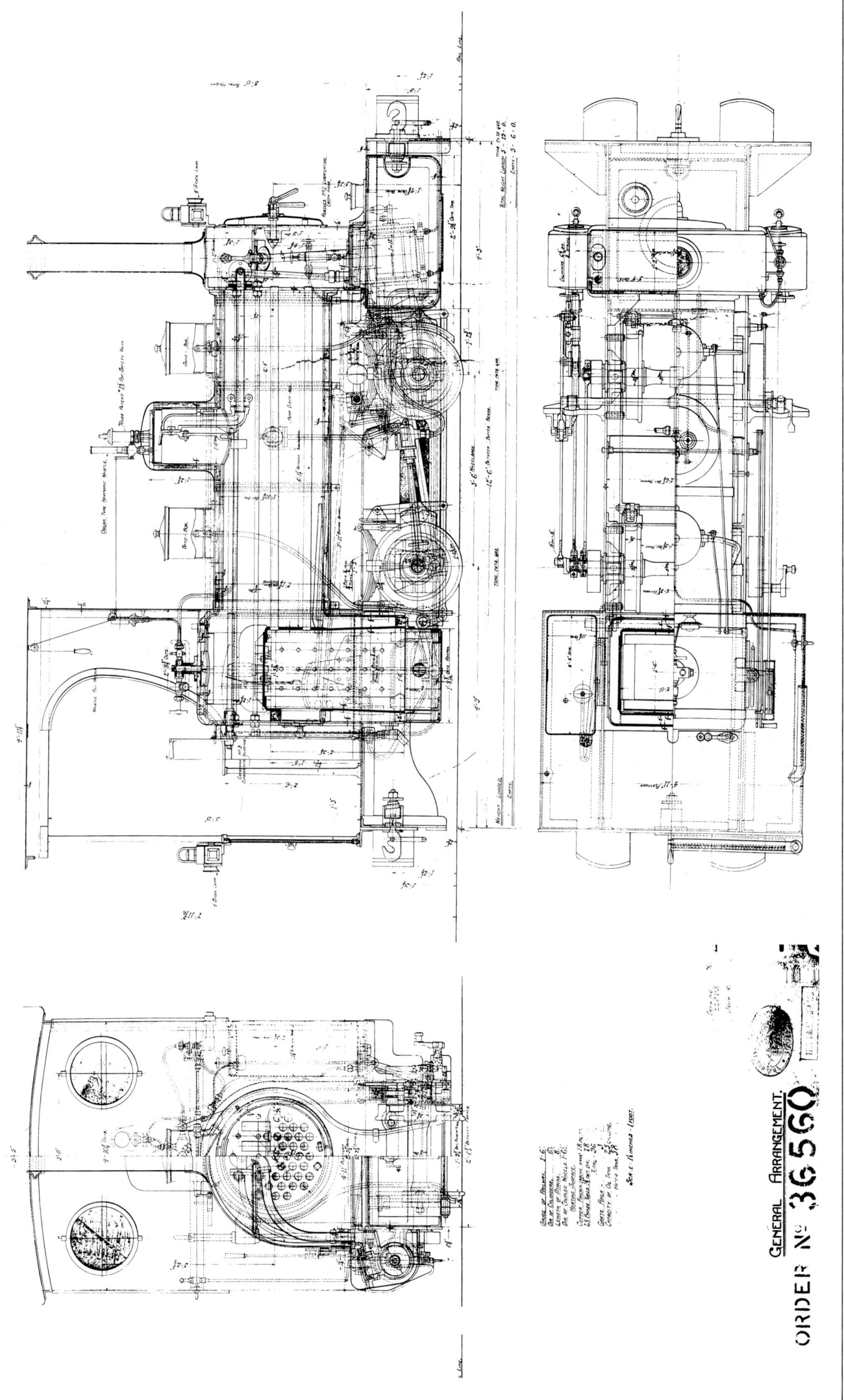

GENERAL ARRANGEMENT.

ORDER No 36560

The Makers' general arrangement drawing of the Hunslet 'Waril' class 0-4-0WT design supplied for use at Deptford Special Reserve Depot.
(Leeds Industrial Museum via G. Horsman)

A view showing part of the narrow gauge Deptford system in the vicinity of the Road Transit Shed.

(Imperial War Museum)

amongst these being their non-standard nature; the decision of the Inspector General of Fortifications in 1896; improvements in the application of internal combustion power to both road and rail; the 1918 Armistice, and the economic climate prevalent during the 1919-1939 period.

The remains of one of the crossings of narrow and standard gauge tracks at Deptford, seen in March 1990.

(Author)

Above: One of the Deptford Hunslets seen during the 1920s after Convoys Ltd had leased the site for paper storage. The Austrian style spark arrester can be seen in this view. Seven of the Hunslets were recorded as still extant in January 1938, although it is believed that they were scrapped shortly afterwards.

(Courtesy W.J. Potter)

A portion of the 18 inch gauge track on the Lower Jetty at Deptford, March 1990. The connections in the background to the two main Jetty running lines do not appear in the Official Plans and are probably later additions.

(Author)

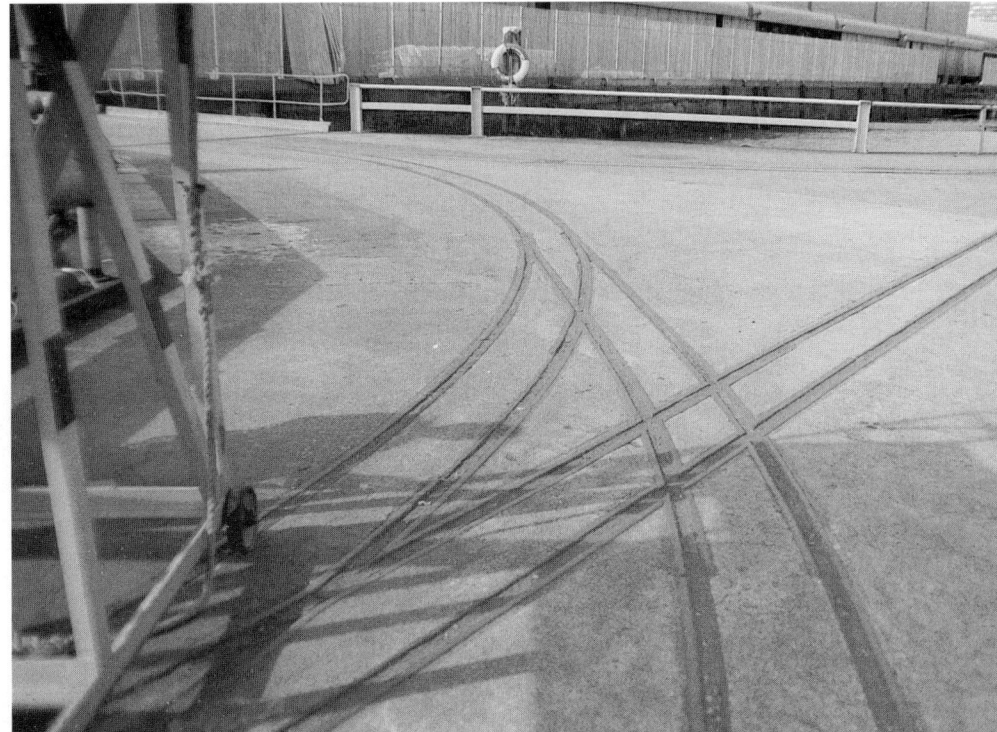

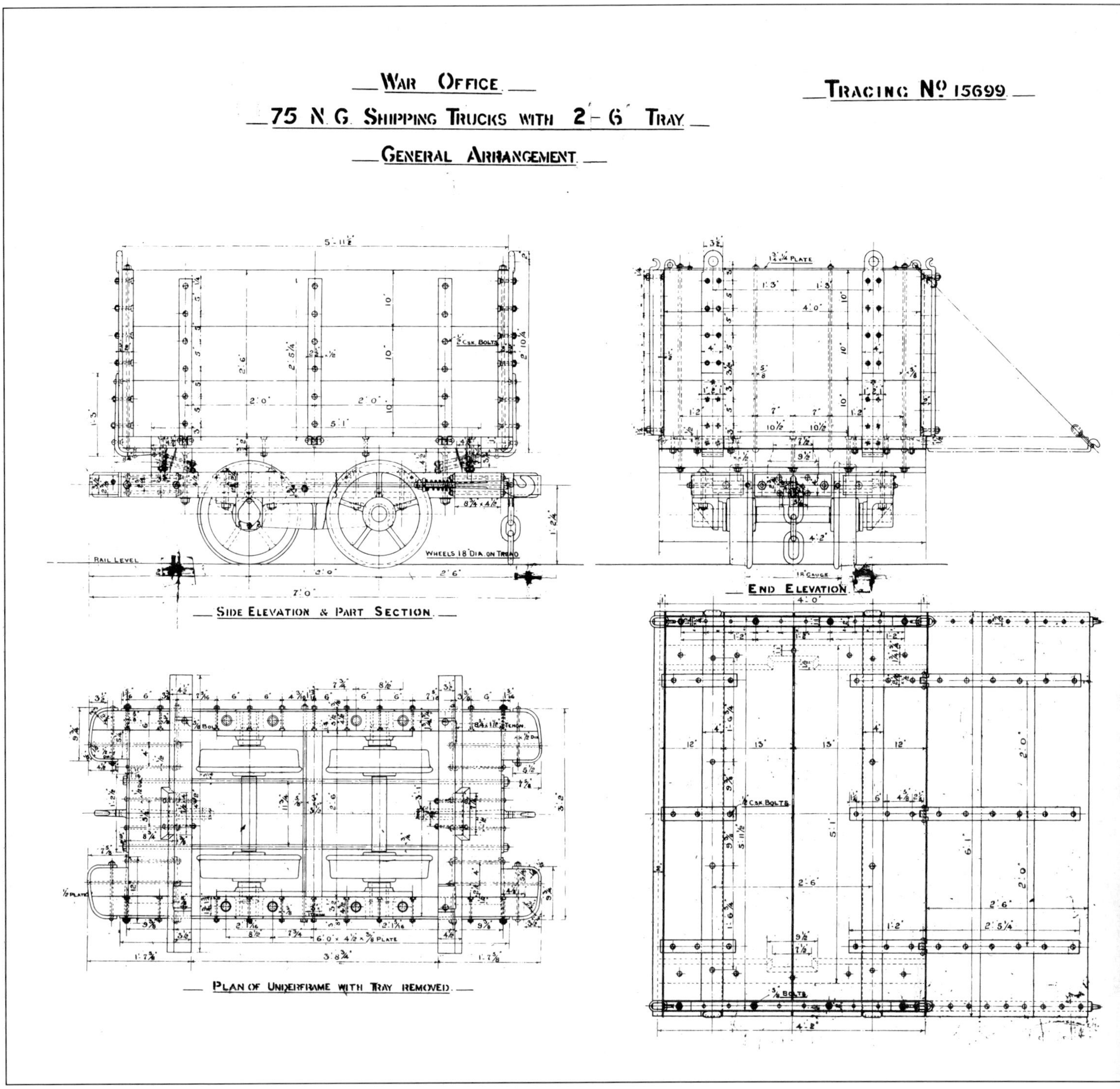
WAR OFFICE
TRACING No 15699
75 N.G. SHIPPING TRUCKS WITH 2'-6" TRAY
GENERAL ARRANGEMENT
SIDE ELEVATION & PART SECTION
END ELEVATION
PLAN OF UNDERFRAME WITH TRAY REMOVED
RAIL LEVEL
WHEELS 18" DIA. ON TREAD

A Maker s general arrangement drawing of the wagons supplied by P. & W. Maclellan Ltd in 1915 for use at Deptford.
(NGRS Library)

A diamond crossing on one of the Jetty portions of the Deptford system, March 1990.
(Author)

The Y-point on the approach to the Upper Jetty at Deptford in March 1990. The site of the lever can be seen to the left of the turnout.

(Author)

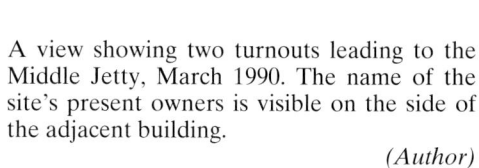

A close-up photograph of one of the turnouts on the Deptford system. The point lever has been removed but its position can still be seen where the road surface has been filled in.

(Author)

A view showing two turnouts leading to the Middle Jetty, March 1990. The name of the site's present owners is visible on the side of the adjacent building.

(Author)

A 'scissors' crossover located between the Lower and Middle Jetties, March 1990. This type of crossover does not appear on this part of the Jetty section of track in the Official Plans and was therefore probably a later addition.

(Author)

3

Estate and Industrial Lines

The Sand Hutton Light Railway

Sir Arthur Heywood's attempts to gain commercial acceptance for 15 inch gauge estate railways were to end in failure, and there was to be one solitary 18 inch gauge steam railway of a purely functional type for estate use, constructed under the auspices of the 1896-1912 Light Railways Acts during the pre-preservation era.

Major Sir Robert J.M. Walker (1890-1930) was the fourth Baronet of Sand Hutton in Yorkshire and he had a virtual lifelong interest in railways. In addition to being a member of the Institute of Transport he laid out a 15 inch gauge line in the grounds of the Sand Hutton Estate in 1912 which was worked by a Bassett-Lowke 4-4-2 locomotive, *Synolda*, an engine which still exists as part of the R&ER museum collection at Ravenglass.

After spending the greater part of World War One in New Zealand undertaking troop instruction, Sir Robert returned home in 1919 and almost immediately resolved to put his 15 inch gauge railway to more serious use. In November 1919 an application was made for a Light Railway Order to authorise a line serving agricultural and commercial interests on the Sand Hutton Estate. The line was to commence at Warthill, a station on the York–Market Weighton portion of the North Eastern Railway, and extend to Scrayingham village approximately 5.3 miles distant in a north-easterly direction. Branches were also to be provided to the goods sidings at Claxton and to Barnby House, the latter being the residence of Mr W. Harrison who was to be one of the railway's directors.

The Light Railway Order was approved by the Light Railway Commissioners, who were the responsible body at the time of the application, in January 1920 and confirmed by the Ministry of Transport with effect from 1st May in the same year. At this stage no thought had been given to alteration of the gauge, despite the fact that Section 12 of the Order effectively authorised the use of any gauge between 15 inches and 2ft

By the end of 1920 progress on the laying of the line, which incorporated some of the metals of the existing pleasure railway, had reached Sand Hutton and the Claxton branch was in place as far as the brickworks. However, at this stage of construction a relatively severe gradient of 1 in 80 was encountered and it was realised that more powerful locomotives than *Synolda*, with its scale model pretensions, would be required. There was at this time a fair amount of 18 inch gauge equipment available from the Ministry of Munitions and it was decided that the Deptford Special Reserve Depot offered the most suitable locomotives and rolling stock for Sand Hutton needs.

The Ministry of Munitions disposal booklet *Surplus* contained an entry in its edition of 15th September 1920 which detailed several 18 inch gauge locomotives for sale. These included four Hunslet 0-4-0 locomotives with 6½in by 8in cylinders at Deptford. A later advertisement of 15th November 1920 identified the locomo-

tives as Hunslet Nos 1207 of 1916 and 1289-1291 of 1917. All four of these locomotives were to end their days at Sand Hutton but they were not all acquired at the same time. It appears from a subsequent *Surplus* insert of 1st March 1921 that Nos 1289 and 1291 (which still carried their Deptford numbers 10 and 12 respectively) had departed from Deptford by this date. No. 1290 (Deptford No. 11) followed shortly afterwards, but No.1207 (Deptford No. 4) did not arrive at Sand Hutton until 1927, having been advertised for sale by R.H. Longbotham & Co. of Northwood in *Contract Journal* during 1924 and 1925. Some 75 of the four-wheeled wagons at Deptford were purchased for use on the SHLR along with the locomotives.

The southern section of the embryonic Sand Hutton Light Railway was relaid with 18 inch gauge permanent way consisting of 20 lb/yd flat-bottomed rail supplied by Robert Hudson Ltd of Leeds. This was secured to wooden sleepers by means of spikes. By April 1922 construction work was complete and the line had been extended to Kissthorns sidings and the Claxton branch finished. The relatively high cost of labour which characterised the years immediately prior to the Depression caused a delay in further construction work and this did not re-commence until May 1923. By December of that year, the line was in operation as far as Bossall and the branch to Barnby House was complete. Cost considerations finally put paid to any prospect of completing the final half mile to Scrayingham as this would have entailed the construction of a bridge over the River Derwent. The northernmost terminus of the Sand Hutton line therefore remained a short projection of track beyond the junction for the Barnby House branch.

At Warthill the SHLR had its exchange sidings with the main NER system and this was achieved by having the standard gauge siding flanked by two of narrow gauge. The most northerly of the two narrow gauge sidings was laid at ground level and this was used for incoming traffic. The other narrow gauge siding was raised on an incline of 1 in 33 so that outgoing loads could be passed downwards manually into standard gauge wagons. By this means the trans-shipment process was made as simple as possible, although it was felt necessary to install a travelling hoist in July 1927. This was supplied by Messrs Herbert Morris Ltd of Loughborough. Despite this latter refinement, no photographs appear to survive to show narrow gauge wagon bodies being lifted by the hoist, a mode of usage for which they had been designed.

From Warthill station the line proceeded eastwards in a direction parallel with the NER route for approximately 650 yards, before crossing a public road on a curve of approximately 45ft radius. It then proceeded in a north-easterly direction and followed a virtually straight course along a public bridle road for about a mile, crossing two 'becks' in the process. At a distance of just under 1.4 miles from the Warthill interchange, White Sike Junction was reached. At this point the

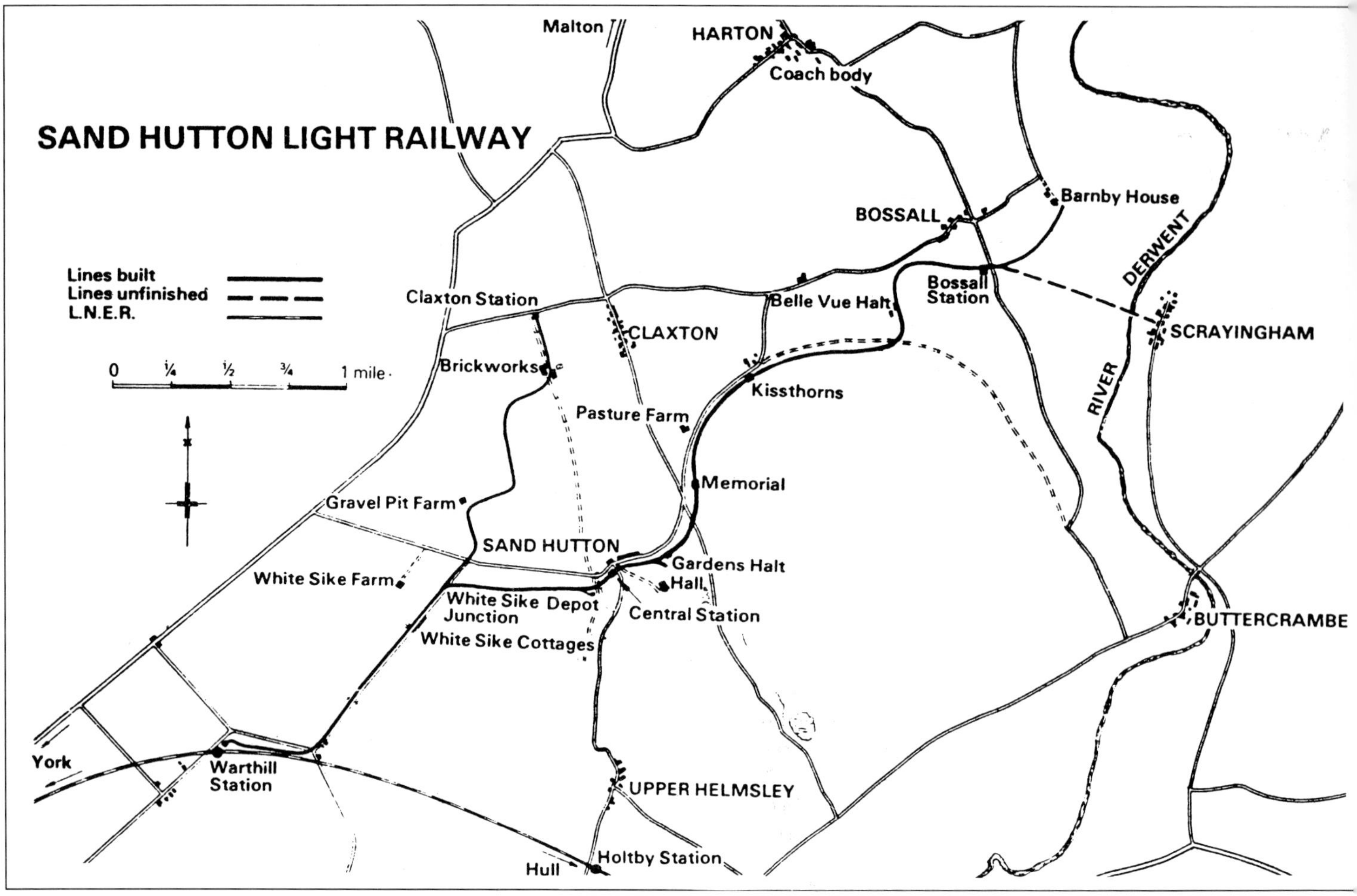

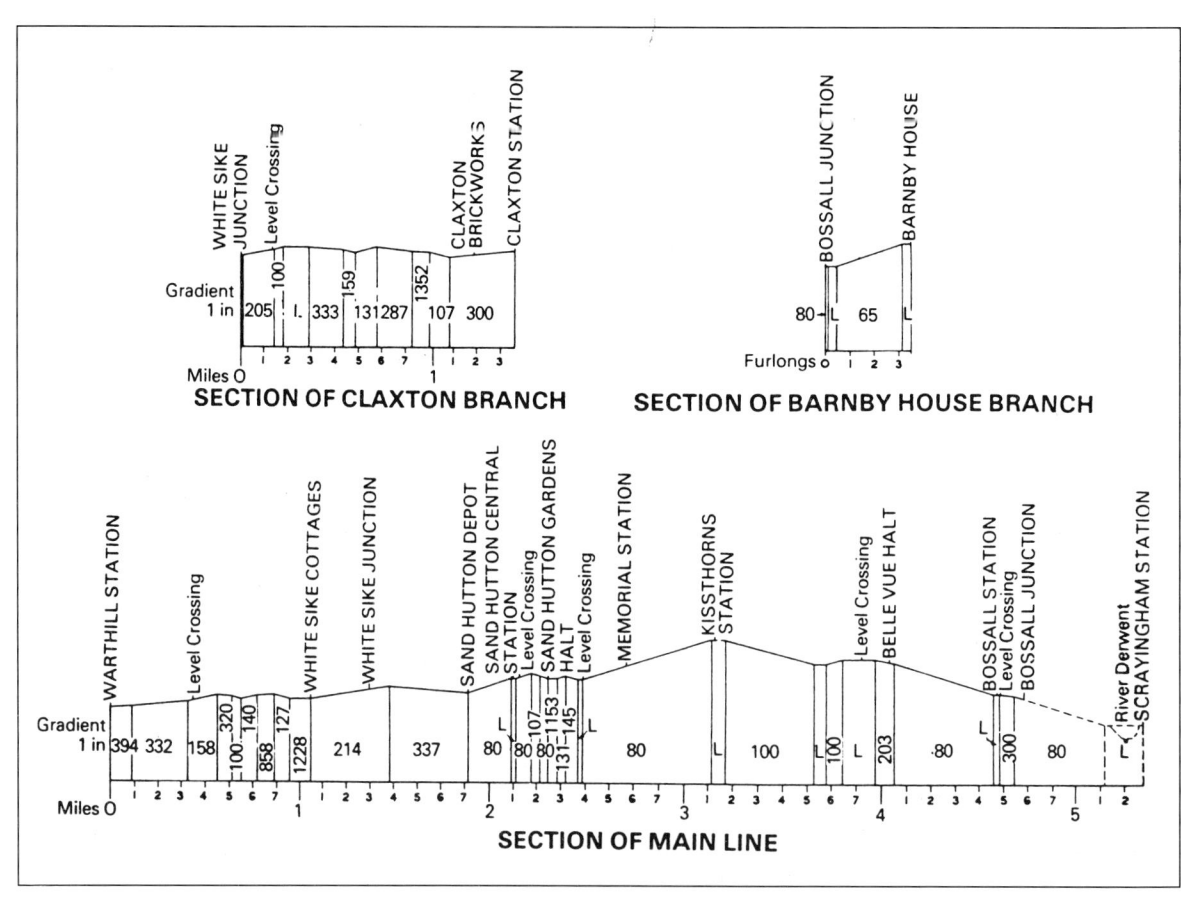

SAND HUTTON LIGHT RAILWAY

Malton

HARTON
Coach body

Barnby House

BOSSALL

Lines built
Lines unfinished
L.N.E.R.

Claxton Station
Belle Vue Halt
Bossall Station

0 ¼ ½ ¾ 1 mile

CLAXTON

Brickworks

SCRAYINGHAM

Pasture Farm
Kissthorns

RIVER DERWENT

Gravel Pit Farm
Memorial

White Sike Farm
SAND HUTTON
Gardens Halt
Hall
BUTTERCRAMBE

White Sike Depot Junction
Central Station

White Sike Cottages

York
Warthill Station

UPPER HELMSLEY

Hull
Holtby Station

A map showing the course of the Sand Hutton Light Railway in its post-1922 form.

SECTION OF CLAXTON BRANCH

WHITE SIKE JUNCTION
Level Crossing
CLAXTON BRICKWORKS
CLAXTON STATION

Gradient 1 in 205 L 333 131 287 107 300
| 100 | | 159 | | | 1352 | |

Miles 0   1   2   3

SECTION OF BARNBY HOUSE BRANCH

BOSSALL JUNCTION
BARNBY HOUSE

80 L 65 L

Furlongs 0 1 2 3

SECTION OF MAIN LINE

WARTHILL STATION
Level Crossing
WHITE SIKE COTTAGES
WHITE SIKE JUNCTION
SAND HUTTON DEPOT
SAND HUTTON CENTRAL STATION
Level Crossing
SAND HUTTON GARDENS HALT
Level Crossing
MEMORIAL STATION
KISSTHORNS STATION
Level Crossing
BELLE VUE HALT
BOSSALL STATION
Level Crossing
BOSSALL JUNCTION
River Derwent
SCRAYINGHAM STATION

Gradient 1 in 394 332 158 100 320 140 858 127 1228 214 337 80 80 80 107 1153 131 45 80 80 100 100 L 203 80 L 300 80

Miles 0   1   2   3   4   5

Gradient profiles of the Sand Hutton 'Main Line' and the Claxton and Barnby House branches.

138

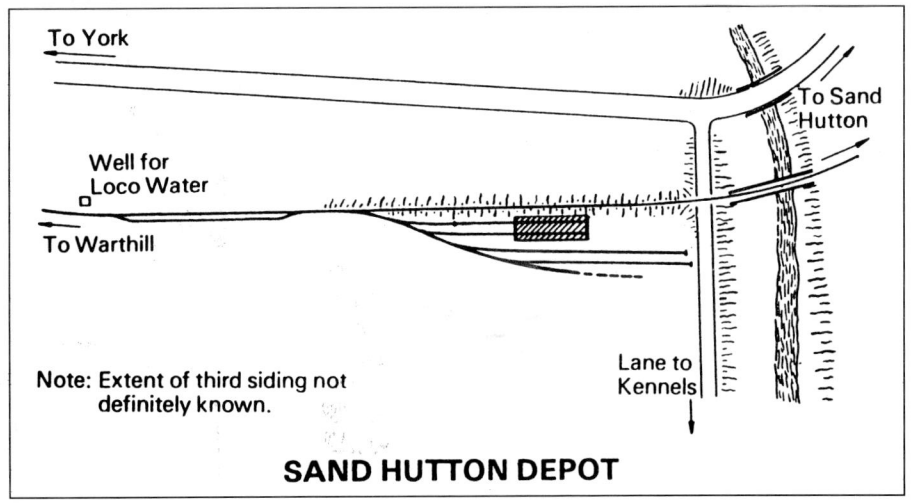

SAND HUTTON DEPOT

To York

Well for Loco Water

To Warthill

Note: Extent of third siding not definitely known.

To Sand Hutton

Lane to Kennels

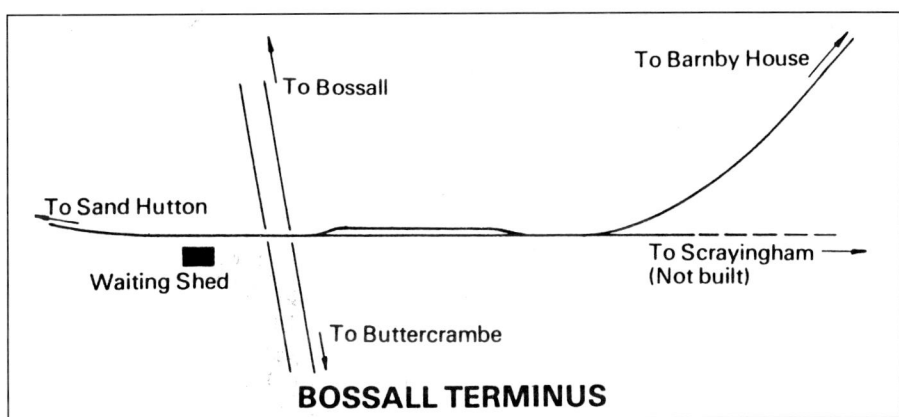

BOSSALL TERMINUS

To Bossall

To Barnby House

To Sand Hutton

Waiting Shed

To Buttercrambe

To Scrayingham (Not built)

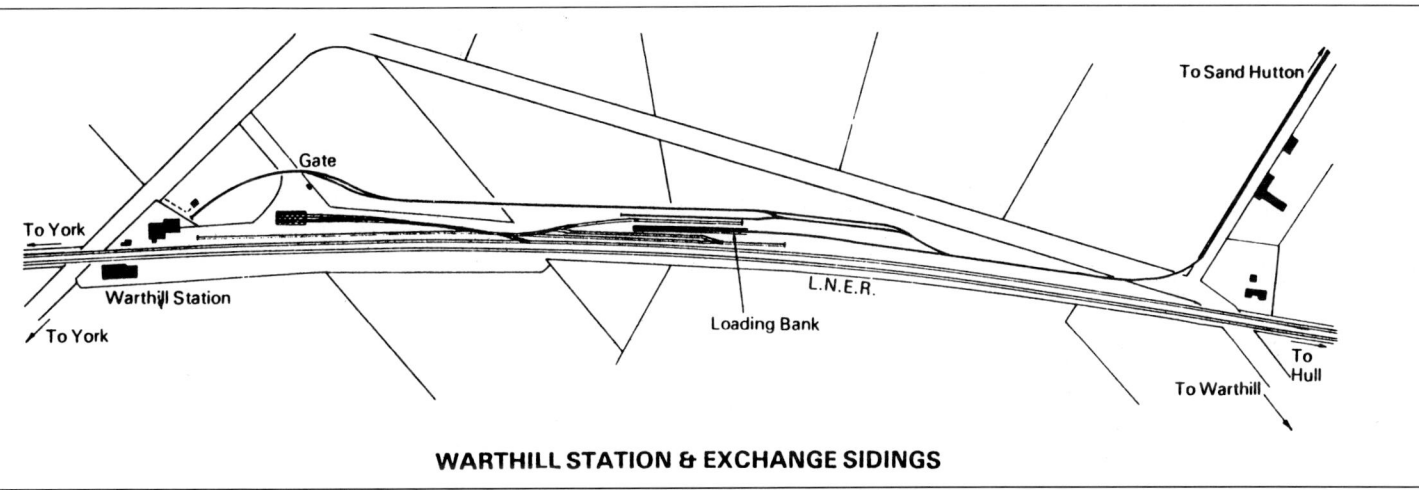

WARTHILL STATION & EXCHANGE SIDINGS

To Sand Hutton

Gate

To York

To York

Warthill Station

Loading Bank

L.N.E.R.

To Hull

To Warthill

Track layout diagrams for the Sand Hutton Light Railway. (This and the two previous illustrations were originally prepared by M. Swift for publication in *The Narrow Gauge* magazine No.95/96. They are reproduced by permission.)

Claxton branch left the 'Main Line'. The Claxton branch was just under 1½ miles long. It was never used for passenger traffic and its two main landmarks were a level crossing close to the junction, and the brickworks which provided the line with much needed revenue until 1929.

From White Sike Junction the 'Main Line' passed through a forest of fir trees and down a steady 1 in 337 gradient to reach Sand Hutton Depot, having passed a gravel pit which provided much of the line's ballast. The engine sheds were situated at Sand Hutton, as were the rather primitive repair facilities and some sidings for agricultural traffic use.

After the depot came the gradient which had been the cause of the decision to change from a gauge of 15 inches to one of 18 inches during the course of the

line's construction. The railway then crossed a large 'beck' on a four-span concrete bridge which was 40 feet in length. After passing a woodyard the railway continued on its course towards Sand Hutton Central station. This was a rather grandiose title for an entity which consisted of a 'platform' of ballast, bounded by wood, and a waiting room which was merely a wooden hut. It has to be said at this juncture that the Light Railway Order did not oblige the SHLR to provide any form of shelter for passengers and the line therefore more than fulfilled its statutory obligations in this area.

Shortly after leaving Sand Hutton Central station the line made its second public road crossing and followed the course of its 15 inch gauge predecessor for approximately 440 yards. From this stretch of line a branch served Sand Hutton Hall and its gardens and the Gardens Halt was a little distance to the east of the junction. At a distance of 2½ miles from Warthill the third public road was crossed and a winding stretch of line was encountered.

To the north of the crossing was Memorial Halt and for a distance of 1,100 yards the line incorporated an ascending gradient of 1 in 80 until, at a point of 142ft above sea level and 74ft above Warthill, Kissthorns station was reached. This station was the line's summit and boasted a siding which served several of the farms on the Sand Hutton Estate, although no waiting shelter was ever provided for the benefit of passengers. After leaving Kissthorns station the line descended for approximately 850 yards on a gradient of 1 in 100 before reaching a short level stretch. This part of the line afforded fine views of the Yorkshire Wolds and after a short upgrade a bridle road crossing was reached, being followed by a cutting and Belle Vue Halt which incorporated another siding. The final stretch of the 'Main Line' from Belle Vue Halt to Bossall station involved the negotiation of the last of the sharp curves, another cutting and a downgrade of 1 in 80. At Bossall station (4.58 miles from Warthill) a waiting shelter was provided along with a well from which water for the locomotives was drawn.

Immediately beyond Bossall station was a junction, the northern fork of which led to the Barnby House branch. Most of this 0.43 mile branch was on an upgrade of 1 in 65, the steepest recorded stretch on the entire SHLR system. The southernmost fork, as has previously been stated, ended in a short stump but was intended to follow a downgrade of 1 in 80 to a point 5.13 miles from Warthill, where a 100ft long bridge would have carried the line over the River Derwent to a station at Scrayingham.

Locomotives and Rolling Stock of the SHLR

Comparatively little modification was made to the four Hunslet well tank locomotives used at Sand Hutton from the condition in which they ran at Deptford. The most obvious change from the mechanical point of view was in the mode of firing. The conditions which existed in the confined environment at Deptford were not evident at Sand Hutton and as a result oil firing was no longer necessary. It was therefore decided to adopt coal firing with the consequential removal of oil burners and the substitution of copper chimney caps for the Austrian style spark arresters with which the engines had been equipped whilst at Deptford.

Whilst at Sand Hutton the locomotives retained their dark green livery and Deptford number plates, the only change being that the name *Esme* (after Sir Robert's second wife) was given to locomotive No. 10. This was accomplished by the fitting of exceptionally small nameplates which were superimposed on the existing number plates. In 1924 this locomotive was fitted with vacuum brake equipment for use with the newly supplied passenger carriage, the apparatus being supplied by Robert Hudson & Co. but fitted by a member of Hunslet's staff.

Apart from the minor modifications detailed above, no major rebuilding work was undertaken on the locomotives and work carried out by Hunslet seems to have been largely confined to routine tasks such as retubing and retyring. The engines gave good service during the lifetime of the railway, their only shortcom-

The Official photograph of the Robert Hudson brake and parcels van constructed for the Sand Hutton Light Railway in 1923.

(Ken Hartley/NGRS Collection)

ings, according to Sir Robert in his *Railway Magazine* article of December 1924, being their relatively low water capacity and lack of a pony truck in order to facilitate a steadier ride.

The goods rolling stock has mostly been described and it remains only to say that Robert Hudson supplied two further items for the line. The earlier of these, supplied in June 1923, was a four-wheeled brake and parcels van with a wheelbase of 6ft and a length of approximately 15ft. The tare weight of this vehicle was

Locomotive No.12 (Hunslet No.1291 of 1917) seen with both Robert Hudson vehicles circa 1928. The driver is Mr George Batty who normally performed the duties of engineer on the railway. In addition to the regular driver, Mr Fred Robinson and certain others, it was not unknown for Sir Robert Walker to take to the footplate of one of the locomotives. This view also shows damage to the front bufferbeam caused by a collision with a tree stump.

(H.G.W. Household)

The Hudson bogie carriage constructed for the Sand Hutton Light Railway in 1924. The design possessed several interesting details and these included hinged upper portions to the first, third and fifth pair of windows from the private saloon entrance. The window glazing was 1/4 in thick and the roof was of 0.375 in plywood covered with canvas. The lack of a ventilator over the semi-open portion gave a rather unbalanced appearance to the roof. The bogies resembled American practice in some respects, although the recessed central section to the uppermost parts of the bogie frames ensured that they could not be truly termed 'diamond framed'. The bogie wheels were 18 in diameter and the suspension consisted of four coil springs per bogie located between the bogie axles. The sides of the vehicle were painted in burnt sienna, with the initials 'S.H.' being applied in brown-edged gold lettering, whilst the roof was painted white and the chassis black. End balconies with ornamental fences were fitted and shortly after delivery to the SHLR, the roof was modified to incorporate cutouts which gave extra headroom over the end balconies.

(Ken Hartley/NGRS Collection)

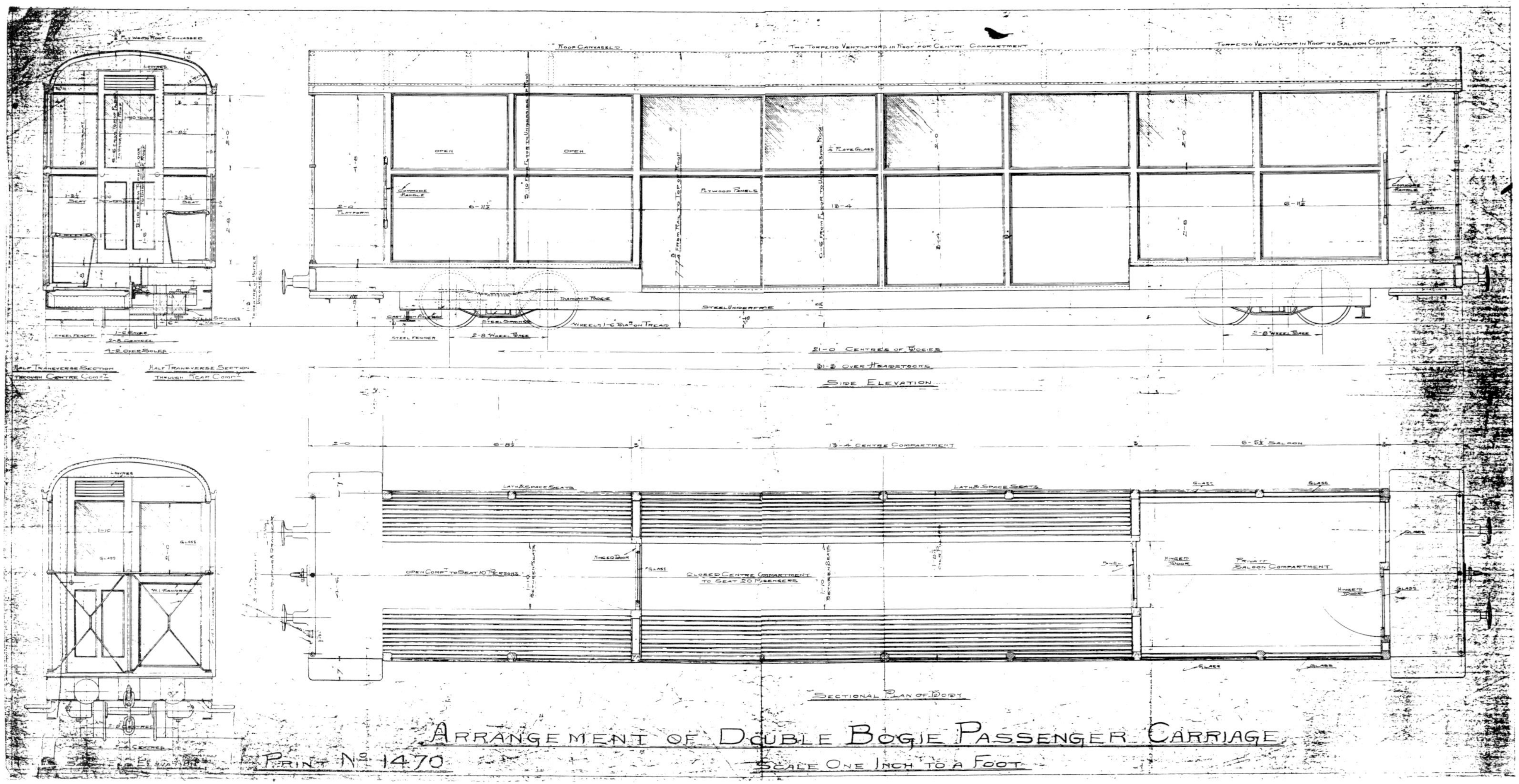

ARRANGEMENT OF DOUBLE BOGIE PASSENGER CARRIAGE

PRINT Nº 1470

The Maker's plans of the Robert Hudson bogie carriage supplied in 1924 for use on the SHLR.

(Courtesy M. Swift)

Esme (Hunslet No.1289 of 1917) at Warthill in July 1925. This view shows the copper capped chimney and vacuum piping.
(Ken Hartley/NGRS Collection)

approximately 1.8 tons and it was able to carry a load of 4 tons. A screw brake was fitted and this acted on all four wheels. The second of the Hudson vehicles was the passenger carriage and this was supplied for the commencement of passenger services in 1924. Its leading dimensions were: overall length 32ft 9in; overall height 7ft 8in; overall width 4ft 8in; bogie wheelbase 2ft 8in and distance between bogie centres 21ft. The weight of the carriage was approximately 6 tons.

As had been the case with the Heywood vehicles, the design of the Sand Hutton carriage was derived from Spooner principles, although the underframe was fabricated from channel section steel components, some of 6in by 3in section and some, including the bufferbeams, of 8in by 3in section. Sprung buffers were fitted along with cast iron axleboxes and the three-compartment body was timber-framed with plywood side panels, the floor timbers being diagonal. The three compartments comprised a 20-seat central saloon, a six-seat private end saloon and a ten-seat open portion with waterproof curtains rather than glazing. Three torpedo roof ventilators were fitted but their design was not shown on the Maker's plans.

A frontal view of *Esme*, taken at the same time as the previous photograph.

(Ken Hartley/NGRS Collection)

Ex-Deptford four-wheeled wagon No.18 at Warthill in July 1925.
(Ken Hartley/NGRS Collection)

This view is believed to show ex-Deptford No.4 (Hunslet No.1207 of 1916) on the ramp at Warthill.

(C.F. Klapper/NGRS Collection)

The SHLR - Legal Aspects, Operation and Closure

The Light Railway Order of 1920 incorporated the SHLR as a limited company with an authorised share capital of £25,000 in £10 shares and borrowing powers of £8,000. By 1924 the Directors were recorded by the *Railway Magazine* as being Major Sir Robert Walker (Chairman); Lady Walker; Major H.A. Watson CBE, MVO; Mr W.T. Grundy and Mr W. Harrison. The Secretary was Mr S.C. Foster whilst Mr G. Batty carried out the duties of maintenance of the railway and its equipment. Major Watson was, immediately before the Grouping, General Superintendent of the North Eastern Railway and much essential help was supplied in the survey and construction stages by this concern, a fact which was acknowledged by Sir Robert Walker.

The extent of the authorised railway was covered by Section 11 of the Order and as was the normal pattern with lines of this kind, the 'Main Line' and the two branches were designated by separate numbers, with the former being Railway No.1, the Claxton branch being Railway No.2 and the Barnby House branch being Railway No.3. Limited powers of deviation from the specified course were granted by the Order, although the minimum radius of curve was limited to 44ft. Gradients of up to 1 in 25 were authorised although, as has been noted, the most severe was the 1 in 65 section on the Barnby House branch.

There was no requirement placed upon the Company to provide gates at level crossings although ungated crossings (in practice all of those on the SHLR system) were to be protected by cattle guards. At points along the line, 200 yards either side of the crossing there was to a legible speed limit placed 5ft above ground level and visible to the engine driver. At points 50 yards along the roadway either side of the crossing there were to be notices warning the public of the presence of trains. The specified speed limit was four miles per hour approaching level crossings, although the warning boards for the locomotive driver do not appear to have carried this figure. The general speed limit for the railway was 12 mph and the normal timetabled running time of 40 minutes allowed for an average speed of approximately 7.1 mph. However unofficially it was commonplace for passenger trains to complete the Warthill-Bossall run in shorter times than the timetable permitted.

There was no general requirement to fence the railway, according to Section 27 of the Order, but there was a requirement to protect unfenced agricultural sections with cattle grids. The opening of the line for passenger traffic was covered in Section 31 and one month's notice to the Minister of Transport of the wish to undergo inspection for this purpose was required, with a penalty of £20 per day's operation in contravention of this provision being payable. In the event, the railway was inspected for the conveyance of passenger traffic in 1924 by Col. J.W. Pringle CB, RE and a passenger service began on 4th October that year.

The bridge over the River Derwent and its associated towpath would have had to have been of the single span variety, and of sufficient height, to give a 15ft clearance above the summer level of the river at the point of crossing. Construction would have had to have been completed within one year of commencement and the river would have had to have remained navigable, along with a 4ft width of towpath, throughout the construction process. In the event, these latter provisions were never to be put into practice, and the requirement for completion within one year, and its associated labour costs, may have helped to ensure that the bridge never materialised.

Section 34 of the Order empowered the company to enter into agreements with the NER for the construction, maintenance and management of the railway, for its use and working and for the conveyance of traffic (and associated rates or tolls). Although assistance had been supplied by the NER to the SHLR at the survey and construction stage, the latter was not destined to follow other well known narrow gauge lines such as the Lynton & Barnstaple and the Vale of Rheidol into main line ownership.

The timetable initially used for passenger services was published in the December 1924 *Railway Magazine* feature. At this stage passenger operation consisted of three trains in each direction on Saturdays

The exchange sidings at Warthill station in 1927.

(*H.G.W. Household/NGRS Collection*)

The travelling hoist used for transshipment at Warthill station, seen in 1927.

(*Ken Hartley/NGRS Collection*)

White Sike Junction with one of the Hunslet 0-4-0WTs and brake/parcels van.

(*H. Speed/NGRS Collection*)

Sand Hutton Depot showing bogie hay wagons improvised using the under frames of ex-Deptford four-wheeled wagons.
(Ken Hartley/NGRS Collection)

only, this being so as to coincide with market days in York. During the subsequent period of passenger operation sundry alterations were made to the timetable, including additional trains on Wednesdays, at least during 1925, the year in which the greatest number of passengers were carried. According to the October 1962 *Railway Magazine* the last day of passenger operation was 7th July 1930 although this is at variance with the official Ministry of Transport Statistics (reproduced in Appendix 2) which show 61 passengers being carried during 1931. It may be that the 1931 passenger workings used wagons rather than the carriage, as is suggested by some photographic evidence of the period.

The receipts from passenger workings were never particularly generous with 1925 being the best year, bringing in a total of £39, of which £1 was for refreshments. The period from 1926 until 1928 was the best in terms of freight receipts, largely deriving from agricultural produce, coal and the products of Claxton Brickworks, but freight traffic declined rapidly during 1929, the main influencing factors being the closure of the brickworks, due to the loss of a reliable and economic source of clay, and improvements in road transportation methods.

In 1930 Sir Robert Walker died and his death proved to be another nail in the coffin of the Sand Hutton Light Railway. The line had made small operating profits during the years up to and including 1929 but it had never brought in enough revenue to cover debenture interest (the debentures, as with 2,488 of the shares, were held by the Trustees of the Sand Hutton Estate). At an Extraordinary General Meeting of SHLR shareholders on 22nd March 1932 at the Estate Offices at Claxton the decision was finally taken to apply to the Ministry of Transport for authorization to abandon the railway. The required Order was granted in June 1932 and traffic ceased on the last day of that month. The company was officially wound up on 24th

October 1932 and at a creditors' meeting on 8th December the summary statement of affairs showed the line's assets as being worth £2,663 16s 3d (£2,663.82) and loan creditors (including debentures) as being £10,756 5s 3d (£10,756.26) which, with the share capital of £25,000 brought the accumulated loss to £33,041 12s 9d (£33,041.64). No liquidator was appointed and the process of winding up the affairs of the company was left in the hands of the Official Receiver.

In the depressed economic climate of the early 1930s the closure of the SHLR was inevitable, particularly in view of the line's accumulated losses by 1932. Demolition work was carried out by Thomas W. Ward Ltd of Sheffield during 1933 with the regular driver, Mr Fred Robinson being instructed by the Ward's foreman in the use of an oxy-acetylene cutter before being assigned to the task of cutting up the locomotives. The ex-Deptford wagons also perished at this stage but the bodies of the two Hudson vehicles survived the closure. The parcels van body ended its days as a chicken shed and its final date of demolition is apparently unrecorded.

The carriage body was acquired for use as a pavilion by Harton Ladies Cricket Club, about 1½ miles distant from the site of Bossall station. The body served in this capacity for a further 34 years until acquired, in a rather ramshackle condition, by an enthusiast based in the South of England. On 17th June 1967 he transferred ownership of the body to the 1ft 11½in gauge Lincolnshire Coast Light Railway at Humberston. Here, thorough restoration of the body was undertaken, including the replacement of rotted plywood panels and the manufacture of new iron handrails and end fences to the original specification. A single floor level was decided upon and so the body sides had their raised portions filled in at each end. A new chassis was built around suitable components salvaged from two WDLR D class bogie wagons. The restored vehicle, which is finished in light brown livery with white roof and black running gear, saw much use on the LCLR but is currently in store with a view to use on a new line at Skegness following the cessation of operations of the railway during the 1980s.

Left hand side view of *Esme* on a fete day train at Kissthorns Siding.
(Ken Hartley/NGRS Collection)

A view showing George Batty on the footplate of *Esme* with Sir Robert and Lady Esme standing in front of the carriage.

(Ken Hartley/NGRS Collection)

This view shows a Hunslet 0-4-0WT at Sand Hutton Depot with the carriage. The lettering on the two central panels of the carriage is shown to advantage.
(Ken Hartley/NGRS Collection)

Ex-Deptford Hunslet 0-4-0WT No.12 (Hunslet No.1291 of 1917).
(Ken Hartley/NGRS Collection)

Was this the last train on the SHLR? Reproduced from a local newspaper photograph of 1932.
(Ken Hartley/NGRS Collection)

The ex-SHLR coach body at Harton in 1962 in use as a Cricket Pavilion. Fortunately this item was rescued for preservation five years later and it is currently mounted on a 1ft 11½in gauge under frame.
(Ken Hartley/NGRS Collection)

Sand Hutton Depot derelict in 1964 after a period of agricultural usage. It was demolished during the following year.

(Ken Hartley/NGRS Collection)

The John Knowles System

Of the steam worked lines of 18 inch gauge in the United Kingdom remaining for consideration, the most historically significant was the John Knowles system which served the Mount Pleasant clay processing works near Woodville in Leicestershire. The origins of the company, whose correct title was recorded as John Knowles & Co. (Wooden Box) Ltd, went back to the year 1847 when John Knowles, a railway engineer by profession, was in the process of excavating a cutting during construction of the local standard gauge railway. He noticed deposits of aluminous fireclay and decided in 1849 to form a company to exploit these for the manufacture of bricks and other clay-based products. Accordingly several clay mines were sunk and a central firing works built in order to facilitate brick manufacture. Many of the workings were equipped with lines of 18 inch gauge, owing to their restricted clearances and these ultimately formed the basis of the locomotive-worked system used by the company from 1898 onwards.

The name 'Wooden Box' in the company title referred to the location of the company premises, which were situated a short distance in a south westerly direction from Woodville Crossroads. In earlier days, when road tolls were levied, the crossroads had been guarded by a wooden sentry box. At no time in its history did the John Knowles company engage in the manufacture of wooden boxes.

The decision to order a steam locomotive for use at the Mount Pleasant Works and its surroundings was taken during the year 1897 and on Christmas Eve of that year, an order was placed with Hunslet Engine Co. of Leeds. This firm was chosen in spite of the fact that they had never before constructed a locomotive for 18

inch gauge, whereas their Leeds rivals, Hudswell, Clarke and Manning, Wardle both had experience in this field.

The locomotive was delivered on the 22nd November 1898 as Hunslet No.684 and it bore the name *Jack*. The basic design was an 0-4-0 with cylinders of 6in bore and 8in stroke, these latter dimensions being the same as for the Manning, Wardle engine *Lord Raglan* built for use at Woolwich Arsenal. The wheelbase was shorter than the Manning, Wardle design at 3ft whilst the wheel diameter was 1ft 6in. The full list of dimensions supplied by the Makers is shown in an accompanying illustration.

One important similarity between *Jack* and most other Leeds built 18 inch gauge steam locomotives was the use of a single injector in conjunction with an axle-driven feedpump. Outside main frames were also utilised but there the similarity ended. Instead of the domeless boiler and sharply raised outer firebox wrapper found on the 'Victoria' and 'Culverin' classes of the Royal Arsenal Railways, a boiler with a slightly raised outer firebox wrapper and a large dome was fitted. In order to keep the centre of gravity of the engine as low as possible, the well tank (Hunslet's referred to this fitment as a 'frame tank'), configuration was decided upon. Outside Walschaerts valve gear was fitted and the cab, which possessed no upper backsheet, was typical of the pattern used by the Makers for several of their narrow gauge products. A single cylindrical sandbox was carried on the boiler between the dome and the chimney and the engine was finished in a similar colour scheme to that used on the later engine, *Gwen* (to be described).

Several modifications were made to *Jack* during the

locomotive's working life. In 1915, the year in which the basic design was adopted in an enlarged form for use at the Special Reserve Depot at Deptford, a new boiler with a copper firebox and brass tubes was fitted. The running gear also received repairs and shortly afterwards a second sand dome, as per the Deptford 'Waril' class, was added behind the steam dome. In 1926 the firebox-mounted Salter safety valves were replaced by a pair of dome-mounted safety valves of the Ross 'pop' variety and two years later an LMS-style whistle, once more fitted to the dome, replaced the original roof-mounted variety. During the later years of the engine's revenue-earning career an upper backsheet was added to the cab and the original Roscoe No.1 displacement cylinder lubricators were replaced by a single mechanical lubricator. In this final condition, *Jack* remained at the Mount Pleasant site until final departure in 1958.

Maker's official photograph of Hunslet 0-4-0WT *Jack* (No.684 of 1898). This view shows to advantage the single sandbox with which the engine was originally supplied, together with the whistle on the cab roof, firebox-mounted Salter safety valves and lamp irons on the smokebox and rear backsheet. As originally constructed, this latter item extended only to waist height. The clack valve visible in this view was supplied from the feedpump.

(Author's Collection)

Jack seen in 1952 with a train of four loaded clay tubs at John Knowles & Co. (Wooden Box) Ltd, Woodville, Leicestershire. The modifications made during the engine's revenue earning career are readily apparent and include the additional sandbox, dome-mounted Ross 'pop' safety valves and whistle, upper backsheet, welded front to the smokebox and removal of the Roscoe pattern displacement lubricator. The pipe linking the feedpump to its anti-vacuum valve is visible just in front of the cab.

(Courtesy J. Peden/IRS Collection 1245B)

Jack, again in 1952, with a train of twelve clay tubs.
(J. Peden/IRS Collection 1245C)

Jack in steam outside the narrow gauge locomotive shed at Woodville. This single-road shed was of sufficient length to accommodate both locomotives *Jack* and *Gwen*, and contained an inspection pit.
(J. Peden/IRS Collection 1245A)

The second steam locomotive to see service on the 18 inch gauge John Knowles system was a Bagnall product, their No. 1907 of 1909. This locomotive, which carried the name *Scout* was fitted with cylinders of 4in bore and 7½in stroke and driving wheels of 1ft 3¼in diameter. It had originally been supplied to D.B. Dobson's Model Poultry Farm in Bolton and John Knowles acquired the locomotive from T. Mitchell & Sons Ltd in May 1913. The engine was not a success at Woodville and it was sold in 1921, with its boiler being put to stationary use by its new owner.

The third and last 18 inch gauge steam locomotive to arrive for use on the Mount Pleasant system was delivered in 1920. In view of the success enjoyed by *Jack*, it was not surprising that the locomotive should have been constructed by Hunslet but the major surprise was that a new locomotive was constructed at all.

Gwen, as the engine was christened, was No.1404 of 1920 and, apart from being a coal burner, it was identical in all substantive respects to the twelve 'Waril' class

locomotives supplied to the Special Reserve Depot at Deptford. When one considers that four of these locomotives had become surplus to requirements during 1919-1920, the cheaper course of action would have been to have purchased one of these engines and removed the oil burning apparatus. It must have been the case that those responsible for placing the order at John Knowles were unaware of the availability of the Deptford locomotives and that Hunslet were either equally unaware or were unwilling, for commercial reasons, to divulge the fact.

One relatively minor difference between *Gwen* and the Deptford locomotives was that the former was fitted with an upper backsheet to the cab when built. The livery, as supplied, was Midland red for the cab, boiler, outer main frames and cylinder covers in conjunction with lining of Naples yellow. The insides to the main frames were vermilion, whilst the smokebox and chimney were, as per normal locomotive practice, plain black.

Gwen, (Hunslet 1404 of 1920) outside the locomotive shed at Woodville on 3rd July 1952. Unlike *Jack*, this locomotive still retained its Roscoe lubricators at this stage, along with a lamp iron on the smokebox front.

(J. Peden/ IRS Collection 1246)

Over the years *Gwen* underwent very little in the way of alterations, although a new welded-front smokebox was supplied after 1946, as was the case with *Jack*. The state of cleanliness of both locomotives deteriorated dramatically during the remaining period of locomotive operation.

The rolling stock in use on the Knowles system was extremely primitive in design and consisted of two basic types of four-wheeled wagon. The more numerous of the two wagon designs was the standard clay tub shown in the accompanying drawing. Although not shown in the drawings, an iron or steel bar passed through the longitudinal centreline under the skip in order to provide eyes for the drawhooks. The earlier examples of the tub wagons were timber framed with

Jack outside the locomotive shed at Woodville in 1952.

(M. Billington)

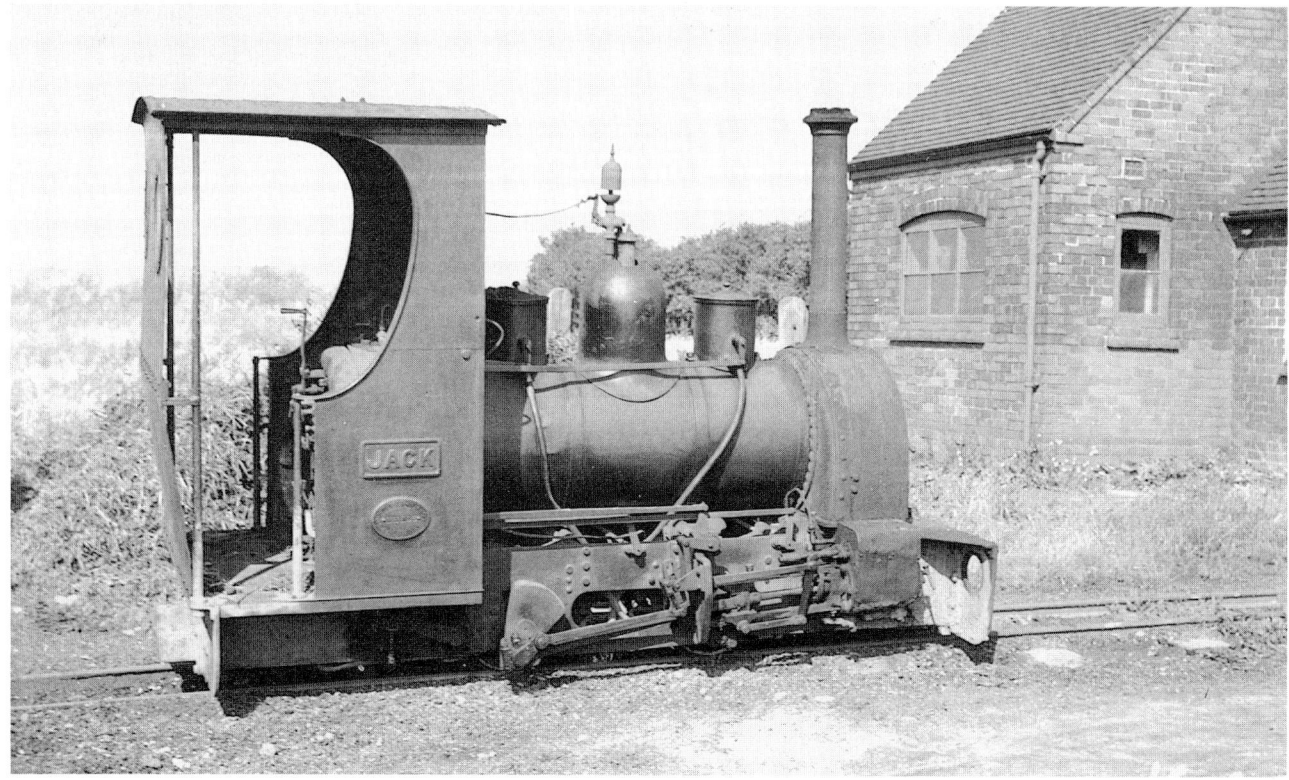

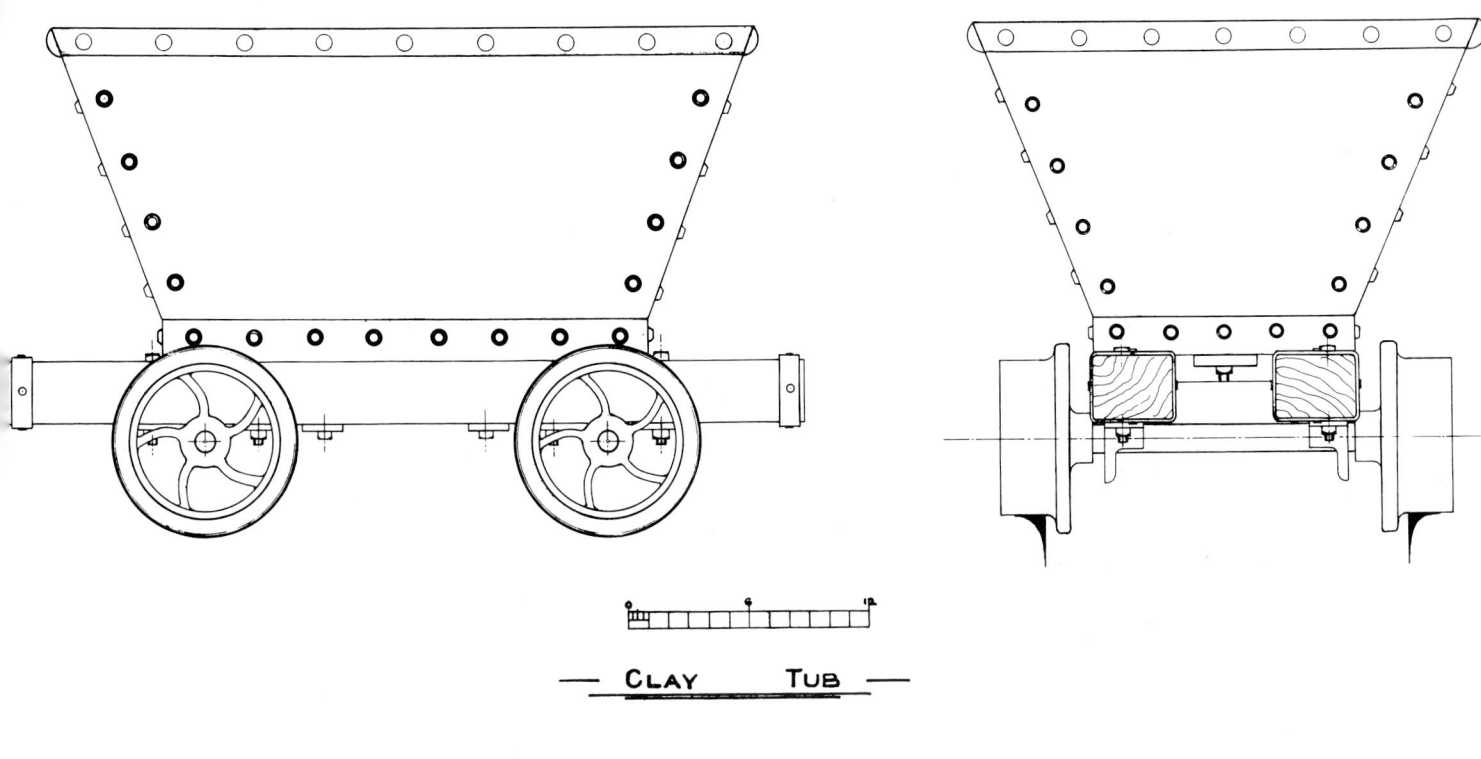

— CLAY TUB —

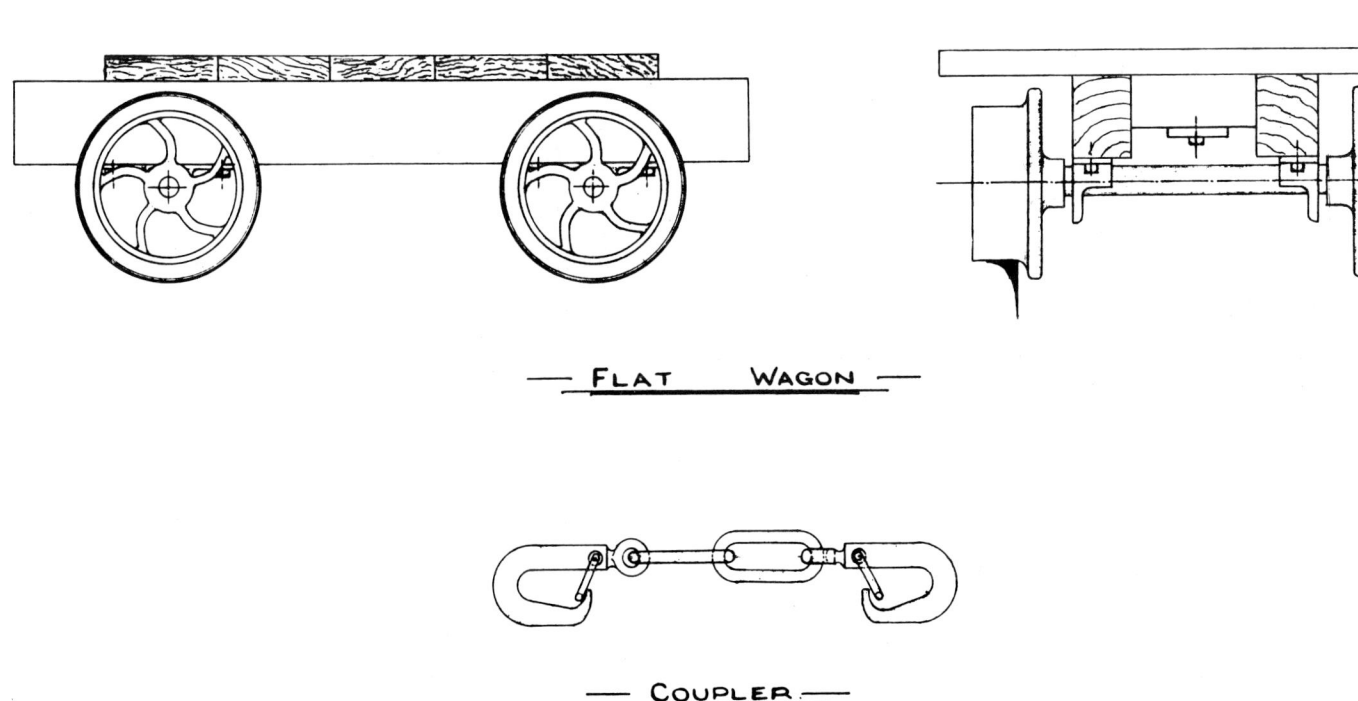

— FLAT WAGON —

— COUPLER —

— 1'-6" GAUGE WAGONS ~ JOHN KNOWLES & Co. Ltd. —

The timber-framed clay tub and flat wagon designs used on the John Knowles system.

(J. Outram via R. Murmann)

riveted iron skips whereas later examples were of welded steel construction.

The other type of wagon in use was a flat wagon constructed on a similar pattern underframe to that used on the earlier tub wagons. The lack of iron or steel hoops to take buffing loads on the underframe as depicted in the drawings suggests that these wagons were designed for manual rather than locomotive propulsion, and were probably intended for the movement of mechanical spares or stores.

By the mid-1950s clay mining at the Mount Pleasant site had been run down to a relatively low level and less than one mile of 18 inch gauge track remained in use, linking a mine shaft with a tipping dock where clay was trans-shipped into standard gauge wagons for ultimate transfer to the main line. A short stretch of the track at this end of the line was comprised of cast iron plates and manually operated tipping devices were employed to transfer the clay into the standard gauge wagons. The track layout was also arranged so as to allow turning of the locomotives without the use of a turntable and photographic evidence reveals that use was made of this facility over the years.

In April 1958 both locomotives were withdrawn from service and the surviving stretch of 18 inch gauge line was converted to cable haulage. In the event clay mining at Mount Pleasant was not destined to survive much longer as flooding of the workings after a spell of heavy rain was to ensure the subsequent loss of much of the necessary equipment. The narrow gauge locomotive shed still survived in a derelict state 25 years after the cessation of locomotive usage, although by that stage most of the Knowles buildings had disappeared.

In September 1958 *Gwen* was sold for £100 for use on the Wild Cat Railroad in California, USA and it is pleasing to record that *Jack* was also saved for preservation after its sixty year period of revenue earning service had expired. After negotiations undertaken by Mr Eric Cope and Mr John Alcock, the Managing Director of Hunslet Engine Co. Ltd, a visit by the Narrow Gauge Railway Society to see *Jack* in steam on 17th July 1956, and further negotiations undertaken by Dr R.P. Lee, an NGRS committee member, *Jack* was moved to Leeds City Museum's Copley Hill Store on 23rd October 1958. The engine's subsequent restoration to working order will be dealt with in the appropriate section of this chapter.

In addition to the locomotives, some of the clay tubs have survived in private ownership and one is on display at the Conwy Valley Railway Museum, Betws-y-Coed, where it is an ideal companion for the four-wheeled ex-Royal Arsenal Railways ammunition wagon also to be found at this museum.

Leading Dimensions for John Knowles Hunslet Locomotives

Jack

Gauge of Railway	1ft 6in
Size of Cylinders: Bore	6in
: Stroke	8in
Diameter of Coupled Wheels	1ft 6in
Rigid Wheelbase	3 ft
Height from Rail to Chimney Top	7ft 9³/₄in
Extreme Width	5ft 5in

Heating Surface: Tubes	72 sqft .
: Firebox	14 sqft
: Total	86 sqft
Grate Area	2.3 sqft
Working Pressure (Original)	130 psi
(Later)	160 psi
Tank Capacity	48 galls
Coal Space	2 cwt
Total Weight (Empty)	4 tons 13 cwt
(Working Order)	5 tons 5 cwts.
Maximum Axle Loading	2 tons 14 cwt
Nominal Maximum Tractive Effort	
At 75% Original Working Pressure	1,518 lb
Adhesive Weight: Tractive Effort Ratio	7.7
Minimum Radius Track Curve	20ft
Lightest Rail Section	20lb/yd
Load Engine will haul: On Level	75 tons
: Up 1 in 100	35 tons
: Up 1 in 50	20 tons

Gwen

Gauge of Railway	1ft 6in
Size of Cylinders: Bore	6¹/₂in
: Stroke	8in
Diameter of Coupled Wheels	1ft 6¹/₂in
Total Wheelbase (Engine)	3ft 6in
Height from Rail to Top of Chimney	8ft
Extreme Width	5ft 5in
Heating Surface: Tubes	78 sqft
: Firebox	18 sqft
: Total	96 sqft
Grate Area	3 sqft
Working Pressure	160 psi
Tank Capacity	58 galls
Fuel Space (Oil)*	25 galls
Weight Empty	5 ton 6 cwt
Weight (Working Order)	5 ton 19 cwt
Maximum Axle Load	3 ton 19 cwts
Nominal Maximum Tractive Effort	
At 75% Working Pressure	2,192 lbs
Adhesive Weight : Tractive Effort Ratio	6.1
Minimum Radius Curve	24 ft
Load Engine will haul: On Level	115 tons
: Up 1 in 100	55 tons
: Up 1 in 50	30 tons

*The dimensions for *Gwen* also applied to the 'Waril' class locomotives used at Deptford Special Reserve Depot, hence the reference to oil firing.

The Bagnall Influence Outside Woolwich

The basic design of narrow gauge 0-4-0 saddle tank locomotive favoured by W.G. Bagnall & Co. Ltd was well adapted to production for 18 inch gauge as its 'drumhead' pattern boiler did not possess a depending firebox to impose limitations upon the spacing of the main frames. Four examples saw use on railways based within the United Kingdom and one of these, *Scout* (No. 1907 of 1909) has already been referred to in connection with the John Knowles system. An engine with similar leading dimensions, No. 1842 of 1907, was supplied to Alfred Herbert Ltd of Coventry and this locomotive appears to have remained in use at these premises for over twenty years, eventually being advertised for sale in *Contract Journal* for 29th February 1928.

In March 1899 a locomotive was supplied to Hastings Corporation for use on a line transporting construction materials from a wharf on the River Brede to the site of a water works then in the course of building. The line remained in use in truncated form after the completion of the works in order to facilitate the supply of coal to the pumping station, although latterly the coal was supplied to a shed by road, from which the railway wagons were loaded, rather than by barge from the River Brede. The engine which ran on this line was Bagnall No. 1560 of 1899, a 0-4-0 saddle tank with 4¹/₂in by 7¹/₂in cylinders, 1ft 7in diameter wheels and Baguley valve gear. A new boiler was supplied on 9th February 1923 at a cost of £160 and the engine underwent sundry other modifications over the years. These included the fitting of a spectacle plate and upper cab side sheets and the replacement of its normal pattern rounded saddle tank by a peculiar straight sided, 40 gallon tank mounted on the rear

154

A photograph of the Bagnall 0-4-0ST (No. 1560 of 1899) supplied for use on the Brede Waterworks Railway. Originally constructed to the Maker's normal pattern and fitted with Baguley valve gear, the engine had acquired several distinctive features as a result of alterations carried out before the period of this photograph, circa 1932. These included the peculiar replacement saddle tank, the spectacle plate with rectangular look-outs and the donkey pump for replenishing the tank, located on the right hand side of the engine. Despite the fact that the locomotive was nearing the end of its career, traces of a lined out livery were still in evidence.

(Courtesy M. Billington)

A map showing the course of the Brede Waterworks 18 inch gauge railway which was in use from 1899 until the mid-1930s. The branch to the well at the south western end of the line was closed after the completion of the Pumping Station by 1904. The section from the easternmost shed to the Wharf fell out of use by the late 1920s when coal was being trans-shipped from road vehicles rather than barges on the River Brede.

(Author, from information supplied by Mr. B. Clarke)

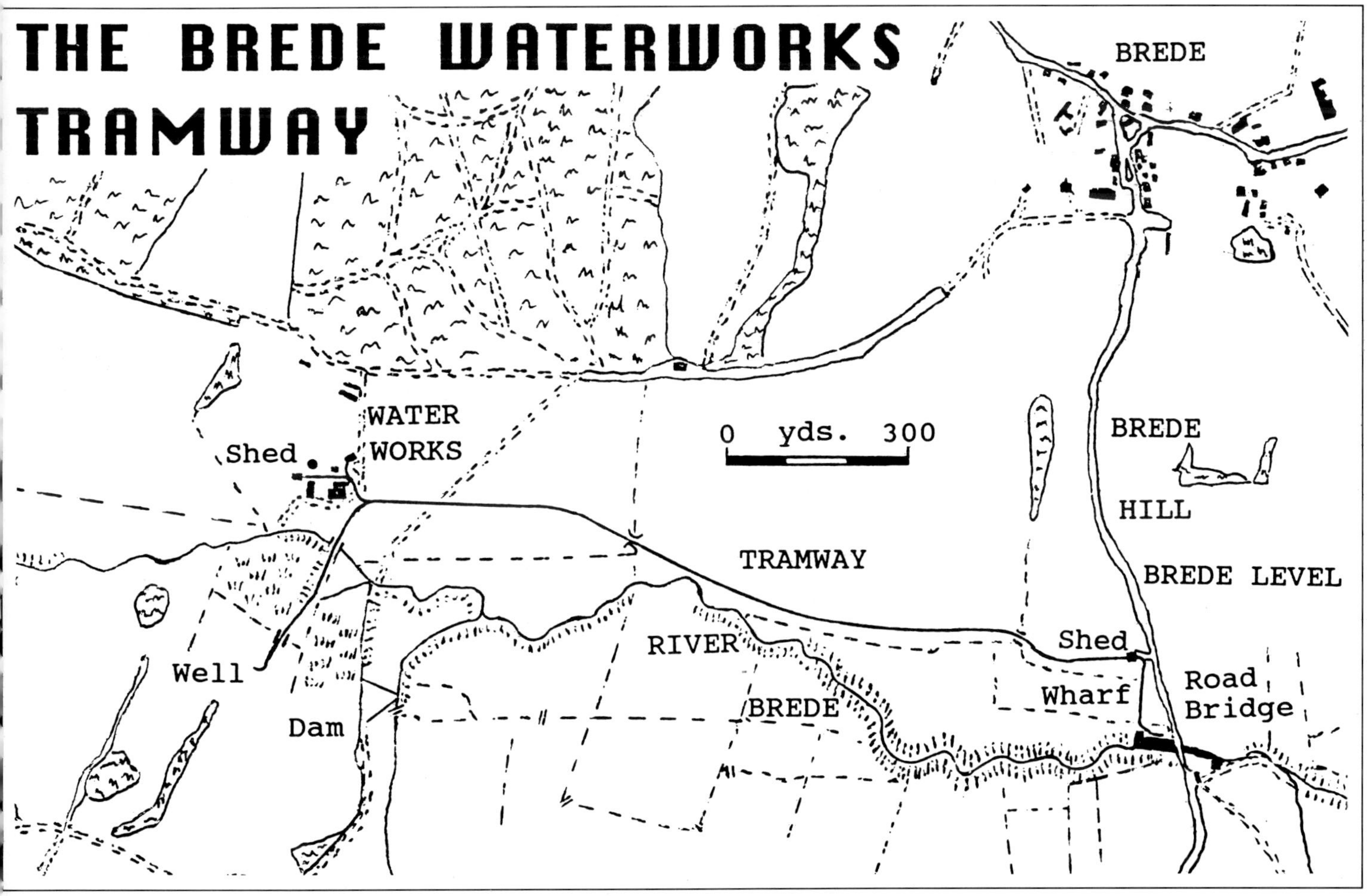

THE BREDE WATERWORKS TRAMWAY

BREDE

WATER WORKS

Shed

BREDE HILL

BREDE LEVEL

0 yds. 300

TRAMWAY

RIVER BREDE

Shed

Wharf

Road Bridge

Well

Dam

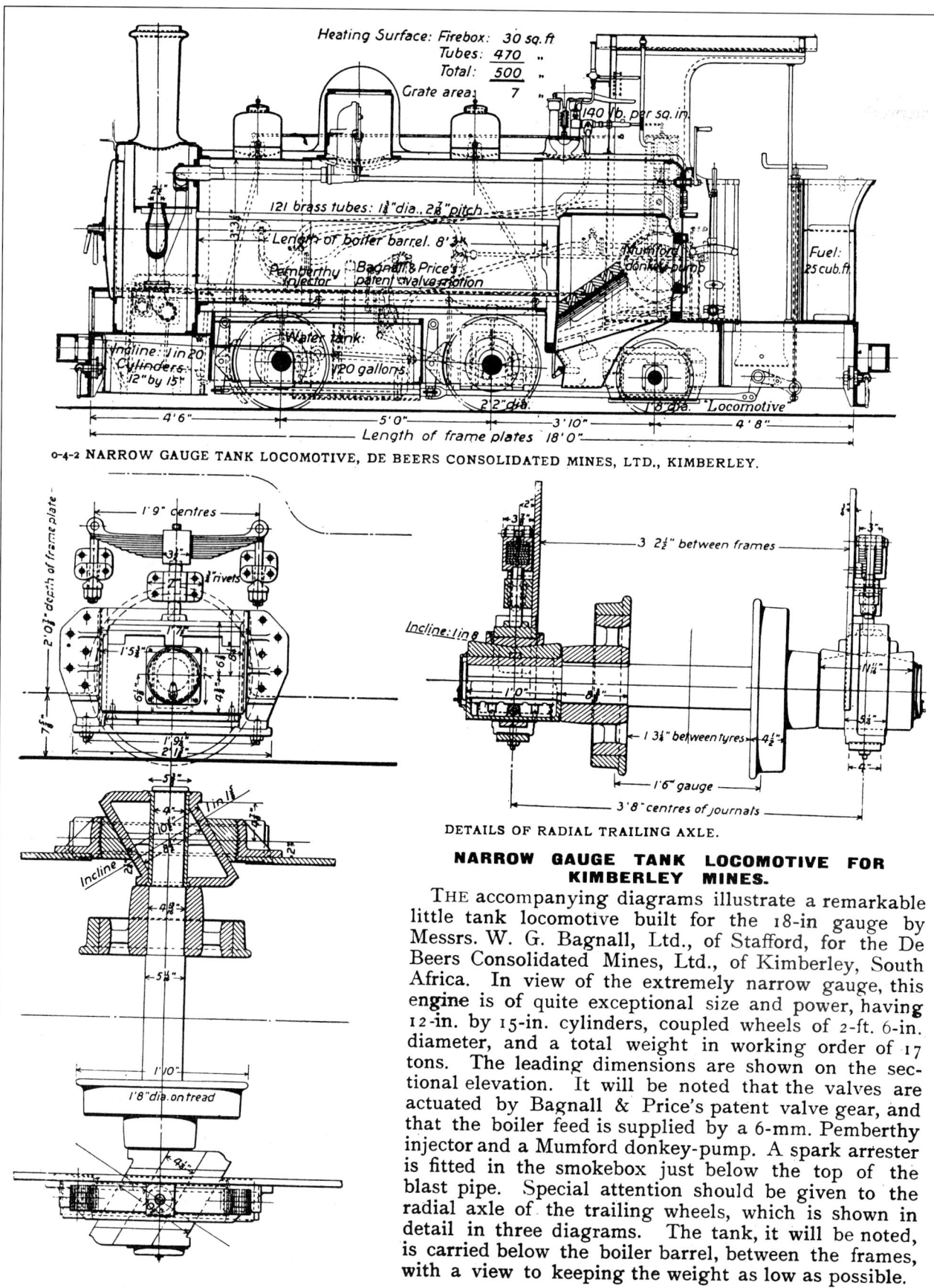

Heating Surface: Firebox: 30 sq.ft
Tubes: 470 "
Total: 500 "
Grate area: 7

140 lb. per sq. in.

121 brass tubes: 1⅛"dia., 2⅜"pitch

Length of boiler barrel 8'2"

Pemberthy injector   Bagnall & Price's patent valve motion

Mumford donkey pump

Fuel: 25 cub.ft.

Incline: 1 in 20
Cylinders 12" by 15"

Water tank: 120 gallons

2'2"dia.

1'8"dia.   Locomotive

4'6"   5'0"   3'10"   4'8"
Length of frame plates 18'0"

0-4-2 NARROW GAUGE TANK LOCOMOTIVE, DE BEERS CONSOLIDATED MINES, LTD., KIMBERLEY.

1'9" centres

2'0" depth of frame plate

Rivets

1'5½"

7½"

1'9¼"
2'11"

1'8" dia. on tread

Incline

Incline: 1 in 8

3 2½" between frames

3"

1'0"

1 3¼" between tyres   4½"

1'6" gauge

3'8" centres of journals

DETAILS OF RADIAL TRAILING AXLE.

NARROW GAUGE TANK LOCOMOTIVE FOR KIMBERLEY MINES.

THE accompanying diagrams illustrate a remarkable little tank locomotive built for the 18-in. gauge by Messrs. W. G. Bagnall, Ltd., of Stafford, for the De Beers Consolidated Mines, Ltd., of Kimberley, South Africa. In view of the extremely narrow gauge, this engine is of quite exceptional size and power, having 12-in. by 15-in. cylinders, coupled wheels of 2-ft. 6-in. diameter, and a total weight in working order of 17 tons. The leading dimensions are shown on the sectional elevation. It will be noted that the valves are actuated by Bagnall & Price's patent valve gear, and that the boiler feed is supplied by a 6-mm. Pemberthy injector and a Mumford donkey-pump. A spark arrester is fitted in the smokebox just below the top of the blast pipe. Special attention should be given to the radial axle of the trailing wheels, which is shown in detail in three diagrams. The tank, it will be noted, is carried below the boiler barrel, between the frames, with a view to keeping the weight as low as possible.

part of the boiler barrel. This locomotive, which was unofficially known as *Brede* was finally withdrawn for scrapping in 1935 and the railway closed at the same time.

The last Bagnall 0-4-0ST to be mentioned in this section was supplied in 1902 to Blackbrook Colliery, Glamorgan, No. 1651. This engine was equipped with 5½in by 7½in cylinders and driving wheels 1ft 3¼in diameter.

Although strictly speaking outside the scope of the present volume, one further Bagnall design deserves a

This class of 0-4-2 well tank built for De Beers Consolidated Mines Ltd is referred to in the main text. These drawings, which appeared in *The Locomotive* for 15th April 1911 show the proportions of the design, together with details of the Cartazzi pattern trailing axleboxes. The engines were fitted with Bagnall-Price valve gear and the boiler feed was facilitated by means of a 6 mm Pemberthy injector and a Mumford donkey-pump. This design is an illustration of what could be utilised on an 18 inch gauge steam railway if traffic demands were sufficiently high. A standard gauge locomotive constructed to these proportions would have a boiler in excess of ten feet in diameter!

brief consideration. The largest commercial export destination for British functional 18 inch gauge locomotives was De Beers Consolidated Diamond Mines at Kimberley, South Africa. Four 0-4-2 well tank locomotives (Nos 1814-1817) were supplied to this customer from Stafford in 1905 and these held the distinction of being the largest functional 18 inch gauge locomotives constructed by any British concern. These engines had boilers 3ft 3¼in diameter, cylinders 12in by 15in, coupled wheels 2ft 6in diameter and they weighed 17 tons

in working order. No. 1814, now named *Olive*, is preserved in the museum at the Kimberley mines by the orginal owners, whilst another member of the class (No. 1817) survives mounted on a plinth at a nearby nunnery.

As a final note to this section De Beers also purchased the last functional 18 inch gauge locomotives constructed in Great Britain, these being four 0-4-2 side tanks with 8in by 12in cylinders completed by John Fowler & Co. Ltd in 1927, Nos 17149-17152.

18 Inch Gauge Steam in Preservation

As has previously been stated, there are a number of surviving relics in preservation to represent a very important and influential chapter in the story of the development of the functional narrow gauge steam railway. The Crewe and Horwich Works locomotives *Pet* and *Wren* are currently to be found at the Narrow Gauge Railway Museum, Tywyn, and the National Railway Museum at York respectively. *Pet* has earned recent fame by making an appearance at the Crewe Heritage Centre as part of the celebrations for the 150th Anniversary of the Grand Junction Railway.

The other static relics of Britain's 18 inch gauge

Two ex-John Knowles clay tubs in private preservation. This view shows the eyes for the drawhooks which are not shown in the accompanying drawing. The vehicle on the left is of the later type than the one on the right, as it is of all-welded steel construction, rather than a riveted superstructure on a timber underframe. Several of these tubs survive in private ownership at the time of writing.

(Peter Nicholson)

steam locomotive practice currently to be found on display in their country of origin are the ex-Beyer, Peacock works locomotive *Dot* (No.2817 of 1887) which has been on display at the Narrow Gauge Railway Museum, Tywyn since 1961, and the partly sectioned boiler of *Mars* (Vulcan Foundry No. 1160 of 1885) which, although incomplete, is an important relic of pre-First World War British military railway practice.

From the point of view of historic rolling stock, there are surviving examples from Crewe Works, Chatham Dockyard, the Royal Arsenal Railways, the Sand Hutton (superstructure only) and the John Knowles systems, although it should be stated that the Crewe and Chatham vehicles in preservation appear to have been designed for manual rather than locomotive propulsion.

The surviving steam locomotives mentioned in this volume which are likely to be of most interest to enthusiasts are the three currently to be found in working order. The older of the two British based examples

Jack in steam on the demonstration line at the Leeds Industrial Museum, Armley Mills during 1990. In its present condition, resplendent in a livery similar to that borne by express locomotives of the Midland Railway, the engine presents a striking contrast with the dilapidated state in which it finished its career on the John Knowles system. The relocated whistle and safety valves, together with the Roscoe pattern lubricators, are evident in this view.

(Peter Nicholson)

is the ex-John Knowles Hunslet 0-4-0WT *Jack*. After over two decades in store following its acquisition for preservation in 1958, *Jack* was moved in October 1980 to the Bradford Industrial Museum's workshops at Moorside Mills. Inspection revealed that whilst the boiler barrel and front tubeplate were basically in good condition, other parts of the boiler, such as tubes and stays, were in a less healthy state. The right hand cylinder was in a particularly poor condition, with steam able to escape into the cavity between the cylinder and the frame plate. There was also a difference between the bores of the left and right hand cylinders of half an inch at this stage. In addition, it was found that there was a considerable amount of wear to the wheel treads and that several boiler fittings including the dome cover and one of the safety valves, had been stolen during two burglaries at the Copley Hill Store.

In restoring the engine to working order, it was decided to retain as many of its existing components as was feasible and that an appearance representative of the period between 1924 and 1928 would be used as a basis for the work. The boiler repairs were undertaken by the Keighley concern, Messrs H.A. McEwan who replaced the inner firebox, tubes and stays with new steel components and corrected minor wastage to the barrel and outer firebox by means of welding. The boiler repairs were completed by 31st March 1981 and on

that date a successful hydraulic test was carried out for insurance purposes, to a pressure of 215 psi.

Whilst the boiler was being repaired at Keighley, other work was being undertaken at Bradford. Corroded parts of the water tank were replaced by new platework and welding, whilst damage to the right hand frame plate was corrected by welding. The front bufferbeam was straightened and two cast iron liners produced to reduce the cylinder diameter on both sides to 5½ inches. The casting of these components was carried out by Messrs Bonar Westcroft Castings of Bradford. New pistons were provided and other repair work was required on the cylinder castings. The plunger on the feedpump was another badly worn component and this was hard chromed and reground to produce the correct fit.

Although the steel tyres on the wheels were badly grooved, it was decided against the fitting of new tyres on cost grounds. The existing tyres were therefore re-machined to the desired profile and although this reduced their effective diameter, the tread thickness was still within the permissible limits.

The original dome cover had been fabricated in three sections which were joined together by dove-tailed joints brazed with spelter. The new dome cover is a brass casting supplied by Messrs Haigh & Co. of Halifax. A new Ross 'pop' safety valve was located to match the surviving one and both were re-sited within the cab. This process involved the production of a new cast brass steam manifold to carry these components, the whistle cock, blower valve and pressure gauge. Other sundry fittings were required and much help was obtained from the Hunslet Engine Company, particularly from Mr Don Townsley and Mr Geoff Horsman, in their location. These fittings included two Roscoe No.1 lubricators, the live steam pipes from the regulator, tallow lubricators for the regulator and cylinders and a stuffing box for the regulator spindle. Repairs

A close-up view of the valve gear of *Jack*, showing the oil cups of a design similar to those used on the Manning, Wardle narrow gauge locomotives at Woolwich Arsenal.

(Author)

Another view of *Jack* as restored.
(Leeds Industrial Museum via R. Fitzgerald)

were also made to the chimney, the Greshams No.3 injector and the regulator valve faces. A replacement water gauge was supplied by Messrs Chanters of Bradford.

Once the necessary mechanical work had been carried out, Jack was mounted on blocks and steamed on 18th August 1982. The restoration was then completed and painting carried out, in authentic Midland red pas-senger livery. This work was undertaken by W.P. Davisworth of Armley, Leeds.

During the period since *Jack's* initial restoration a mixed (18/24 inch) gauge demonstration track has been constructed at the Leeds Industrial Museum, Armley Mills, and with the aid of the necessary maintenance work, *Jack* has been in steam on many occasions. The locomotive now forms an important part of the muse-

Ex-John Knowles 0-4-0WT *Gwen* (Hunslet No. 1404 of 1920) seen in June 1992 following restoration in California, USA. During the previous year *Gwen* appeared at the Sacramento Railfair. The owner, Mr Richard Farmer is on the footplate with his sons on the left.

(Courtesy M. Swift)

um's collection covering the contribution made by manufacturers within the City of Leeds to Britain's private railway equipment industry from its formative years to the present day.

Jack's larger and later sister, *Gwen* has enjoyed a chequered history since departing for the United States in 1958. The engine was sold initially to Mr W. Jones of Los Gatos, California. Here it operated on the Wildcat Railroad at Los Gatos until sale following Mr Jones' death. *Gwen* subsequently gravitated to being a static exhibit on a plinth adjacent to a public highway. On 12th March 1983 *Gwen* was amongst the items included in an auction of assets of the estate of a Mr Quentin Jervis at San Pedro, California. Mr Richard Farmer and his wife of Chatsworth, some forty miles distant from San Pedro made a successful bid for the locomotive and *Gwen* has since been restored to full working order, no mean achievement considering the loss of many fittings, including the original injector, during the period leading up to sale during the 1983 auction.

As was stated earlier, the ex-RAR locomotive *Woolwich* now survives at the Bicton Woodland Railway at Bicton Park, East Budleigh in Devon. The decision to construct this line was made by the propri-

etors of Bicton Gardens in October 1961 after it had been decided to open the gardens to the public. A preliminary survey showed that the line would incorporate gradients of a greater severity than 1 in 30, along with several sharp curves and therefore, as had been the case with the SHLR, a 'functional' pattern 18 inch gauge line was to be constructed in preference to a 'miniature' style 15 inch gauge one, notwithstanding the fact that tourists constitute the regular payload.

After departure from the Royal Arsenal, *Woolwich* had gravitated to the yard of Messrs E.L. Pitt & Co. Ltd of Brackley, Northamptonshire and it was inspected on 27th November 1961 with a view to possible purchase for use at Bicton. Messrs J. & W. Gower of Bedford undertook to put the engine back into working order, a task accomplished by 9th April 1962. On 11th April of that year, *Woolwich* arrived at Bicton, having had its spark arrester removed but still retaining its ex-RAR livery of green with yellow lining.

On 3rd May 1962 track laying began at Bicton Gardens station and, as then envisaged, this was completed on 10th August that year, with the last spike being driven into place by Lord Clinton. The permanent way consisted of flat bottomed rail of 30 lb/yd

Ex-RAR Avonside 0-4-0T *Woolwich* (No.1748 of 1916) at Bicton Woodland Railway, Devon on 2nd August 1964, after repainting in lined blue livery.

(Courtesy M. Billington)

Woolwich leaving Bicton Gardens station with a train whose leading vehicle is an open carriage on an ex-RAR underframe.

(M. Billington)

Woolwich at Bicton Gardens station in company with No. 2 *Bicton*, an ex-RAR 16/20hp Ruston & Hornsby diesel which has been fitted with a new body at Bicton.

(BWR/NGRS Library)

The oldest of the ex-RAR bogie under frames, an Oldbury product of 1901 which was incorporated into a Buffet Car during the early period at Bicton. In April 1966 it was converted into a closed passenger carriage.

(BWR/NGRS Library)

calibre, supplied by Messrs M.E. Engineering Ltd, with timber sleepers.

The original length of permanent way was 1,359 yards, but because of the need to traverse the Bicton Gardens station–Pines Junction section twice in each journey, the actual length of run was 1,617 yards. The normal practice in operation was to use the eastern section of the loop for the 'down' run and the western section for the 'up', or return run.

In June 1962 a complete bogie open wagon, together with six bogie under frames, which had formerly been the running gear for red explosives vans, were acquired from the Arsenal. The superstructures of the explosives vans had been burned at Woolwich in accordance with safety regulations. The under frames, together with others acquired from elsewhere, have proved invaluable for incorporation into passenger rolling stock at Bicton and those originally of RAR ownership comprise five built in the Darnall Railway Carriage & Wagon Works by Cravens Ltd of Sheffield (two in 1911, two in 1913 and one in 1915), and one built by

the Oldbury Railway Carriage & Wagon Co. Ltd in 1901. The open wagon was constructed by Dick, Kerr & Co. Ltd. in 1914. Other miscellaneous ex-R.A.R. components also survive at Bicton.

Although initial working was on a 'one engine in steam' basis, it was felt that interest would be added to the line if signal posts were incorporated. Some ex-LSWR signalling equipment became available in September 1962 following the closure of Lympstone

A map of the Bicton Woodland Railway in Devon as at 1st June 1990.

(Author)

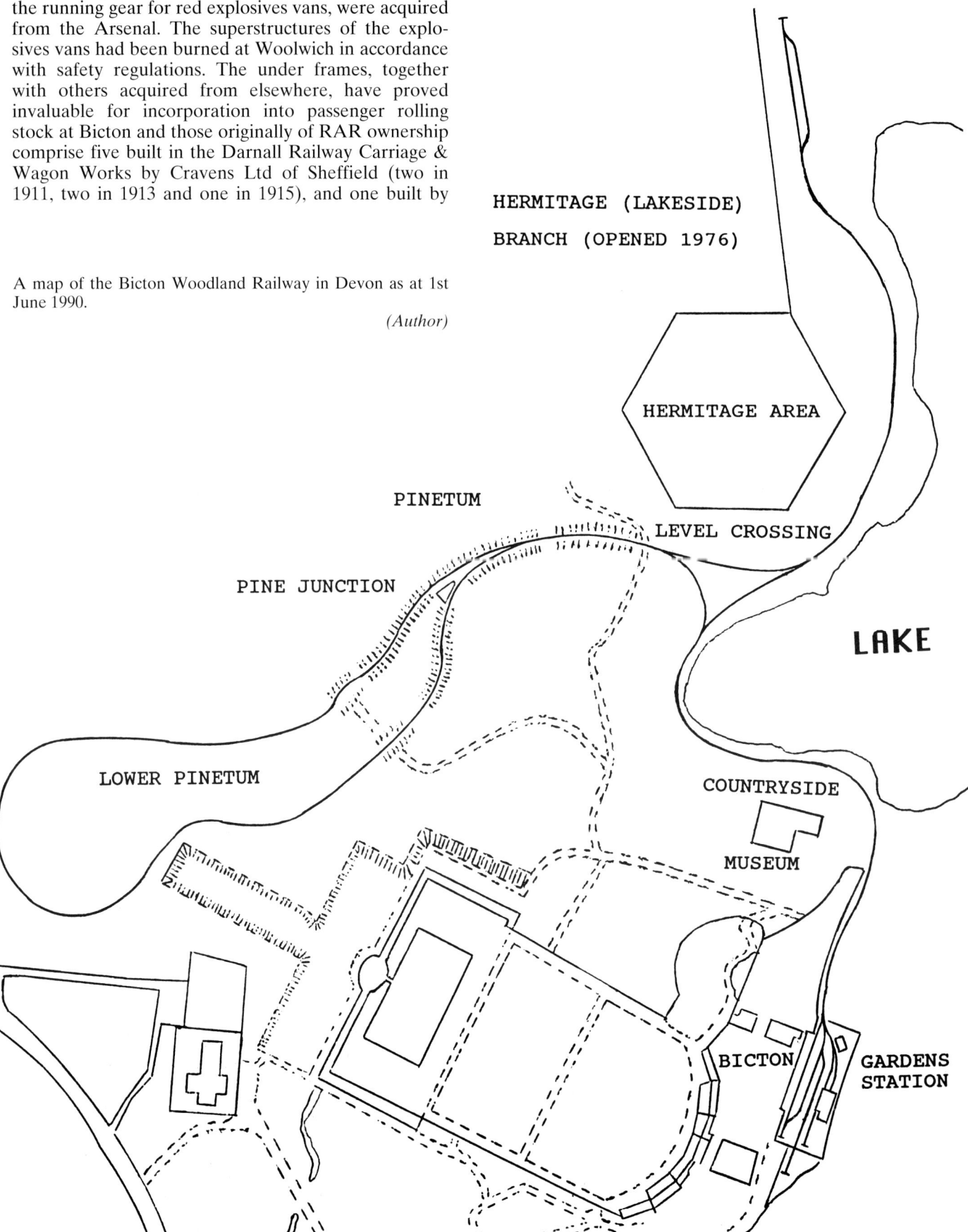

Carnegie, the unique 0-4-4-0 diesel ex-Woolwich Arsenal, 88hp Hunslet 4524 of 1954, as it is today. Restored in apple green livery it is a regular performer on the Bicton Woodland Railway, Devon.

(Peter Nicholson)

signal box on the Exeter–Exmouth line and this was acquired for use at Bicton shortly afterwards.

Woolwich was in steam on several occasions during the 1962 track-laying operations and during the latter part of that year the engine was repainted in a royal blue livery with black smokebox and running boards with red under frames and bufferbeams.

The official date of opening to the general public was on 6th April 1963 with *Woolwich* being in steam once again. Since 1963 the railway has undergone several changes, amongst which has been the acquisition of additional motive power of the diesel variety. The most important of these acquisitions from the historical and technical point of view is *Carnegie* (Hunslet 4524 of 1954) a double-bogie rod-coupled diesel-mechanical locomotive with a McLaren 88 horse power engine, electrically powered starter, lighting and heating, pneumatic braking and two gears in forward and reverse. This locomotive was the last new 18 inch gauge locomotive delivered for use on the RAR and was a much modified development of the 75 horse power machine *Albert* (Hunslet 1722 of 1934), which had finally been scrapped by R.N. Bradbury Ltd of Warrington in October 1961 after sale by the Arsenal.

In order to accommodate the later additions to the locomotive fleet, the engine shed, which was constructed in 1962, was extended in 1966 and to facilitate two-train working an island platform was constructed at Bicton Gardens station. The track layout there has undergone sundry alterations over the years although the most ambitious additions to the permanent way were made in readiness for an additional branch of 537

yards constructed so as to skirt the Hermitage and ornamental lake. This was opened on 22nd March 1976 in the presence of Lady Clinton.

During the 1980s, *Woolwich* has undergone overhauls at the Exeter premises of Phoenix Associates and at the Festiniog Railway's Boston Lodge Works. It is currently normal practice to steam the locomotive on one operating day per week and the only major change in its external appearance from 1963 has been two changes of livery. The loss of the lined out livery of the cab and side tanks in favour of an unlined blue colour scheme is much in evidence in the accompanying 1990 view, but in 1991 this was replaced by a new, light green livery.

The left hand sandbox on *Woolwich* showing the rod which operates the sand valve on the opposite sandbox.

(Author)

The right hand rear crank-web of *Woolwich*, displaying a configuration not shown on the general arrangement drawing.
(Author)

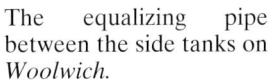

The equalizing pipe between the side tanks on *Woolwich*.
(Author)

This view shows an important modification made to *Woolwich*, namely the fitting of a continuous braking capability which is supplied from a compressed air reservoir in the rear of the cab. The air pipes can be seen above the bufferbeam.
(Author)

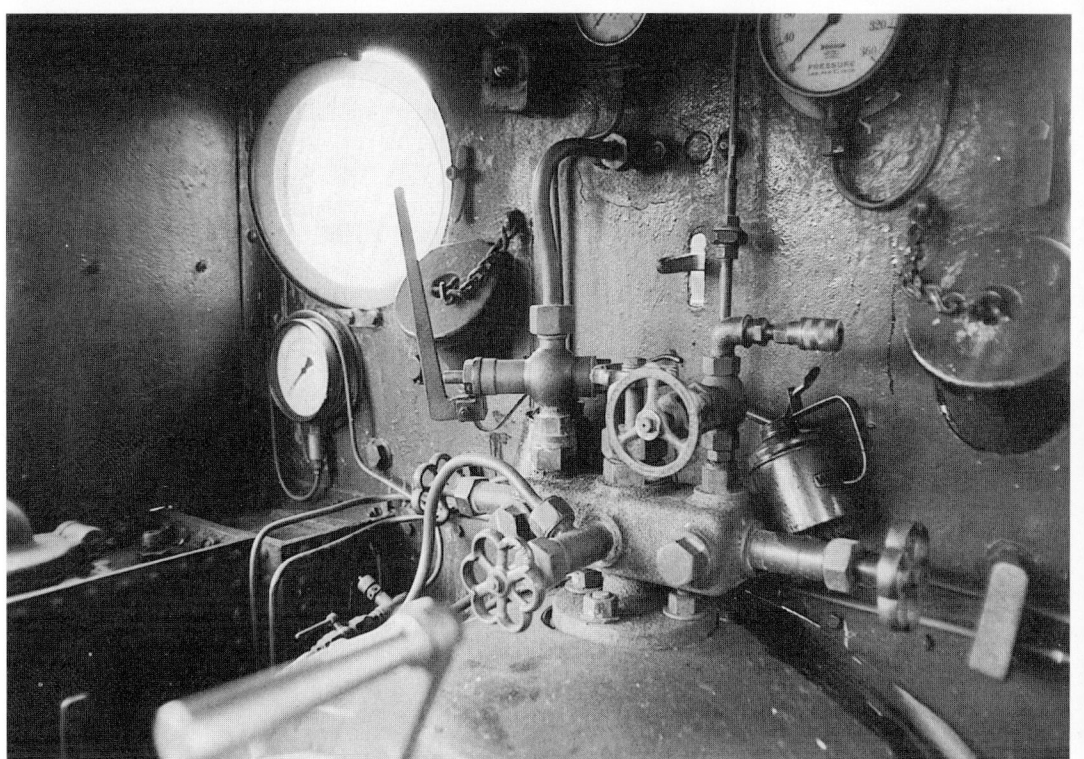

These three views show respectively the steam manifold above the firebox wrapper, the firehole door and water gauges and the steam and oil pipes supplying the burner nozzle.

(Author)

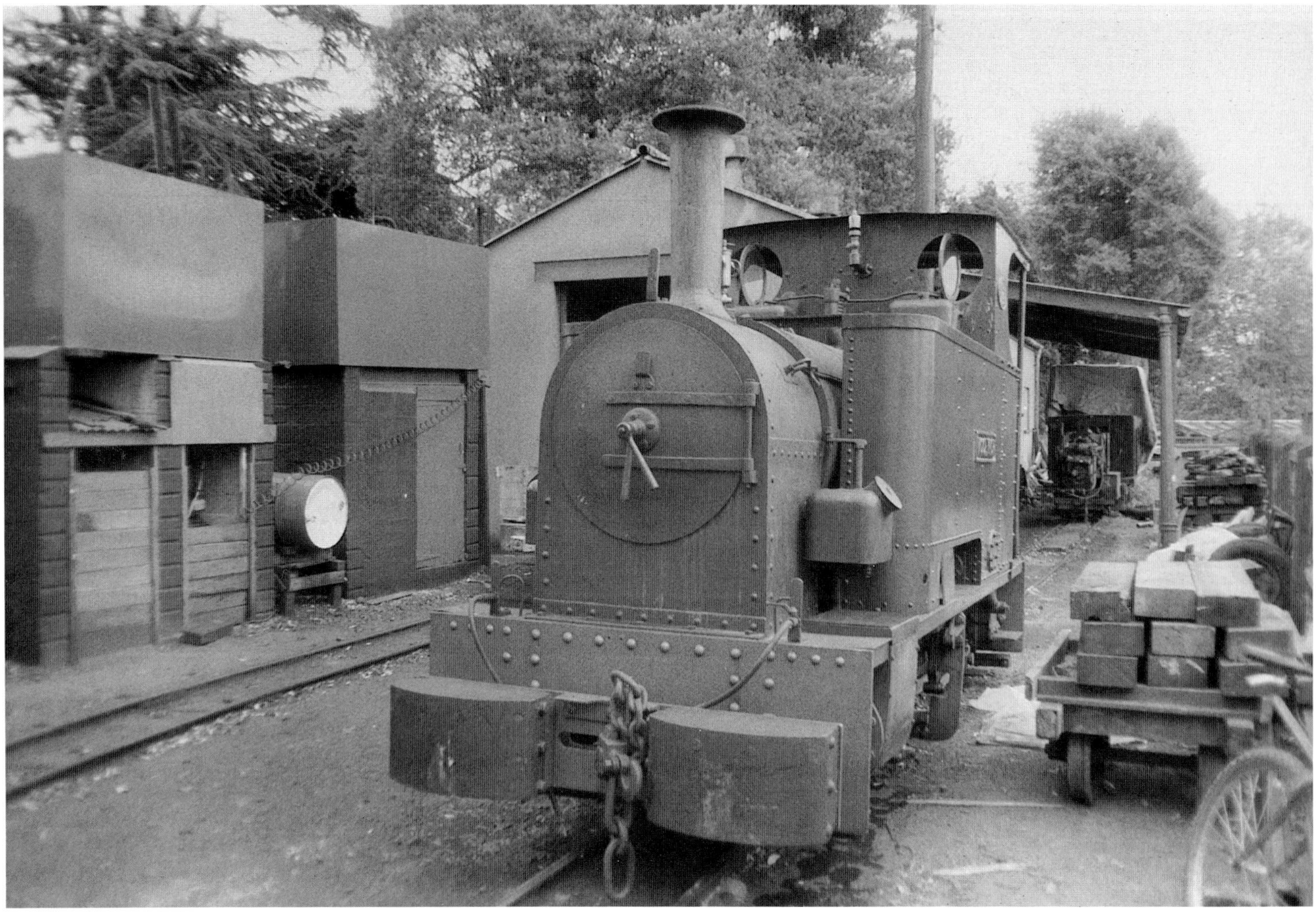

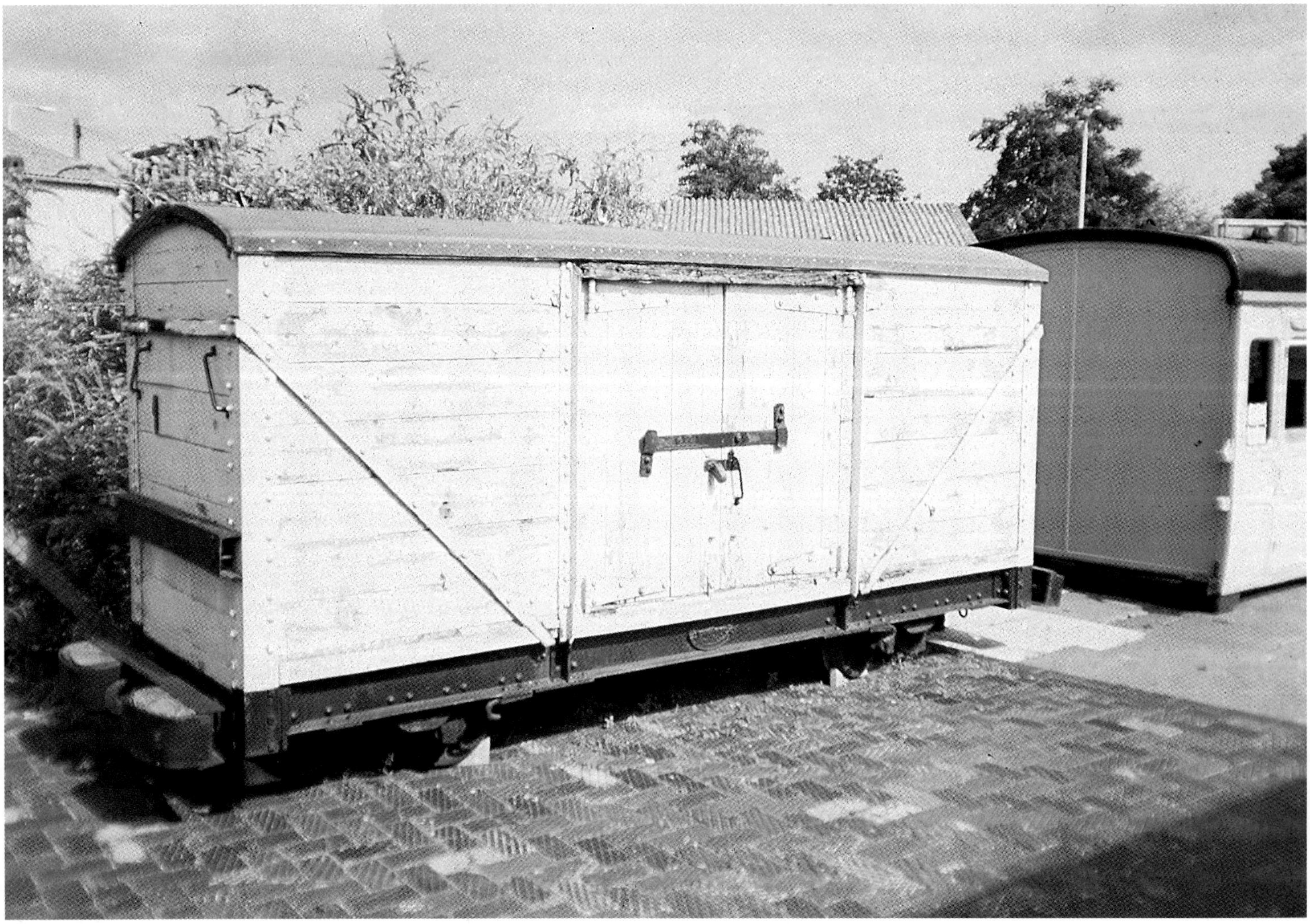

Left: Another of *Woolwich* near the engine shed at Bicton in June 1990. The locomotive had reverted to an unlined blue colour scheme, similar to its original BWR repainting in 1962 but has since been repainted in a bright green livery. It is shown alongside a wagon acquired from BR at Wolverton Works, which had formerly been used on the hand-worked system there.

(Author)

Below: This wagon from the Chatham Dockyard 18 inch gauge railway is now on display in the Dockyard Visitor Centre. Its design differs little from the wooden four-wheeled wagons shown in *Engineering* but, contrary to normal practice in the Dockyard, it is fitted with drawhooks.

(Author)

Left: The last item of ex-RAR rolling stock to leave the Arsenal was this 7-ton capacity covered, red bogie ammunition wagon. This vehicle, which was built by Cravens in 1913, was moved in the summer of 1990 to North Woolwich Old Station Museum where it is now displayed, along with sections of cast iron permanent way used at Chatham Dockyard.

(Author)

Above: Carnegie, the second of the two double-bogie Hunslet diesels supplied for use at the Royal Arsenal is also now to be seen at Bicton. This view emphasises the scenic nature of the engine's present surroundings.

(Peter Nicholson)

Possible Future Developments

From the point of view of possible future developments in railway preservation, the recreation of a section of the old RAR system as part of a heritage project would have much to commend it as a tourist attraction. This is particularly true in the light of recent announcements to the effect that the MoD will be vacating the remains of the Arsenal by the mid-1990s. The classic 18 inch gauge designs of the Royal Arsenal Railways would have much to offer those who wish to see more replicas constructed of historically important but extinct steam locomotive classes. The 6-inch Manning, Wardle design, as represented by *Albert Edward* or *Arquebus*, would be the most historically valuable of the RAR classes to reproduce, although new component drawings would be required as the originals were destroyed by fire. Another particularly deserving candidate would be the very successful 'Culverin' class, which featured in the official film of March 1918, now in the possession of the Imperial War Museum, and in the 1921 feature on the Royal Arsenal Railways in *The Locomotive* magazine.

As regards suitable passenger rolling stock to accompany a replica of any of the RAR locomotives, the obvious candidates for reproduction would be the distinctive Superintendent Saloon design, along with the two-compartment bogie carriage. At the time of writing, however, no authentic builder's plans of these vehicles have come to light and therefore any replicas of RAR passenger stock could currently be constructed only on the basis of photographic evidence.

A few previously unmentioned 18 inch gauge track formations survive at historic military installations in Britain, such as Hurst Castle in Hampshire and Fort Victoria near Yarmouth on the Isle of Wight, but although these systems appear to have been fairly extensive in their prime, they do not appear to have ever utilised any steam locomotives.

Before bringing this history of British 18 inch gauge steam railways to a close, mention must be made of one particularly interesting survival which it is hoped can at least be preserved in its present condition, if not restored to a reasonable approximation of its former glory. On the western approaches to Cork Harbour, in what is now the Irish Republic, stands Camden Fort. This was garrisoned from its completion in 1871 until 1938 (some 17 years after the Partition) by the Royal Engineers and Coast Artillery. A derelict, but virtually complete 18 inch gauge track formation, probably dating from the mid-1880s, survives at this location, having probably been out of use since the mid-1920s. The formation extends to about a mile in length and is on two levels linked by a crane. According to a caretaker who had worked at the fort and had spoken to the local historian, Mr Walter McGrath, a steam locomotive had definitely worked on the Camden Fort line and this was trans-shipped between levels by means of the crane as stores movements required.

Although the identity of the locomotive which worked on this railway has not currently been ascertained, circumstantial evidence points very much in the direction of Fox, Walker No. 386 of 1878, the engine mentioned previously in connection with the Crewe Works system. Such a locomotive would have proved adequate for the relatively light stores traffic which would have been encountered at the Fort, and would also have been suitable for relatively easy cranage. An engine of equivalent size could certainly be constructed today for use on a revived line at the fort, should the wish for restoration prevail.

Appendix 1

Royal Arsenal Railways 18 Inch Gauge Locomotives

This list is compiled from Makers' and RAR records, along with sales advertisements in *The Engineer*, *Surplus*, *Contract Journal* and *Colliery Guardian* and other information. These records are not exhaustive and consequently some errors may be present. Internal combustion locomotives are included for the sake of completeness.

Manning Wardle Locomotives (All 0-4-0ST)

No. 353 *Lord Raglan* - delivered 9/3/1871. This locomotive was a 'Special' constructed under Order No. 5750 (drawings no longer extant). Scrapped within the Arsenal during the period 1/4/1915 to 31/3/1917.

No. 477 *Victoria* (re-named *Boxer* circa 1901) - delivered 3/11/1873. Advertised for sale in *The Engineer* for 20/4/1917, sold to J.F. Wake, Geneva Works, Darlington and still at their premises 27/6/1923. It is presumed that the engine was scrapped shortly afterwards.

No. 482 *Albert Edward* - delivered 29/12/1873. Advertised for sale in *The Engineer*, *Surplus* and *Contract Journal* during July 1919 and sold to J.F. Wake, being re-advertised in *Contract Journal* for 8/10/1919. To an unknown purchaser after this date and new firebars supplied by the Makers under Order No.81231 on 9/11/1920. Scrapping date unknown.

No. 555 R.L. No.2 (re-named *Rocket* after 1891) - delivered 27/4/1875. This engine was scrapped within the Arsenal during the year ended 31/3/1915.

No. 605 R.C.D 2 (re-named *Norman Ramsey* after 1891) - delivered 21/3/1876. Scrapped within the Arsenal during the year ended 31/3/1915.

No. 612 *Trumpeter* - delivered 21/3/1876. Scrapped within the Arsenal by 31/3/1911.

No. 613 R.L. No.3, (re-named *Shrapnel*) - delivered 15/6/1876. For disposal see No. 477.

No. 685 *Vauban* - delivered 26/11/1877. For disposal see No. 477.

No. 696 *Coehorn* - delivered 18/3/1878. Scrapped during year ended 31/3/1917.

No. 939 R.L. No.4 (re-named *Fusee* after 1891) - delivered 21/7/1884. Sold November 1918 to J.F.Wake and thence to Swanwick Collieries, Derbyshire. Advertised again for sale in *Colliery Guardian* for 19/12/1924.

No. 986 R.C.D No.5 (re-named *Gordon* after 1891) - delivered 1/3/1886. To J.F. Wake in 1919 and still at Darlington 27/6/1923 with scrapping presumed shortly afterwards.

No. 1043 R.L. No.5 (re-named *Torpedo* after 1891) - delivered 23/9/1887. Sold November 1918 to J.F. Wake and still at Darlington 27/6/1923, probably being scrapped shortly afterwards.

No. 1130 *Arquebus* - delivered 23/3/1889. For disposal see No. 477.

Vulcan Foundry Locomotive

No. 838 of 1878 0-4-0ST *R.C.D No.3* (re-named *Iron Duke* after 1891) - scrapped during year ended 31/3/1915.

Fox, Walker Locomotive

Ex-'Handyside' 0-4-2 (formerly 2-4-2) Back Tank, one of Nos 399-404 of 1878, fitted with a cab and with winch and front pony truck removed. Disposed of before 31/3/1911.

Bagnall Locomotives

No. 710 of 1885 0-4-2T *Osiris* - sold 1920 to J.F. Wake, probably scrapped shortly afterwards.

No. 711 of 1885 0-4-2T *Serapis* - scrapped during year ended 31/3/1912.

No. 712 of 1885 0-4-2T *Anubis* - disposal as for No. 710. No. 713 of 1885 0-4-2T *Isis* - disposal as for No. 710.

No. 714 of 1885 0-4-2T *Apis* - disposal as for No. 710.

No. 1442 of 1895 0-4-0T *Ajax* - included in auctions of 9/6/1920, 29/9/1920 and 15/11/1921. Probably scrapped shortly after the last-mentioned of these auctions.

John Fowler Locomotives (All 0-4-2T)

No. 5058 of 1885 *Cormorant* - included in auctions of 9/6/1920, 29/9/1920 and 15/11/1921. Probably scrapped after the last-mentioned of these auctions.

No. 5059 of 1885 *Vulture* - for disposal see No. 5058.

No. 5060 of 1885 *Ostrich* - for disposal see No. 5058.

No. 5061 of 1885 *Quail* - for disposal see No. 5058.

Nos 5063 and 5064 of 1885; *Owl* and *Pelican* - for disposal see No. 5058.

No. 5062 of 1885 *Flamingo* - to Longmoor 1905 and scrapped 1919.

Hudswell, Clarke Locomotives (All 0-4-0ST)

No. 268 of 1884 *Carronade* - included in one of 1922 auctions (21/3, 5/5 or 19/9) - scrapping date unknown.

No. 269 of 1884 *Culverin* - for disposal see No.268.

No. 273 of 1885 *Hector* - for disposal see No.268.

No. 274 of 1885 *Achilles* - included in auctions of 15/9/1920 and 15/11/1921 - scrapping date unknown.

No. 280 of 1885 *Scipio* - for disposal see No.274.

No. 281 of 1885 *Hannibal* - for disposal see No.274.

No. 288 of 1886 *Basilisk* - for disposal see No.274.

No. 295 of 1887 *R.L. No.6* (re-named *Grenade* after 1891) -for disposal see No.268.

No. 345 of 1889 *Militades* - for disposal see No.268.

No. 1144 of 1915 *London* - sold in 1922 and re-advertised for sale in Machinery Market for 7/7/1922.

No. 1145 of 1915 *Carnarvon* - for disposal see No. 1144.

No. 1146 of 1915 *Kent* - for disposal see No. 1144.

No. 1147 of 1915 *Cornwall* - for disposal see No. 1144.

No. 1148 of 1915 *Essex* - for disposal see No.1144.

Experimental Crampton Locomotive

This locomotive was a rebuild undertaken within the Arsenal in 1886, probably utilising the boiler, frames and wheels of either *Vulcan* or *Mercury* from the Suakin Expedition. The engine is believed to have run in this form for less than two years.

Kerr, Stuart Locomotives (All 0-4-0ST)

No. 761 of 1901 *Pluto* - sold during auction of 15/11/1921, having previously been auctioned at Erith. To Taquah Mining & Exploration Co. Ltd, Gold Coast.

No. 762 of 1901 *Polumephus* - included in one of the auctions of 1922 (21/3, 5/5 or 19/9) - scrapping date unknown.

No. 763 of 1901 *Phaeton* - for disposal see No. 761.

No. 807 of 1902 *Pegasus* - for disposal see No. 761. A new firebox tubeplate supplied by the Makers 12/5/1927.

No. 808 of 1902 *Prometheus* - for disposal see No. 762.

No. 809 of 1902 *Phoenix* - for disposal see No. 762.

No. 1266 of 1912 *Regulus* - for disposal see No. 762.

No. 1267 of 1912 *Pompey* - for disposal see No. 762.

No. 1268 of 1912 *Brutus* - for disposal see No. 762.

No. 2400 of 1914 *Petrolea* - for disposal see No. 762.

Avonside Locomotives (All 0-4-0T)

No. 1715 of 1915 *Bristol* - either sold during one of the auctions of 1922 (21/3, 5/5 or 19/9) or to George Cohen (Canning Town Depot) in January 1933.

No. 1716 of 1915 *Glasgow* - for disposal see No. 1715.

No. 1717 of 1915 *Liverpool* - for disposal see No. 1715.

No. 1718 of 1915 *Newcastle* - scrapped by 1947.

No. 1747 of 1916 *Derby* - for disposal see No. 1715.

No. 1748 of 1916 *Woolwich* - to E.L. Pitt & Co. Ltd, dealers by 1960, resold to Bicton Woodland Railway 1962. Still extant 1993.

No. 1749 of 1916 *Waltham* - for disposal see No. 1715.

No. 1750 of 1916 *Birmingham* - for disposal see No. 1715.

No. 1751 of 1916 *Sheffield* - for disposal see No. 1715.

No. 1752 of 1916 *Charlton* - for disposal see No. 1715.

No. 1753 of 1916 *Leeds* - for disposal see No. 1715.

No. 1754 of 1916 *Manchester* - out of use by 1947, scrapped by 1951.

No. 1755 of 1916 *Colchester* - scrapped by 1947.

No. 1756 of 1916 *Cardiff* - for disposal see No. 1715.

No. 1757 of 1916 *Berkeley* - for disposal see No. 1715.

No. 1758 of 1916 *Enfield* - for disposal see No. 1715.

NB Four members of this class were sold in 1922 and a further six passed to Messrs George Cohen & Sons in 1933, being re-advertised for sale in that year.

Compressed Air Locomotive

In 1877(?) a compressed air locomotive designed by Colonel F.E. Beaumont was completed. It is thought to have run for approximately two years but was underpowered in service.

Internal Combustion Locomotives

Hornsby Oil-Mechanical (Paraffin)

0-4-0

No. 1705 of 1896 *Lachesis* - to J.F. Wake 1920 and still at Darlington 27/6/1923. Presumed scrapped shortly afterwards.

2-4-0

No. 4535 of 1900 *Clotho* - scrapped year-ended 31/3/1917.

No. 5245 of 1901 *Atropos* - scrapped year-ended 31/3/1919.

No. 5883 of 1902 *Hecate* - scrapped shortly after 31/3/1919.

No. 7226 of 1904 *Alecto* - for disposal see No. 1705.

Ruston Hornsby 4-wheel Diesel Mechanical

11/13 hp

No. 192886 of 1939 - to Taurus Nicholls, dealer, Greenwich 1971 - scrapped after this date.

16/20 hp

No. 213839 of 1942 - to Lemon Burton, dealer, London, thence to Bicton Woodland Railway via M.E. Engineering Ltd in 1963. Still extant 1993.

No. 213840 of 1942 - to Stanfield Nurseries, Littlehampton 4/1971, thence to the Great Bush Railway, East Sussex (re-gauged to 2 ft). Still extant 1993.

Baguley/McEwan-Pratt 0-4-0 Petrol-Mechanical

No. 630 *Megaera* acquired 1914 and sold at the auction of 15/11/1921 to Lewes Portland Cement & Lime Co. Ltd. Re-gauged to 2ft after sale and scrapped in 1931.

Hunslet 0-4-4-0 Diesel-Mechanical

75 hp

No. 1722 of 1934 *Albert* - to R.N. Bradbury, Warrington for scrap 10/1961.

88 hp

No. 4524 of 1954 *Carnegie* - to F. & J. Darnell, North Ockenden, Essex and re-sold 2/1966 to Bicton Woodland Railway. Still extant 1993.

Appendix 2

Royal Arsenal, Woolwich (March 1915)
Mechanical Engineers Department
Staff & Duties (Locomotive Section)

	Shop Manager	Foremen	Assistant Foremen	Duties
Locomotive Running	Mr F. Turner	Mr Neath		Locomotive Staff & Motor Lorries
Locomotive Repairs	As Above	As Above	Repairs to	Locomotives. & Lorries
Rolling Stock Shop	As Above	Mr Staig		Manufacture & Repair of Rolling Stock
Smiths Shop	As Above	Mr Polkinghorn		Smiths work for Rolling Stock, Locomotive and Machinery Shops & Permanent Way Services
Boiler Shop	As Above	Mr Mackenzie	Mr Brooker	Boiler & Structural Steel Work

RAR Hornsby No. 1705 0-4-0 oil-engined locomotive *Lachesis* at Grantham when new in 1896. This view shows, from left to right, the handbrake column, clutch and reverse controls, the single cylinder, twin flywheels, gear train and clutch, jackshaft and the water cooling tower utilizing induced draught provided by the exhaust. The two pipes leading from the cylinder to the cooling tower are the water pipe (thinner) and the exhaust (thicker).

(Courtesy R. Hooley)

Two views of *Clotho*, Hornsby 2-4-0 oil-engined locomotive No. 4535 on a Great Northern Railway 10-ton flat wagon at Grantham, when new in 1900. The design was similar to *Lachesis* except for the leading pony truck and increased wheelbase (5ft + 3ft 6in). Features of particular interest include the asymmetrical cab and eccentric driven water pump.

(Courtesy R. Hooley)

Appendix 3

Traffic Information for the Sand Hutton Light Railway

Year	No. of 3rd Class Passengers	Goods Carried (Tons)			Goods & Materials Carried (Tons) (Originating on S.H.L.R. System)		
		General Materials	Coal, Coke Etc.	Total Freight	General Materials	Coal, Coke Etc.	Total Freight
1924	579	2,256	694	2,950	1,560	-	1,560
1925	2,185	3,175	1,453	4,628	1,264	-	1,264
1926	1,568	10,030	2,522	12,552	9,393	187	9,580
1927	1,534	10,306	3,039	13,345	9,903	29	9,932
1928	948	11,010	2,640	13,650	10,727	-	10,727
1929	791	3,946	2,300	6,246	3,522	-	3,522
1930	65	1,887	1,552	3,439	1,677	-	1,677
1931	61	570	295	865	493	-	493
1932	-	166	152	318	98	-	98

Engine Mileage:	Passenger	Freight	Light Running Etc	Total
1924	529	3,143	146	3,818
1925	1,918	3,480	153	5,551
1926	1,548	3,908	169	5,625
1927	1,485	4,225	252	5,962
1928	1,550	4,249	265	6,064
1929	1,460	3,856	232	5,548
1930	262	3,210	280	3,752
1931	18	2074	249	2,341
1932	-	692	98	790

Source: Ministry of Transport Railway Returns for the period 1924-1932.

Appendix 4

SHLR Revenue and Expenditure Details

Year	Gross Freight	Traffic Passenger	Receipts Total	Miscellaneous Income/(Expenditure)	Gross Income Carried Forward
1924	502	12	514	(14)	500
1925	882	39	921	14	935
1926	1,121	27	1,148	6	1,154
1927	1,211	26	1,237	5	1,242
1928	1,247	17	1,264	-	1,264
1929	851	15	866	-	866
1930	503	1	504	-	504
1931	193	2	195	-	195
1932	65	-	65	-	65

Year	Gross Income Brought Forward	Revenue Expenditure	Net Receipts	Adjustment for Depreciation Etc. (Shortfall) +/(-) (A)	Debenture Balance Interest +/(-)	Carried Forward
1924	500	459	41	101	254	(112)
1925	935	863	72	44	309	(305)
1926	1,154	1,107	47	51	350	(557)
1927	1,242	1,153	89	49	360	(779)
1928	1,264	1,104	160	52	360	(927)
1929	866	855	11	152	360	(1,124)
1930	504	703	(199)	(51)	360	(1,734)
1931	195	392	(197)	52	360	(2,239)
1932	65	172	(107)	?*	293*	-*

* The Company was officially wound up on 24th October 1932.
Source: Ministry of Transport Railway Returns for 1924-32. (A): added by the author.

Index